TOO SMART TO BE SENTIMENTAL

TOO SMART
TO BE
SENTIMENTAL

*Contemporary Irish American
Women Writers*

Edited by

Sally Barr Ebest

and

Kathleen McInerney

Foreword by Caledonia Kearns

University of Notre Dame Press
Notre Dame, Indiana

Designed by Wendy McMillen
Set in 10.2/13.3 Goudy by Four Star Books
Printed on 55# Nature's Recycle Paper in the U.S.A. by Versa Press

Library of Congress Cataloging-in-Publication Data

Too smart to be sentimental : contemporary Irish American women writers /
edited by Sally Barr Ebest and Kathleen McInerney ;
foreword by Caledonia Kearns.
p.   cm.
Includes bibliographical references and index.
ISBN-13: 978-0-268-02773-5 (pbk. : alk. paper)
ISBN-10: 0-268-02773-0 (pbk. : alk. paper)
1. American literature—Irish American authors—History and criticism.
2. American literature—Women authors—History and criticism.
3. American literature—20th century—History and criticism.
4. Irish Americans in literature.   5. Irish Americans—Ethnic identity.
I. Ebest, Sally Barr.   II. McInerney, Kathleen H.
PS153.I78T66   2007
810.9'9287—dc22

2007038704

For our favorite Irish Americans:

Ron Ebest

and

Morgan and Caitlin Halstead

Contents

ORAL TRADITIONS

SEXUALITY

FEMINISM, CULTURE, AND CRITIQUE

Foreword

Caledonia Kearns

Eileen Myles, the poet and novelist, is quoted within these pages as explaining why she writes: "Writing is just making a mark. It's your mortality, your need to exist. It's probably totally linked to feeling endangered." When I discovered there was writing by Irish American women that was in danger of being forgotten, I began to collect their work. This became a collection of fiction by Irish American women entitled *Cabbage and Bones*.

In compiling this collection I learned that much of the writing by Irish American women at the beginning of the twentieth century was out of print and unknown even to American literature scholars. Consequently, I decided to arrange the collection chronologically, placing out-of-print work alongside writing by contemporary authors to show there was a valid and historical tradition of writing by women of Irish American descent throughout the twentieth century as, indeed, there was.

It is, therefore, most important that a decade after the publication of *Cabbage and Bones* this collection of criticism on the writing of Irish American women is being published. Organized around common themes such as sexuality, religion, and feminism, the fine scholarship in *Too Smart to Be Sentimental* makes a vital contribution, for it not only takes Irish American literature one step further but also establishes a place for the writing of Irish American *women* in the canon of American literature.

We have Sally Barr Ebest and Kathleen McInerney to thank for this. This collection, which includes their own fine essays on Mary McCarthy, Elizabeth Cullinan, and Erin McGraw, also offers new essays on writers such as Maeve Brennan, Maureen Howard, Mary Gordon, Alice McDermott, and Mary McGarry Morris. Ebest and McInerney chose to organize the collection using *The Field Day Anthology of Irish Literature: Irish Women's Writing and Traditions* as a model "to demonstrate their parallels with their Irish sisters" rather than drawing on a "literary tradition that tends to overlook women."

While this is an admirable organizational structure, I would like to add that you cannot read an anthology of writing or criticism by women of any ethnicity without having at the forefront of one's mind that most literary traditions overlook women. It is an obvious truism that if women's literature was not overlooked, collections of writing by women would not need to exist. This is why the publication of *Too Smart to Be Sentimental* must be celebrated. It is one thing to collect writing and publish it in an anthology; criticism, however, is the next vital step for acceptance into the halls of academia, providing necessary validation for the work of Irish American women writers.

I have long admired the work of Mary Helen Washington in anthologizing the fiction of African American women, and I turn to her again. At the root of her vocation is the desire to learn from women's writing. She looks to it for sustenance. In the introduction to her important collection *Black Eyed Susans, Midnight Birds*, she comments on the beginning of her research: "I began to immerse myself in collecting the stories of black women. I know that I felt an immediate sense of community and continuity and joy in the discovery of these writers as though I had found something of my ancestry, my future and my own voice" (4).

It seems obvious that in editing *Too Smart to Be Sentimental* Ebest and McInerney also felt the joy that comes from the kind of recognition that placing the work of Irish American women writers within a critical context brings. The sum is larger than its parts. We can see how one literary work can and does inform and inspire another and, in doing so, establishes a literary tradition. At the *New Yorker* Maeve Brennan's Irish voice made way for Elizabeth Cullinan's Irish American one; Mary McCarthy, with her fierce intellectual rigor, cleared a path for Maureen Howard; and Mary Gordon's fictional explorations of religion and identity served to initiate Erin McGraw; and so it continues. *Too Smart to Be Sentimental* makes it clear that there is a trajectory of Irish American women's writing; it is both the voices of those who came before and those of contemporary writers that have moved the genre into the twenty-first century.

In her essay Patricia Keefe Durso writes that Maureen Howard's work is frequently mentioned as containing echoes of Joyce. In her interview with Durso, Howard says that Joyce "was enormously conscious" that "writing was a performing art." Howard cites her own belief in this as well. After reading these essays in concert, it becomes clear that for all these writers, their work is a kind of performance. It is on this stage, using pen and paper, that the writing of Irish American women breaks open cultural silences that have long been kept and releases emotions that have long been repressed. Whether highlighting Elizabeth Cullinan's debunking of the stereotypical good Irish mother or Mary McGarry Morris's renegade misfit Fiona Range, *Too Smart to Be Sentimental* brings common themes to light while emphasizing what is unique about the work of the women included in this volume.

It is interesting to note that not all the contributors to this collection are Irish American, nor do they all specialize in Irish or Irish American studies. As McInerney writes in her essay on Elizabeth Cullinan, the work by the writers discussed in *Too Smart to Be Sentimental* is part of the larger genre of Diaspora writing by women. I would have to concur. As debates about immigration and immigrants continue to rage, it is particularly important that the experience of "assimilated" white Americans is not forgotten simply because we have become removed from the immigration experience by multiple generations; it is too easily forgotten that excepting those native to the Americas and the slaves forcibly brought here, our families were all immigrants to the United States. Collections of writing about and criticism of this experience, and these writers and their connection to Ireland, will take on even greater importance in the future as it is compared with writing by more recent immigrants, such as women of Mexican or Russian American descent.

I will be proud to place *Too Smart to Be Sentimental* on my bookshelf next to Hasia Diner's fine history of Irish American women, *Erin's Daughters in America*, and my own collection, *Cabbage and Bones*. I see the three as a trio of sorts, companion volumes giving voice to and validating the history, literature, intellectual life, and experience of Irish American women in the United States, word by precious word.

Works Cited

Washington, Mary Helen, ed. *Black Eyed Susans, Midnight Birds: Stories by and about Black Women*. New York: Anchor Books, 1990.

Acknowledgments

A brief glance at the index, introduction, or any of the articles in this collection quickly reveals the person who laid the groundwork for this study: Charles Fanning. Charlie's 1990 edition of *The Irish Voice in America* was the first to recognize and pay scholarly attention to a wide range of Irish American women writers; the second edition went even further, introducing women whose works had been published in the intervening decade. Without Charlie, we would not have the readily available background information on these women, nor the context in which they published. We want to thank him for his prescient and impressive scholarly work.

Similarly, we thank Caledonia Kearns not only for her fine foreword, but also for recognizing the need and taking the initiative to publish the first two—indeed, the only two—anthologies of Irish American women's writing. *Cabbage and Bones* and *Motherland* took Fanning's scholarly assessments and, in a sense, made them flesh by publishing short stories and excerpts by the women he introduced. Taken together, Fanning's and Kearns's works represent the foundation upon which subsequent Irish American women's scholarship was built.

Anyone reading Charlie's or Caledonia's works would recognize a third person deserving acknowledgment, one of our foremost foremothers: Maureen Howard. Practically every essay quotes her foreword to Kearns's *Cabbage and Bones*. Indeed, our own title is taken from that same text, for Howard's words best encapsulate our sense of Irish American women's fiction. They are, as she puts it, "realistic, too smart to give in to the sentimental."

We would also like to thank organizers of the Midwest Regional and National American Conferences on Irish Studies (ACIS). They provided a forum for us to present our research across the United States in St. Louis, Bloomington/Normal, St. Paul, Milwaukee, and Omaha, and in Great Britain at the International ACIS in Liverpool. These conferences not only led to our collaboration but also helped us solicit contributors and resulted in invaluable feedback, which helped us shape and refine this collection. Finally, we would not have been able to teach or travel to some of these conferences without support from the faculty at our institutions. From the University of Missouri–St. Louis, thanks to Eamonn Wall, Jefferson Smurfitt Chair of Irish Studies; Joel Glassman, director of the Center for International Studies; Robert Bliss, dean of the Honors College; and Farida Jalalzai, colloquium chair for the Institute for Women's and Gender Studies. From Chicago State University, thanks to Maria Teresa Garreton, program director of Bilingual Education, and to Lawrence J. Caffrey, professor emeritus at Loyola University of Chicago, for their support and steady encouragement.

Of course, this volume could not have happened without the fine writing and cooperation of our contributors. They have waited patiently and responded quickly to our feedback. We thank them for their wisdom, their scholarship, and their contributions to the small but growing body of research on Irish American women writers.

Sally Barr Ebest and Kathleen McInerney

Introduction

Writing Green Thoughts

SALLY BARR EBEST

When the first wave of Irish immigrants arrived on our shores 250 years ago, they brought with them the Irish literary tradition. With this, they created Irish American literature—"one of the oldest and largest bodies of ethnic writing produced by members and descendants of a single American immigrant group" (Fanning 1). According to Charles Fanning, nineteenth-century Irish American literature reflected immigration patterns: the first wave included writers who arrived before the "Great Hunger" in the 1840s, the second wave those who fled the Famine years from 1850 to 1875, and the third wave those who described the gradual assimilation and acceptance of the Irish during the final years of the nineteenth century (1).

With the dawn of the twentieth century, a new generation of Irish American writers emerged. Ron Ebest describes their stories and novels as *Private Histories*, for they reflect Irish Americans' cultural and socioeconomic milieu by detailing the rituals surrounding their lives from birth through death. As Ebest's title suggests, many of these works continued what Fanning terms the "sentimental conventions of plot and character" (3). With the 1932 publication of James T. Farrell's *Young Lonigan: A Boyhood in Chicago Streets*, however, this approach was shattered (at least for male writers) and the way paved for the realism characterizing subsequent twentieth-century Irish American literature (Fanning 3).

Toward the end of the 1990s Irish American literature further shifted its boundaries and perspectives. Thanks to increased transatlantic travel, Irish American writers "now cross oceans and boundaries at will" (Fanning 369). The effects are evident in what Fanning calls the "Irish inflections" in the works of Irish American poets and fiction writers. At the same time, immigration to America by the "New Irish" has yielded large numbers of Irish writers who view America through Irish eyes (370). Fanning argues that this confluence does not wholly account for Irish American writing; nevertheless, it "reinforce[s] the decisive fact that there continues to *be* an Irish-American experience, a living culture on which writers feel compelled to draw." Regardless of birth country, these writers convey "ethnicity as liberating doubleness," a characteristic Fanning has traced to pre-Famine literature (371).

The above analyses, along with Daniel Casey and Robert Rhodes's *Irish-American Fiction: Essays in Criticism*, represent the first in-depth efforts to analyze the Irish American literary tradition. For this, scholars of Irish American literature owe them a great debt. At the same time, however, these works continue the tradition established by the founders of the literary canon: the majority of their discussions center on the works of Irish American *males*. Throughout most of the twentieth century, the only scholars to recognize the contributions of contemporary Irish American females were Caledonia Kearns and Charles Fanning. Kearns published *Cabbage and Bones* and *Motherland*, the first (and only) anthologies of Irish American women's writing, whereas Fanning's *The Irish Voice in America* was the first comprehensive acknowledgment of women's role in this tradition.

In the first edition of *The Irish Voice* Fanning noted the emergence of a significant number of Irish American women writers in the 1990s (378). Along with the usual Irish American foremothers—Mary Doyle Curran, Mary McCarthy, Flannery O'Connor,[1] Maureen Howard, Elizabeth Cullinan, and Mary Gordon—Fanning mentions Joan Bagnell, Carol O'Brien

Blum, and Caryl Rivers and discusses the works of Elizabeth Savage, Elaine Ford, Susanna Moore, Diana O'Hehir, and Ellen Currie. In the second edition Fanning added Ann T. Jones, Maura Stanton, Joan Mathieu, Maureen Waters, Ann Beattie, Bobbie Ann Mason, Alice Fulton, Kathleen Ford, Helena Mulkerns, Eileen Fitzgerald, Eileen Myles, Anna Quindlen, Kristina McGrath, and Alice McDermott. While this list features some of the best-known Irish American women writers, it is not exhaustive. Maeve Brennan, Mary McGarry Morris, Jean McGarry, Erin McGraw, and Joyce Carol Oates also deserve notice.

The purpose of this collection is to introduce some of these writers, for despite Fanning's recognition they remain a surprisingly ignored cohort within the field of Irish studies. For years, Irish studies conferences rarely included papers or panels discussing Irish American women. Until 2001 Kathleen McInerney's work on Elizabeth Cullinan was a notable exception, unique amidst the exegeses of Irish and Irish American males. At that point, Sally Barr Ebest introduced an array of contemporary Irish American women writers in a paper at the Midwest Regional American Conference on Irish Studies.[2] This presentation caught the interest of Mary Ann Ryan, who began researching the roots of Tess Gallagher. However, not until a call for papers was circulated internationally did other scholars emerge. The contributors in this collection hail from across the United States, but they also come from as far away as England and Hong Kong. Clearly, interest in the writing of Irish American women existed; it simply lacked a unifying nexus. *Too Smart to Be Sentimental* provides that space.

In this collection the term *Irish American* is defined by geography as well as birth. Maeve Brennen, for example, was born in Ireland and then moved to America, whereas the other authors can trace their Irish lineage through their forebears. This ethnic doubleness allows the authors to draw on what Vincent Buckley calls their "source-country"—"a source in the sense that the psyche grows from and in it, and remains profoundly attuned to it . . . provid[ing] an artist with images, history, language, manners, myths, ways of perceiving, and ways of communicating"—regardless of residence (qtd. in Fanning 358). William Kennedy provides a gloss on this definition when noting that if Irish Americans "set out to discover themselves, to wonder about why they are what they are, then they'll run into a psychological inheritance that's even more than psychological. That may also be genetic, or biopsycho-genetic. . . . But whether from North or

South, whether Catholic or Protestant, some element of life, of consciousness, that is different from being Hispanic, or Oriental, or WASP. These traits endure" (qtd. in Fanning 312).

As Irish Americans assimilated to life in the United States, measuring these traits became more difficult; nevertheless, these writers' literary works remain recognizably Irish. Thematically, they can be identified by the presence of "explicit images, places, names, historical events, legends, folklore, patterns and customs both familiar and cultural; and stylistically by virtue of an implicit 'mode' . . . habits of perception, language retained or remembered" (Fanning 359). Many of these traits can be traced to James T. Farrell, whose "regional realis[m] created a solid base of Irish-American fiction" (Fanning 359). Throughout the twentieth century and into the twenty-first, writers such as Maureen Howard, Elizabeth Cullinan, and Erin McGraw continue this tradition as they write about the Catholic Church and explore working-class life (Fanning 377).

This summary of Irish American literary characteristics may strike some readers as definitive, while others might question the notion of a static definition. In his introduction to *Private Histories: The Writing of Irish Americans, 1900–1935*, Ron Ebest addresses this issue. Noting that recent scholars "have regarded ethnic identity as fluid, situational, and subjective; a question of collective identification" (7), he argues that ethnic identity has thus evolved into "self-identification." Those writers who identify as Irish American choose to do so. This does not mean that their identity is "arbitrary or fictional; not anyone, after all, can be Irish; ancestry, no matter how elastic intermarriage may make the definition, remains the crucial element. What it does mean is that to some degree . . . Irish-American ethnicity is an expression neither of nationality, nor of religion, nor of class, nor of race. It is an expression of desire" (7). Self-identification is evident in the works of Mary McCarthy, Mary Gordon, and Eileen Myles.

What about those writers who neither draw on their source country nor self-identify? Fanning maintains that they too may be characterized as Irish American if their work contains the following traits:

> The dominant mother in her fortress house; the first son marching off to the priesthood; the convent-educated daughter playing the piano in the parlor; parochial schoolmates turning into leaders of the Young Men's Sodality or incorrigible criminals; lives affected by extremes of

dissipation, abstinence, profligacy, and piety; lives organized around ideas of religion, family, nationhood for Ireland, hard work, home-ownership, the rise to respectability; tableaus of ritual gathering at deathbeds and christenings, weddings and wakes; the gift of humor and invective in public speech joined to an inability to express love and compassion in private; a penchant stylistically for formal experimentation, linguistic exuberance, and satiric modes. (3)

Alice McDermott prefers assimilation to self-identification. Her novel *At Weddings and Wakes*, however, not only takes its title from the above definition but also includes many of its identifying traits. So does her award-winning *Charming Billy*, whose plot emanates from Billy's death from alcoholism—an Irish and Irish American theme touched on by Mary McCarthy and running throughout the works of Joyce Carol Oates, Tess Gallagher, and Eileen Myles. Interestingly, how the disease is addressed seems to depend on their characters' relationships with the alcoholic: exploring the Irish American community's response, McDermott includes every point of view; taking the daughter's stance, Gallagher and Myles offer a more benign portrait; conversely, viewing alcoholism from the wife's point of view, McCarthy and Oates detail physical violence and broken domestic relationships. Nevertheless, in the majority of Oates's novels and short stories, she neither identifies herself as Irish American nor focuses on her heritage. Similarly, the works of other "non-identifiers"—Mary McGarry Morris, Jean McGarry, and Tess Gallagher—exhibit clear-cut "regional realism" in their settings; possess explicitly Irish names such as Fiona Range and Martha Horgan, Peggy Curran and Joe Keefe, Mr. Gallivan and Bernadine, respectively; and are propelled by plots hinging upon fatalism, forgiveness, and redemption.

In sum, the Irish American women introduced in this collection represent an amalgamation of the traits identified by Fanning. Maureen Howard describes these writers as "realistic, too smart to give in to the sentimental"—a phrase so apt we decided to make it our title. "If there is a vision that draws together Irish-American women writers," Howard continues, "it is a culture of commerce as much as the duties and privileges of home and of proud, self-defining rebellion. . . . We seem a sturdy lot—sworn to both love and duty—though we can never cut free of our promise to others or to ourselves but can only write as best we can: green thoughts" (qtd. in Kearns, *Cabbage and Bones* xiii).

Updating the Irish American Literary Tradition

Maureen Howard's "green thoughts" bring to mind things Irish, one obvious reason why these writers deserve recognition in the field of Irish Studies. Irish American women represent one half—the female half—of the Irish literary tradition in America. In *The Irish Voice in America* Fanning categorized this tradition as comprising four areas: "past lives, public lives, private lives, and stylized lives" (313). Past lives refers to historical novels and public lives to novels describing the "world of work"; novels of private lives focus on domestic issues, while stylized lives tend to follow the modernist tradition by emphasizing style. Fanning cites Thomas Flanagan as the author best representing novels of past lives, Edwin O'Connor as the central figure in novels of public lives, Elizabeth Cullinan as the epitome of novels of private lives, and William Kennedy as the most prominent chronicler of stylized lives. Yet Irish American women could just as easily represent every category. The works of these women underscore the many ways these traits endure.

Rather than draw on a literary tradition that tends to overlook women, perhaps a better way to categorize Irish American women writers is to demonstrate their parallels with their Irish sisters. Volumes 4 and 5 of *The Field Day Anthology of Irish Literature: Irish Women's Writing and Traditions* are organized around the following themes: Religion, Science, Technology, and Ethics; Sexuality; Oral Traditions; Politics; Women in Society; Women's Writing; and Feminism, Culture, and Critique. Although this rubric encompasses Irish women's writing from 600 to 2001, when applied to contemporary Irish American women, it places them firmly within the Irish literary tradition while simultaneously providing them with a thematic "room of their own."

Obviously, we could not include every contemporary Irish American female fiction writer in this collection. Instead, we have chosen studies that best reflect the Irish American version of the above themes. To demonstrate the parallels between Irish and Irish American women writers, the chapters are grouped according to the relevant *Field Day* categories, adapted for an American context: Women in Irish American Society; Religion and Ethics; Oral Traditions; Sexuality; and Feminism, Culture, and Critique. Each chapter describes the author's key works by drawing on relevant criticism, discussing how she is representative of Irish American voices, and contextualizing these findings with biographical information. Just as Irish

American identity is fluid, so too are the categories used to organize this volume. As the following discussion reveals, thematically most authors could be placed into more than one area; moreover, most of their work reflects some aspect of Fanning's Irish American paradigm. The abundance of such identifiers places these women firmly within the Irish American literary tradition.

Women in Irish American Society

In her introduction to the section entitled "Women in Irish Society, 1200–2000" in the *Field Day Anthology*, co-editor Maria Luddy writes that

> The restrictions placed on women's lives have always tended to be more repressive than those placed on the lives of men. These restrictions often reflected the traditional beliefs of men, and sometimes, women, regarding what women could or should be, or do in society. This is not to say, however, that they should be viewed as helpless victims. As the writing of women's history over the last three decades of the twentieth century demonstrated, women were in many instances active agents of their own fate. (5: 461)

Although Luddy is describing women in Irish society, her words apply equally to their Irish American counterparts. In *Modern Feminist Thought* Imelda Whelehan describes the period of 1970–90 as "a movement from creativity to sophistication" in American radical feminist politics (130). In Irish American women's writing, however, this political ferment can be traced to the 1940s. Mary McCarthy's novels and short stories mark the literary inception of this movement.

In her first collection of short stories, *The Company She Keeps* (1942), McCarthy's alter-ego Meg Sargent breaks her wedding vows and her subsequent engagement, arguing that sexual freedom applies to both men and women even as she second guesses her choices. Although adultery becomes a subplot in *A Charmed Life* (1955), the same beliefs can be seen in the seduction of Martha/Mary McCarthy by Miles/Edmund Wilson. In *The Group* (1963), McCarthy's breakout novel about the lives of seven Vassar graduates from the class of 1933, the reader listens to each of the women declare her intellectual independence, only to watch this independence be eroded by society's expectations as embodied in their husbands and lovers. In chapter 1 Sally Barr Ebest demonstrates how such behavior parallels McCarthy's own as she moved among four husbands and numerous lovers. McCarthy dealt with this dichotomy by exploring the reasons for such behavior in her memoirs—*Memories of a Catholic Girlhood, How I Grew,* and the posthumous *Intellectual Memoirs*—and by distancing herself via satire. While satire represents a long-respected literary tradition among McCarthy's male Irish forebears, her usage garnered anger and disdain from her male contemporaries. Yet rather than shrink from their epithets, McCarthy generated a body of critical reviews, political treatises, satirical novels, and short stories unique among women of her generation. She was indeed an "active agent" of her own fate.

The 1975 publication of Maureen Howard's memoir, *Facts of Life,* suggests continuing agency among Irish American writers. In chapter 2 Patricia Keefe Durso reveals the complicated and multilayered psychological journey through and beyond the personal territory of the Irish American "family core." According to Durso, Howard stretches the familiar domestic scene to address the "violence underneath . . . the emotional violence and tragedy and displacement." By employing an unconventional and intricate narrative approach, Howard's fiction reflects and structures her characters' psychic dislocation. Winner of the National Book Critics Circle Award, reviewers compared the cinematic qualities of *Facts of Life* to James Joyce. Howard herself, writes Durso, describes her own commitment to writing—like Joyce's—as performance. In *Natural History,* Durso argues, Howard integrates the "language of theater and film, sideshow and circus, show tunes . . . . [P]erformative effects are achieved not with a sleight of hand but a sleight of words, not with death-defying acts but with convention-defying narratives." Indeed, the "Double Entry" section of *Natural History* delineates the characters' complicated relationship with their Irish histories and their current displacements. Ireland, called "The Other Side," is unreachable and distant, with the protagonist "confined" to the "left side of the page . . . as marginalia, diddling with apocrypha"—the stories and memories of Ireland. Durso notes that nostalgia for home similarly "contaminates" the characters in *Big as Life* and *A Lover's Almanac:* the sentimentalizing of a past through myth and fairy tale distorts our vision of home in the "natural world" and cripples our ability to see the "necessary detail."

In contrast, John Menaghan's chapter, "Moments of Kindness, Moments of Recognition: The Achievement of Maeve Brennan" (chapter 3), locates the cultural pressures on Brennan as an adolescent émigré in the United States. After growing up in Dublin during one of the most volatile periods in Irish history, as an adult Brennan chose to live, for the most part, in New York City. Yet she places most of her characters in Ireland. Through her novels the tropes of Irish and Irish American political and psychological exile offer an early example of "ethnic doubleness." Menaghan observes that mapping Brennan's fiction is complicated, and he argues that the usual understanding of exile as Joycean in her fiction is less than accurate, because she is "a writer who brought her fierce intelligence, sharp eye and stunning command of language to bear on the two worlds she knew best, and who in the process became, again like Joyce but distinct from him, a writer both quintessentially Irish and at the same time international in her vision, scope and . . . impact on writers and readers around the world." In fact, Menaghan suggests that Brennan's writing more accurately reflects the attentions of her mentor at the *New Yorker*, William Maxwell. While distinctly unsentimental in her representation of the Irish and Irish American experience, Brennan offers a compassionate view of the exiled who "have . . . lost their way in the world," clearly an appropriate theme in the twenty-first century.

Religion and Ethics

Margaret MacCurtain, editor of the *Field Day*'s section on "Religion, Science, Theology, and Ethics, 1500–2000," notes that Irish women began to find their voice concerning these subjects in the last quarter of the twentieth century. Again, among Irish American women this voice was raised earlier, in part because of the Catholic Church's political activities. During the 1960s and 1970s groups such as the Sister Formation Movement, the Grail, and the Catholic Family Movement (CFM) sought to promote a feminist agenda along with social action and ran afoul of church authorities. Members of the Grail were chastised and evicted from church property for their independent activities (Kalven). The CFM eventually broke with the church after dissident members of the Papal Commission persuaded the pope to reaffirm the ban on artificial birth control in the 1968 *Humanae Vitae* (Ruether 6–7). According to feminist theologian Rosemary Radford Ruether, "For Catholic women Vatican II correlated with trends in American society and culture in a way that had an explosively transformative effect," leading to agitation for "social criticism and reform in American society" via the civil rights movement in the 1960s and, in 1965, through the "rebirth of feminism that had been left truncated by the Depression and the Second World War" (7).

Although Mary McCarthy was one of the first contemporary Irish American female writers to criticize the Catholic Church, apart from explorations regarding her loss of faith in *Memories of a Catholic Girlhood* (1957), she did not explicitly concern herself with religion. Similarly, although Maureen Howard's *Bridgeport Bus* (1961) rejects the hypocrisy of the church, her subsequent novels are more concerned with secular issues. With the publication of Elizabeth Cullinan's *House of Gold* (1970), however, the gloves came off through the story of a mother who stifles her children's lives through Catholic guilt.

Fanning argues that *House of Gold* "exemplifies contemporary Irish-American domestic fiction at its best . . . a definitive portrait of crippling psychic damage that can occur within Irish-American families" (335). The protagonist of the novel, Elizabeth Carroll, and her siblings gather for an event familiar to readers of Irish and Irish American fiction: the dying of the matriarch. In chapter 4 Kathleen McInerney explains how through the lens of the dutiful daughter, Elizabeth reveals the power of the Irish American mother over her children's and grandchildren's lives and the pervasive effort of the matriarch to silence and control those around her. With characteristically Irish and Irish American gallows humor, Cullinan illuminates the psychic debts accrued by Irish Catholic women whose families seek respectability in the United States. In her autobiographical fiction, Cullinan's characters struggle to resist the oppressive obedience fortified by an immigrant culture of anxiety and to give voice to the psychological experience of creating an identity within, and despite, the constrictions of the Irish American culture of church and family. But Cullinan is not alone.

In "Confessions of a Reluctant Catholic," Alice McDermott describes the genesis of her narrative style and focus:

> Gradually, as the pattern of my own work began to come clear, I began to understand that this repetition of what might be called Catholic themes, Catholic language, had meaning that I did not at first recognize, meaning that went far beyond matters of craft and convenience and material at hand. Gradually—no lightning bolts here—I began

to realize that the language of the church, my church, was not only a means to an end in my fiction but an essential part of my own understanding of the world.

Catholicism, she continues, "was the native language of my spirit" (16). The theme of faith increasingly pervades McDermott's novels, most notably in At Weddings and Wakes, Charming Billy, and Child of My Heart.

In "Storyteller's Work: Alice McDermott's Narrators" (chapter 4), Beatrice Jacobson claims that McDermott's trademark combination of character and narrator reflects authorial duality: although she eschews labels such as feminist, Catholic, or Irish American, McDermott's novels explore the impact of these roles (and the expectations they convey) on her female characters. The unnamed female narrator in Charming Billy, like Theresa in Child of My Heart, reflects the fledgling feminist characteristics of independence and directness, just as McDermott's Catholic language, themes, and settings reveal "the native language of [her] spirit." Such duality reflects the Irish American woman writer's attempts to reconcile past and present, Ireland and America, feminism and Catholicism, writer and mother, realism and postmodernism. Thus, while McDermott underscores her family's insistent assimilation and her own (earlier) rejection of the church, her female narrators display characteristically Irish storytelling skills as they construct and deconstruct family lore and interweave secular, mystical, and spiritual beliefs.

Cullinan and McDermott provide readers with two different visions of religion and ethics among contemporary Irish Americans. While Cullinan offers satirical warnings regarding the imposition of religion on one's children, McDermott asks us to consider the role and necessity of faith in a near-apocalyptic world.

Oral Traditions

In her introduction to the section on oral traditions, Field Day co-editor Angela Bourke suggests that addressing oral traditions in a collection of written work might strike some readers as "anomalous." Nevertheless, she continues, such texts often trace their genesis to works that were originally "spoken, recited, chanted or sung" (4: 1191). These can be categorized as life stories, folktales, traditions of storytelling, legends of the supernatural, songs lamenting the dead, expressions of spirituality and religion, work and play—and the writing that resulted from them. In Ireland oral traditions were initially collected and written by males; however, this changed in the late 1900s when Lady Gregory was introduced to the oral tradition after reading Yeats's *Celtic Twilight*. This experience led her to become what Patricia Lysaght calls "an important and assiduous female collector and compiler of works on Irish folklore" (*Field Day Anthology* 4: 1434), which ultimately, in 1945, led to J. H. Delargy's recognition that "women excelled in the branch of tradition called *seanchas*, which included 'many tales of a short realistic type about fairies, ghosts, and other supernatural beings'" (*Field Day Anthology* 4: 1435).

One characteristic of the Irish oral tradition is its reliance on legends. According to Bourke and Lysaght, legends most often came out of rural Ireland, where the Catholic residents believed in heaven and hell and the triune God. These stories dealt with the supernatural, "subtly moulded to fill in the spaces left in Christian discourse or to mediate its occasional contradictions" (*Field Day Anthology* 4: 1435). Unlike folk or fairytales, legends "deal with a more-or-less recent past; instead of princes, princesses, widows' daughters, and giants, they deal with 'real' people, often very similar to the members of their audience . . . [and] their central 'plot' is usually an extraordinary encounter of some kind," quite often involving an animal (*Field Day Anthology* 4: 1435).

Tess Gallagher and Joyce Carol Oates clearly draw on this tradition. One characteristic of Gallagher's writing is the practice of "borrowing," a concept by which Irish storytellers claim others' stories as their own. The eponymous story in Gallagher's short story collection *The Lover of Horses* underscores her mastery of legend. In addition to elaborating on the legend of the narrator's grandfather, a horse whisperer, Gallagher's story draws on the oral tradition of lamenting the dead, "a central theatre of women's expression in the Irish language," most often concerning the death of a man (*Field Day Anthology* 4: 1365–66). Like her foremothers, Gallagher's narrator finds herself keening "a soft crooning of syllables that was satisfying to my ears, but ultimately useless and absurd" (*Lover of Horses* 16). In this case, Gallagher's narrator is lamenting the imminent death of her father, a man known for his drinking and gambling, both of which likely contributed to his demise. Here, too, the story resembles the oral tradition in that "the messages conveyed could be coded" (*Field Day Anthology* 4: 1367)—in this case, caveats regarding the perils of drink, a theme reprised in many of Gallagher's other stories.

As Mary Ann Ryan demonstrates in chapter 6, Tess Gallagher's roots place her firmly within the Irish American community, and her travels to Ireland lend her a sense of ethnic doubleness. Her fiction reveals not only her awareness of these ancestral bonds but also her lyrical, stylistic facility. Although her reputation was gained through her poetry, Gallagher displays the same virtuosity in the short story through what Kathryn Robinson calls "brilliant wordplay" as well as her combination of "plain speech and large vision."[3] In *The Lover of Horses* and *At the Owl Woman Saloon*, Gallagher draws on the physical beauty of the Pacific Northwest to explore themes common to both the Irish and Irish Americans—the power of memory and imagination, the loss of language, the effects of mistranslation, the need for faith, and the effects of these on identity.

It is probably not coincidental that Charles Fanning's best-known work is entitled *The Irish Voice in America*. One characteristic of the Irish voice is satire; another is "blarney," the "gift of gab." In discussing Irish American novels of public lives—"novels largely concerned with Irish-American experience on the job and outside the home, novels about priests, politicians, businessmen, policemen and firemen, and other public servants"—Fanning notes that they embody "an important, and very Irish, thread . . . a fascination with the spoken word, with talk" (316–17). Fanning finds this fascination most evident in Edwin O'Connor's political novel *The Last Hurrah*. The novel's success, Fanning writes, derives "mostly through talk." The same may be said for O'Connor's *The Edge of Sadness* (1961), in which once again "talk itself is of paramount concern" (319). These same traits characterize Joyce Carol Oates's most Irish novel, *What I Lived For*.

As Susana Araujo observes in chapter 7, *What I Lived For* satirizes the very public life of Jerome "Corky" Corcoran, a successful real estate broker with a promising career in local politics. Araujo notes that Corky possesses the stereotypical Irish traits of drinking, fighting, and blarney, which not surprisingly get him into trouble. Indeed, the juxtaposition of Corky's pursuit of the American dream while subordinating his lower-class roots provides the tragicomic axis of the novel. Throughout, Oates plays the Irish sense of fatalism and American optimism against one another; however, the novel rises above stereotypes to explore what Araujo describes as "the complex realities running through these two staples of national identities, creating a self-reflexive and multifaceted tragicomedy."

Like Edwin O'Connor, Oates's novel "celebrates the Irish-American gift of gab"; she does so through a similar, if not superior, "command of traditional narrative techniques and a good ear for the rhythms of . . . talk"

(Fanning 324). Unlike O'Connor, Oates has emerged as one of the twentieth century's most prolific and preeminent authors. Recipient of the National Book Award, the PEN/Malamud Award for Excellence in Short Fiction, the Common Wealth Award for Distinguished Service in Literature, the *New York Times Book Review* Notable Book of the Year, and the *Kenyon Review* Award for Literary Achievement; nominated for the Pulitzer Prize; member of the American Academy of Arts and Letters; and author of numerous novels, novellas, short story collections, children's books, plays, memoirs, and other nonfiction works, Joyce Carol Oates is a welcome addition to the Irish American canon.

Sexuality

When Edna O'Brien published *The Country Girls* in 1965, Ireland banned it because of its unprecedented depictions of female sexuality. According to Irish journalist Mary Kenny, "Edna became the first Irishwoman to assert her own sexuality boldly and to demand, as a right, the sexual freedom that men have traditionally enjoyed" (240). Not surprisingly, O'Brien's novels and stories were "regarded as breaking new ground for women" (Kenny 240). But more than two decades before O'Brien raised the ire of the Irish, Mary McCarthy was raising Irish American eyebrows with graphic descriptions of her adulterous, seductive, and easily seduced heroines. On both sides of the ocean, these authors' portrayals of heterosexual love and longing were unheard of in the post-Eisenhower, prefeminist years. They opened the bedroom doors to reveal women's sexuality—and the men who prey on it.

These themes pervade the novels of Mary McGarry Morris. According to Patricia Gott in chapter 8, "the bad girls and boys of Mary McGarry Morris's fiction"—*Vanished* (1988), *A Dangerous Woman* (1991), *Songs in Ordinary Time* (1995), *Fiona Range* (2000), *A Hole in the Universe* (2004), and *The Lost Mother* (2005)—are presented in stark, unsentimental terms as they negotiate a cruel and unfair world. Morris's female characters often find themselves betrayed by their own sex, which in this context denotes their gender, behavior, and companions. In *A Dangerous Woman* Martha Horgan is branded a misfit as a child and later ridiculed and assaulted by a group of teenaged boys. Through her story, Morris shows the damaging effects of repression, hypocrisy, and betrayal. In *Songs in Ordinary Time*

Marie and her mother Alice are victims of deceit and manipulation by men, including a predatory priest. Invoking parallels to Joyce, Gott observes that Morris's "characters' Irish ethnicity and the latent Catholicism . . . lurk below the surface to indicate some of the familial and social pressures they face." In *Fiona Range* Morris concerns herself less with grotesque figures, evolving into a "sympathetic contemporary chronicler of lonely, dispossessed women." This time the "bad girl" who resists family and cultural pressures emerges by novel's end with her identity reinvented and her character redeemed by exposing the sexual depravity of the family patriarch.

While Irish and Irish American readers have perhaps grown complacent about heterosexual relationships, homosexuality is another matter. Siobhan Kilfeather, co-editor of the *Field Day* section on "The Erosion of Heterosexual Consensus, 1940–2001," reveals that from 1900 to 1975 "Irish writing on homosexuality was characterized by indirection and oblique reference." However, the end of the century witnessed an increasingly "in your face gay aesthetic" by male and female writers alike (4: 1040). This is one area in which Irish women writers have clearly preceded their Irish American counterparts. Indeed, in her research on the subject, Emma Donoghue discovered "at least two dozen Irish writers, from the late eighteenth century to the late twentieth [who] have touched on lesbian themes in their works" (*Field Day Anthology* 4: 1090). Contemporary writers Mary Dorcey, Emma Donoghue, and Medbh McGuckian are no doubt familiar to readers of Irish literature, but Irish Americans may be hard-pressed to name even one Irish American writer who has explored lesbian themes in her work. Enter Eileen Myles.

A contemporary of Emma Donoghue, Myles may be the first Irish American woman writer to exit the closet. Like Donoghue's *Stir-Fry* (1994), Myles's nonfiction novel, *Cool for You* (2000), traces her coming of age amidst growing recognition of her sexual preferences. Unlike Donoghue, Myles rejects the traditional narrative approach in favor of a series of vignettes. As Kathleen Kremins's title for chapter 9, "Blurring Boundaries," suggests, Myles's novels, *Chelsea Girls* and *Cool for You*, resist convention by blending genres and by presenting herself sometimes as narrator, sometimes as character. This duality allows her to develop traditional Irish American themes of isolation and the paradox of memory, recounted in ironic and mocking tones, while at the same time exploring formerly verboten issues surrounding sex and sexual identity. Myles herself is a hybrid:

half Polish and half Irish American, Irish Catholic and lesbian, sometimes middle class and sometimes lower class depending on the severity of her father's alcoholism. Needless to say, alcoholism is a staple of Irish and Irish American writing, but here, too, Myles blurs boundaries, describing her father as a "better" alcoholic than others she knew—kind and loving rather than angry and loud. Perhaps because of this she tends to identify more with him than with her mother, who in turn perpetuates the stereotype of the distant Irish matriarch. Such portraits move Myles's works well beyond the boundaries of the *bildungsroman*, taking Irish American women's writing into the twenty-first century.

Feminism, Culture, and Critique

As most readers are no doubt aware, the 1991 publication of *The Field Day Anthology* raised an outcry when women discovered that its editor, Seamus Deane, had ignored the contributions of Irish women writers. The resulting outrage was so overwhelming that the publishers agreed to publish subsequent volumes to rectify this blatant "oversight." Clair Wills, editor of the *Field Day*'s section on "Feminism, Culture and Critique in English," suggests that the subsequent editorial acquiescence and the 2002 publication of volumes 4 and 5 "are testament to the impact feminism has made on Irish cultural and intellectual life, and the vitality of contemporary feminist debate in Ireland" (5: 1578). Can the same be said about Irish American feminist writing?

As noted earlier, Mary McCarthy's novels and short stories, published in the 1940s, represent perhaps the first Irish American feminist works. These were followed by the *bildungsromane* of the 1960s, 1970s, and 1980s, best exemplified in Irish American novels such as Maureen Howard's *Bridgeport Bus* (1961) and Mary Gordon's *Final Payments* (1978). Interestingly, Charles Fanning has nothing but praise for Howard, yet he dismisses Mary Gordon's *Final Payments* as "fueled by personal rage and bitterness at the perceived excesses, distortions, and injustices of Irish-American Catholic family life." Fanning views Gordon's characters as caricatures—intolerant extremists, hateful whiners, and "mawkish alcoholics" (329). "There is no scrap of community here," he writes, "only embarrassing nets to be escaped. And escape Isabel does—to ill-considered sex, a reactionary self-immolation as Margaret Casey's servant, and a final movement up and out toward a new life" (330).

Even a feminist reading of the book would find Isabel's father extreme, Margaret hateful, and Isabel's sexual escapades ill-advised. However, this stance also provides a different perspective. Jeana Delrosso argues that Catholic girlhood narratives—which *Final Payments* most certainly is— probe "the intersections of gender and Catholicism . . . [to] expose the diverse, often seemingly contradictory positions from which women write about Catholicism today, in which they variously view the church as vehicle of repression, of subversion, or of liberation" (5: 1394). In detailing Isabel's coming-of-age, Gordon presents the church as both repressive and eventually liberating.

In chapter 10 Susana Hoeness-Krupsaw analyzes Gordon's feminist side. She observes that Mary Gordon writes frequently of parent-child relationships as well as shame and guilt as psychic artifacts of an Irish American Catholic girlhood. As in Howard's *Bridgeport Bus*, Mary Gordon's characters are often challenged by the moral issues of caring, or not caring enough, for a dying parent. In *Final Payments* Isabel Moore struggles with reinventing her life and identity after years of sacrificing herself to her father. Felicitas, in *The Company of Women*, learns to resist the obedience demanded by Father Cyprion, but she is psychologically equipped to do so only after the birth of her own child. Gathering around the dying matriarch in *The Other Side*, the children rewrite their family narrative as a way of understanding and coming to terms with their collective history as immigrants. Revealing ethnic and class consciousness in addition to gendered themes, Gordon's fiction, poetry, and critical essays speak directly to the power relationships between men and women within the family and the church, creating a vision of Irish American women's identity affirmed within communities of supportive women.

In the late 1980s and early 1990s the U.S. feminist movement seemed to be treading water. In the public sector its stasis was due largely to the efforts of the New Right, who enjoyed the full support of the Reagan administration to dismantle or disrupt the gains made in the previous twenty years (see Faludi). In the private sector, particularly in academia, internal bickering between various feminist factions similarly precluded any progress. What had appeared to be solidarity in the 1970s was revealed to be "primarily, the province of highly educated, white middle-class heterosexual women." As these disagreements became public, "women found they had less, not more, in common and a bitterness developed in the will to discover who had the most 'authentic' voice for the women's movement" (Whelehan 129–30).

Jean McGarry's fiction embodies this understanding. Rather than raise specifically feminist issues, her characters reenact the early immigrants' sense of isolation and loneliness as they move from small town to big city only to find that no place is home. In chapter 11 Amy Lee traces the evolution of McGarry's fiction from short stories to novels. Lee argues that the early collections serve as a proving ground for McGarry's subsequent novels, for *Airs of Providence* (1985) and *The Very Rich Hours* (1987) are notable for their interrelated stories about death and dying, disappointment and disillusion. These themes are then reprised in her short story collections, *The Courage of Girls* (1992), *Home at Last* (1994), *Gallagher's Travels* (1997), and *Dream Date* (2002). This emphasis on dreams and dreaming allows McGarry to carry these familiar tropes beyond the Irish American community and apply these same yearnings to late twentieth-century alienation.

McGarry's themes suggest the refraction of both American and Irish American feminism at the dawn of the twenty-first century; however, just as she rejects purely feminist themes, her contemporary, Erin McGraw, embraces them. In *Lies of the Saints* (1996) McGraw's characters question women's roles in the family and on the job, implicitly arguing for equality. With the publication of *The Baby Tree* (2002) she raises the issue of abortion rights. To demonstrate her frustration with the Catholic Church's refusal to allow women to the priesthood, McGraw makes her protagonist, Kate Gussey, a Methodist minister.[4] Yet this novel is neither a diatribe nor a fairy tale. McGraw uses her heroine as a vehicle to explore the difficulties of maintaining a congregation and a marriage, of believing in a woman's right to choose but recognizing that such freedom bears responsibilities. Light years from the messages conveyed by McGraw's Irish American foremothers, the novel retains traditional Irish American traits in its focus on motherhood, relationships, and life in the public eye while subtly questioning the Catholic Church's stance on female clergy. It is only fitting that a study of McGraw conclude this collection, for she epitomizes the Irish American literary tradition while moving its boundaries ever farther.

The Contributions of Contemporary Irish American Women Writers

When asked why he failed to include Irish women in the original three volumes of *The Field Day Anthology*, Seamus Deane implied that it simply did not occur to him. Nuala Ni Dhomhnaill notes that those original volumes, as well as volumes 4 and 5 devoted to women's literature, which were "conceived as an afterthought . . . epitomize the territorial attitudes and 'gender-blindness'" Irish women scholars have fought throughout their careers (4). Granted, American writers have enjoyed a modicum of scholarly attention in the past thirty years; however, Irish American women writers have been similarly overlooked. Although Charles Fanning introduced them, Caitriona Maloney and Helen Thompson interviewed six (out of seventeen), and Caledonia Kearns has published two collections of their work, to date no scholars have seen fit to pursue in-depth studies of Irish American women's writing. But if "green thoughts" equal fresh ideas, then these women deserve recognition, for they have both continued and expanded the Irish American literary tradition.

Before 1942 "Women in Irish American Society" would have been an impossible theme, for the denizens of Irish American women's fiction did not venture beyond their homes. In the early twentieth century Gertrude M. O'Reilly and Elinor Macartney Lane continued the sentimental literary tradition centered around home and family, and although Kathleen Norris and Clara Laughlin attempted realism, they soon "abandoned the enterprise" (Fanning 242). Between 1900 and 1930 Anne O'Hagan, Kathleen Conway, and Myra Kelly maintained a similar focus (R. Ebest). The 1930s and 1940s found Kathleen Coyle, Margaret Marchand, Mary Deasy, Ellin MacKay Berlin, and Mary Doyle Curran exploring tensions between first- and second-generation Irish immigrants "betwixt and between" cultures; nevertheless, these authors maintained the focus on domestic issues (Fanning 298).

To a certain extent, this tradition has been continued in the works of contemporary Irish American women writers, for much of their work often revolves around what Fanning has termed "private lives" (328). This focus is only natural, he argues, for "Ethnic identity is first of all a family affair; it grows from customs and attitudes, stated and unstated, that are grounded in family life" (328). Certainly Elizabeth Cullinan, Alice McDermott, and Mary Gordon fall directly into this category even as they question the mores traditionally associated with home and family.

At the same time, Mary McCarthy, Maureen Howard, Maeve Brennan, Joyce Carol Oates, and Erin McGraw have expanded this tradition into the realm of what Fanning describes as "public lives"—the "Irish-American experience on the job and outside the home" (316). Long considered the domain of male writers, the female characters developed by contemporary Irish American women have left their homes and their churches to explore working life and its effects on themselves and those they have left at home.

"Religion and Ethics" have traditionally been associated with the writing of Irish American women, epitomized by nineteenth-century writer Mary Ann Sadlier. According to Ron Ebest, Sadlier (and her male counterparts) "idealized Irish-American womanhood as the living vessel of traditional Celtic ethno-religious values. Fidelity to one's mother meant fidelity to Ireland and the Church" (108). Although idealization of the literary matriarch began to fade at the beginning of the twentieth century, Irish American women's positive associations with the church continued. In her early novels Alice McDermott implicitly reaffirmed the importance of faith. In the aftermath of 9/11, however, McDermott, like Tess Gallagher, has moved religion and ethics beyond the church into nature and toward spirituality. At the same time, Irish American women's writing is identifiable by its questioning of traditional religious figures and their faith. McCarthy's ultimate loss of faith, explored in *Memories of a Catholic Girlhood*, opened the sanctuary door. Throughout the twentieth century and into the twenty-first, Irish American women have critiqued the Catholic Church: Mary McCarthy, Maureen Howard, Elizabeth Cullinan, and Erin McGraw attack its hypocrisy, while Mary Gordon and Jean McGarry sometimes question its necessity.

Conversely, the Irish oral tradition remains a staple. After their immigration Irish Americans continued this tradition in the form of "American Celticism," which Fanning traces from the 1700s through the late 1800s. Father Hugh Quigley incorporated Irish folktales into his 1854 novel *The Prophet of the Ruined Abbey*. In that same year Robert Shelton collected "Irish stories and legends" into *Bits of Blarney*, followed shortly thereafter by Robert Dwyer's *Legends of the Wars in Ireland* (1868); Patrick Donahoe's *Irish Fireside Tales* (1871) and *Ballads of Irish Chivalry* (1872); P. M. Haverty's *Legends and Fairy Tales of Ireland* (1872), *Deirdre* (1876), and *Blanid* (1879); and Jeremiah Curtin's *Myths and Folklore of Ireland* (1890). Unfortunately, such literature also led some to "unhealthy romanticizing of even the least attractive aspects of Irish life" and others to ignore or denigrate the contribution of Irish American literature (Fanning 171). Even more unfortunately, the worst perpetuator of the negative aspects of American Celticism was a woman, Louise Imogen Guiney, whose biographical sketches of Irish martyrs and heroes "rationalized, justified, and praised" defeat (Fanning 172). However, Fanning acknowledges that Anna C. Scanlan's *Der-*

vorgilla; or, The Downfall of Ireland (1895), whose Irish Helen of Troy supposedly contributed to the British invasion in 1170, "describes in great detail the customs, poetry and music of Gaelic Ireland before the invasion, to establish the sophistication of that culture" (173). As Fanning chronicles, late nineteenth-century and early twentieth-century Irish American fiction moved from folktales and morality tracts eventually to "realism and respectability." Nevertheless, some aspects of these early traits endure.

Mary McCarthy considered *The Group* "an experiment in marrying style with content, language with concept. Hence the clichés, the trivia, the group-speak" (qtd. in Brightman 492). Elizabeth Cullinan's *House of Gold* revolves around family interchanges, while Erin McGraw's Kate Gussey makes her ideas known from the pulpit in *The Baby Tree*. Joyce Carol Oates uses *How I Lived* to highlight Corky's blarney, just as Tess Gallagher's characters in *At the Owl Woman Saloon* and *The Lover of Horses* excel in storytelling. Still, not every Irish American woman continues this tradition. On the whole, they have been more likely to move beyond tradition to consider altogether new themes.

Neither "Sexuality" nor "Feminism, Culture, and Critique" have been considered traditional Irish American themes. Certainly Fanning does not address them. Caitriona Maloney and Helen Thompson, who raised these issues during their interviews with Irish and Irish American women writers, found that younger women tend to view feminism indifferently because that generation tends to misunderstand or deny its necessity (142). Nevertheless, regardless of age and political affiliation, the works of contemporary Irish American women writers fit the rubric of feminist novels.

The purpose of feminist novels is to "change the world." Gender and politics are intertwined in an attempt to reflect this arena of political struggle, while connection, community, and the "struggle against patriarchy" are often prominent themes leading to feelings of optimism about the prospect of future change. In these novels, male characters are no longer the most interesting, and powerful women are neither monstrous nor unfeminine. Instead, female experiences and value systems are examined and more likely to be reified, leading women readers to identify more easily with the characters and plots. The text/story is viewed as a manifestation of the author's voice because these novels rely on a personal voice conveying a sense of "interiority"—that is, the authors provide an inside look at the character's "heart and mind," which in turn often triggers a desire to "connect" with the text (Schweikert). Feminist novels by Irish American women in the past four decades reflect most if not all of these traits.

Despite her rejection of feminism, Mary McCarthy's focus on women's private lives, concerns, and actions places her among the first feminist writers of the twentieth century. In the 1970s and 1980s the *bildungsromane* of Mary Gordon and Maureen Howard portrayed the stirrings of the contemporary feminist movement in heroines who ignore the tradition of self-immolation through service to one's parent and learn to live independently. In the early 1990s novels by Mary McGarry Morris and Joyce Carol Oates repeatedly emphasize the need for connection and community as well as the ongoing struggle against patriarchy. In the late 1990s novels by Alice McDermott increasingly serve as a manifestation of the author's voice as she looks into her characters' hearts and minds, while the novels and short stories of the new millennium by Jean McGarry, Tess Gallagher, and Erin McGraw continue the focus on women's experiences and value systems by examining women's expanding roles as well as the price paid for that growth: isolation and alienation, anger and despair. Meanwhile, third-wave feminist Eileen Myles puts a new spin on the *bildungsroman* by examining the rites of passage experienced by lesbian protagonists. Through their writing, these women have expanded the thematic horizons of Irish American literature.

Just as Irish American women's novels have broken new political ground, they have also crafted their own literary tradition, revealed in what Alice McDermott has described as "Catholic themes, Catholic language," representing "the native language of [their] spirit" (12–16). Running throughout these novels are themes of guilt and repression, suffering and penance, transcendence and redemption, prayer and forgiveness, fatalism and free will, exploration and often rejection of traditional women's roles as daughter, wife, and mother. These themes alone might be enough to pronounce Irish American women's novels unique and deserving of attention, but ultimately the quality of writing determines their stature and commands our respect.

Writing for the *Nation*, Robert Kiely praised Mary McCarthy's *The Group* for its "virtuoso display of 'narrative mimicry'" set within a Jamesian comedy of manners (qtd. in Brightman 483). Elizabeth Cullinan's writing has been described as "remarkable for its combination of precise craftsmanship and authenticity to felt experience" (Fanning 334), while Maureen Howard "strain[s] at the boundaries of conventional narrative by means of abrupt shifts of tense and point of view and brief, epigrammatic shards" (345–46). Alice McDermott, winner of the National Book Award, has been praised for her lyrical narrative style. Similarly, Mary Gordon has won numerous awards, including a Guggenheim. The novels of Mary Mc-Garry Morris have been praised by none other than McDermott, who maintains that "Morris does not devise plots, but traps: steel-toothed, inescapable traps of circumstances and personality against which her characters struggle . . . and fail" ("Mary McGarry Morris"). Obviously, Joyce Carol Oates's reputation is both prodigious and above reproach, but newer writers such as Erin McGraw are also deserving of attention and praise. Although Tess Gallagher is known primarily as a poet, her two volumes of short stories are distinguished by her "lyrical prose" and "brilliant wordplay" as well as her "wholly original characters." Jean McGarry's novels and short stories are equally distinctive through her clever evocations of Irish American home life.

Clearly, these writers' contributions to the Irish American canon should be recognized, but so should those lesser-known but equally talented writers such as Maeve Brennan and Eileen Myles. *Too Smart to Be Sentimental* attempts to do so by introducing contemporary women into "one of the oldest and largest bodies of ethnic writing produced by members and descendants of a single American immigrant group" (Fanning 1).

Notes

1. As Fanning points out in *The Irish Voice in America*, Flannery O'Connor preferred to be regionally rather than ethnically labeled; consequently, her work is not addressed in this collection.

2. This paper was subsequently published as "These Traits Also Endure," *New Hibernia Review* 7.2 (Summer 2003): 55–72.

3. These Quotes appear on the cover of the 1986 edition of *The Lover of Horses*.

4. McGraw confirmed this interpretation in an email to Sally Barr Ebest in June 2004.

Works Cited

Brightman, Carol. *Writing Dangerously: Mary McCarthy and Her World*. New York: Clarkson Potter, 1992.

Casey, Daniel J., and Robert Rhodes. *Irish-American Fiction: Essays in Criticism*. New York: AMS Press, 1979.

Delrosso, Jeana. *Veiled Threats: Contemporary International Catholic Girlhood Narratives*. Diss. University of Maryland, College Park, 2000.

Ebest, Ron. *Private Histories: The Writing of Irish Americans, 1900–1935*. Notre Dame, IN: University of Notre Dame Press, 2005.

Faludi, Susan. *Backlash: The Undeclared War Against American Women*. New York: Doubleday, 1991.

Fanning, Charles. *The Irish Voice in America*. 2nd ed. Lexington: University of Kentucky Press, 2000.

Field Day Anthology of Irish Women's Writing and Traditions. Ed. Angela Bourke, Siobhan Kilfeather, Maria Luddy, Margaret Mac Curtain, Geraldine Meaney, Mairin Ni Dhonnchadha, Mary O'Dowd, and Clair Wills. Volumes 4 and 5. New York: New York University Press, 2002.

Gallagher, Tess. *The Lover of Horses*. New York: Harper and Row, 1986.

Kalven, Janet. "Feminism and Catholicism." *Reconciling Catholicism and Feminism?* Ed. Sally Barr Ebest and Ron Ebest. Notre Dame, IN: University of Notre Dame Press, 2003. 32–46.

Kearns, Caledonia, ed. *Cabbage and Bones: An Anthology of Irish American Women's Fiction*. New York: Holt, 1997.

———. *Motherland*. New York: William Morrow, 1999.

Kenny, Mary. *Goodbye to Catholic Ireland*. Dublin: New Island Books, 2000.

Maloney, Caitriona, and Helen Thompson. *Irish Women Writers Speak Out*. Syracuse: State University of New York Press, 2003.

"Mary McGarry Morris." Andover Authors. 20 Jul. 2003. 1 Aug. 2004 <http://www.mhl.org/community/authors.htm#mary>.

McDermott, Alice. "Confessions of a Reluctant Catholic." *Commonweal* 22 Feb. 2000: 12–16.

Ni Dhomhnaill, Nuala. "A Spectacular Flowering." *Irish Times* 29 May 1999: The Arts, 4.

Ruether, Rosemary Radford. "American Catholic Feminism: A History." *Reconciling Catholicism and Feminism?* Ed. Sally Barr Ebest and Ron Ebest. Notre Dame, IN: University of Notre Dame Press, 2003. 3–12.

Schweikert, Patrocinio. "Reading Ourselves: Toward a Feminist Theory of Reading." *Feminisms*. Ed. Robyn R. Warhol and Diane Price Herndl. New Brunswick, NJ: Rutgers University Press, 1991.

Whelehan, Imelda. *Modern Feminist Thought: From the Second Wave to "Post-Feminism."* New York: New York University Press, 1995.

WOMEN IN IRISH AMERICAN SOCIETY

CHAPTER 1

Mary McCarthy

Too Smart to Be Sentimental

SALLY BARR EBEST

It is only fitting that we begin this volume with Mary McCarthy, for she single-handedly reformulated the Irish American literary tradition characterizing her female predecessors. Charles Fanning describes the nineteenth- and twentieth-century Irish American literary tradition in the following terms:

> The dominant mother in her fortress house; the first son marching off to the priesthood; the convent-educated daughter playing the piano in the parlor; parochial schoolmates turning into leaders of the Young Men's Sodality or incorrigible criminals; lives affected by extremes of dissipation, abstinence, profligacy, and piety; lives organized around ideas of religion, family, nationhood for Ireland, hard work, home-ownership, the rise to respectability; tableaus of ritual gathering at deathbeds and christenings, weddings and wakes; the gift of humor

27

and invective in public speech joined to an inability to express love and compassion in private; a penchant stylistically for formal experimentation, linguistic exuberance, and satiric modes. (3)

While Mary McCarthy continued many of these traditions, she also updated them. In McCarthy's world, mothers have become their daughters' confidants, daughters are Vassar educated and work in business or politics, women are often promiscuous or adulterous, religion is secondary to politics, motherhood is frustrating, weddings perpetuate male dominance, marriages end in divorce,[1] and wakes commemorate suicides. At the same time, McCarthy's fiction continues the Irish American tendency toward "formal experimentation, linguistic exuberance, and satiric modes" (Fanning 3). But here, too, she breaks tradition: McCarthy is the first contemporary Irish American *woman* to be recognized for her satiric fiction. Her influence can be traced in the works of the Irish American women writers who followed.

Like McCarthy, novelists Mary McGarry Morris, Alice McDermott, Joyce Carol Oates, and Erin McGraw hesitate to associate themselves with Irish Catholicism, even though their fiction, like hers, reveals the church's influence through the themes of guilt and repression, suffering and penance, fatalism and free will. In developing these themes, McCarthy explores topics such as promiscuity, birth control, impotence, mental illness, and domestic abuse—topics previously taboo among her male and female predecessors. McCarthy's influence on later writers is evident: Elizabeth Cullinan and Maureen Howard debunk the mythical saintly Irish mother, Mary Gordon questions the self-immolation of daughters in service to their parents, Eileen Myles discusses lesbianism, and Erin McGraw features a prochoice female "priest."

Like Maureen Howard, Tess Gallagher, and Eileen Myles, McCarthy is best known for her writing style. Whereas Gallagher, like Alice McDermott, earned praise for her lyrical prose, McCarthy established her reputation via the "habit of satire." Defined by Fanning as "the use of the English language for the purpose of linguistic subversion" (6), satire, notes David Krause, comes naturally to the Irish: "In the oral and written Irish tradition, language itself, the power of words, is a great offensive weapon, a potent and public act of comic aggression that fortifies one against one's enemies" (34). McCarthy's "habit of satire"—a style previously dominated by male writers[2]—paved the way for Howard's scathing *Bridgeport Bus* and Cullinan's more subtle *House of Gold*.

With the publication of *Memories of a Catholic Girlhood*, McCarthy opened yet another door for Irish American women: she became the first woman[3] to pen what Fanning characterizes as "the significant subgenre of late-twentieth-century Irish-American autobiography," with an approach that "brought exemplary sophistication and craftsmanship to Irish-American materials in this period of regional realism" (301). *Memories* (1957) was followed by such notable memoirs as Frank Conroy's *Stop Time* (1967), Maureen Howard's *Facts of Life* (1978), McCarthy's second effort, *How I Grew* (1986), John Gregory Dunne's *Harp* (1989), and McCarthy's posthumous *Intellectual Memoirs: New York 1936–38*, among others.

As her novels and memoirs reveal, McCarthy was too smart to be sentimental. Her semi-autobiographical heroines are painfully realistic as they struggle against the restrictions placed upon women while dealing with the resulting guilt. *The Group* paved the way for Maureen Howard's independent Mary Agnes Keely, Mary Gordon's passionate Isabel Moore, Mary McGarry Morris's stubborn Martha Horgan, Joyce Carol Oates's resilient Marianne Mulvaney, Alice McDermott's loyal Maeve Lynch, and Erin McGraw's feisty Kate Gussey. Mary McCarthy laid the groundwork for subsequent Irish American women writers to develop flawed heroines and to upset stereotypical conventions regarding marriage and motherhood—in sum, to enter the man's world of writing and publishing and succeed on her own terms. In this realm, and despite her denials, McCarthy broke the bounds of Irish American literary conventions by leading her female counterparts into second wave, twentieth-century feminism.[4]

McCarthy was a talented and prolific writer: she was book and drama critic for the *Partisan Review* as well as a contributor to *Ideas and the Novel* (1980), *Theatre Chronicles, 1936–62* (1964), and *Sights and Spectacles: Theatre Chronicles 1937–56* (1957); author of short stories in *The Company She Keeps* (1942), *Cast a Cold Eye* (1950), and *The Hounds of Summer and Other Stories* (1981); social critic in *A Charmed Life* (1955); political satirist in *The Oasis* (1949), *The Groves of Academe* (1952), *Birds of America* (1971), and *Cannibals and Missionaries* (1979); commentator on Italian art and architecture in *Venice Observed* (1956) and *The Stones of Florence* (1957); best-selling novelist with *The Group* (1963); and political reporter in *Vietnam* (1967), *Hanoi* (1968), *Medina* (1972), *The Seventeenth Degree* (1974)—which united the previous three volumes—and *The Mask of State: Watergate Portraits* (1974). Such a varied and prodigious output was unique among women of her era.

In recognition of her groundbreaking work, McCarthy has been the subject of numerous studies and biographies. In *The New York Intellectuals: From Vanguard to Institution* (1995), Hugh Wilford analyzed her literary politics. McCarthy's personal, philosophical, and intellectual musings have been explored in *Between Friends: The Correspondence of Hannah Arendt and Mary McCarthy, 1949–75* (1995), edited by biographer Carol Brightman. In *Mary McCarthy* (1967) Barbara McKenzie examined McCarthy's use of satire through 1967, while Bard College published the proceedings of a conference devoted to McCarthy in *Twenty-Four Ways of Looking at Mary McCarthy* (Stwertka and Viscusi). More recently, Sabrina Fuchs Abrams has analyzed McCarthy "as a fiction writer and a cultural critic" in *Mary McCarthy: Gender, Politics, and the Postwar Intellectual* (2004). Finally, at least six very different biographies have lent insight into other aspects of McCarthy's life: Doris Grumbach's *The Company She Kept* (1967), Barbara McKenzie's *Mary McCarthy* (1967), Willene Hardy's *Mary McCarthy* (1981), Carol Brightman's *Writing Dangerously* (1992), Carol Gelderman's *Mary McCarthy: A Life* (1988), and Francis Kiernan's *Seeing Mary Plain* (2000) (Abrams x).

Despite this range of scholarly attention, McCarthy is rarely described as representative of, if not key to, the development of Irish American women's literary tradition in the second half of the twentieth century. In this chapter I attempt to address this oversight. While I acknowledge McCarthy's nonfiction prose, I focus on her fiction and memoirs. To organize the discussion, I borrow (and improvise upon) the rubric established by the editors of volumes 4 and 5 of the *Field Day Anthology of Irish Writing* to demonstrate Irish women's influence on and parallels with their contemporary Irish American sisters.

Religion and Ethics

Although she rejected her faith at age eleven, Mary McCarthy's early Catholic training is evident throughout her *oeuvre*. Stacey Lee Donohue argues that McCarthy's conflicted attitudes and behavior, and that of her characters, can be directly traced to her heritage: "Mary McCarthy is identifiably a Catholic writer, writing in the Irish-American literary tradition. . . . She broke away from an anti-intellectual, puritan, sexist Irish-Catholicism succeeding as a writer, participating in the sexual, political and intellectual freedom of the 1930s and 1940s, but still struggling with the Church's restrictive definition of women, and a historically and culturally Irish fatalism" (87). Because of these innate beliefs, McCarthy's heroines "are often foiled by a stereotypically Irish-Catholic idealization of suffering and penance as well as the desire to be seen as good girls" (Donohue 88).

Although McCarthy grew further and further from the mores of her Catholic girlhood throughout her life, she could not escape herself. An "infamously autobiographical writer," her heroines inevitably reflect her beliefs, for "All are effectively Catholic" (Donohue 91). According to Donohue, "all of McCarthy's characters are unable to mediate between the traditional definitions of femininity embraced by the church, and the modern revisioning, an Irish Catholic fatalism and a belief in free will. . . . the women of *The Group* all succumb to different but equally unappealing fates, while the structure of the novel forebodes determinism, beginning with Kay's wedding and ending with her wake" (91). McCarthy would deny it, but such characterizations are, Donohue argues, "oddly . . . still a rather feminist position in the way [she] acknowledges the tension of women torn between two conflicting ideals. Her heroines declare their sexual freedom, intellectual independence, and are willing to compete in the world with men, but ultimately they are undermined by self doubt, shame and an internalization of Catholicism, which lead to a desperate search for someone to tell them what to do, and some structure to tell them how to do it" (93).

McCarthy might counter that she merely reflected the women of her generation, who were raised to view men as the authorities and to ignore their own needs (Donohue 93). Yet of all the characters in *The Group*, Polly, whose ancestry bears a "Catholic strain," receives the most treatment in the novel and has the happiest life. Moreover, throughout her writing, McCarthy relies on "Catholic allusions and metaphors" (Donohue 96). Donohue states that this stance reflects McCarthy's ingrained "Catholic sensibility," manifested in her belief in "social change, political change, and freedom for women to reach their potential"—unless these changes threatened the status quo (97).

Such views are explained by historian John Cogley. Discussing early twentieth-century parochial schools, he remarked: "Nowhere else in the world were so many Catholic children drilled in the catechism as thoroughly as in American parochial schools; nowhere did the notion of Catholicism as embodying a tidy system of rules and regulations covering practically every aspect of life gain stronger hold on the faithful . . . and the 'siege mentality' the schools inculcated was often carried over to life outside the classroom" (qtd. in R. Ebest 140). Maureen Howard argues that McCarthy's work embodied these Catholic ideals: "I see her as the missionary, the very missionary we Catholic girls laughed at, stern and diligent among heathens, believing in truth . . . the undeniable facts that drew her to the upper story of almost blessed intelligence which made her work valid. As for the secular act of writing, there was in her own performance a sense that writing was to her a touch sacred" (198). Mary McCarthy's early education marked her forever; she may have renounced her Catholic faith, but she could not rid herself of its tenets.

Politics

In her essay "Politics and the Novel," McCarthy writes that once she read John Dos Passos's *The 42nd Parallel*, "I never looked back. Like a Japanese paper flower dropped into a glass of water, my political persona unfolded, magically" (qtd. in Brightman, *Writing Dangerously* 83). This persona inadvertently intensified a few years later because of a conversation with James T. Farrell. When Farrell asked McCarthy if she thought Trotsky (about whom she was ignorant) deserved a fair trial, she blithely answered yes—after which Farrell added her name to a missive demanding justice for the agitator. Although Stalinist friends urged her to remove her name, McCarthy did not capitulate. "I let my name stay," she writes, "a pivotal decision, perhaps *the* pivotal decision of my life" (*Intellectual Memoirs* 57–58).

Sabrina Fuchs Abrams suggests that "As a satirist, McCarthy's art cannot be separated from her politics and is often an ironic comment on the political scene" (2). McCarthy initially explored this conjunction in a series of lesser-known novels. In *The Oasis* she satirizes the "intellectual passivity and alienation of radical and liberal intellectuals" following her divorce from Edmund Wilson and her subsequent break with coworkers at the *Partisan Review* (Abrams 55). Although McCarthy defended the rights of Communists and their sympathizers to teach in U.S. high schools and universities in her 1952 speech to the American Federation of Teachers, she also critiqued unquestioning liberalism (Abrams 11). In *The Groves of*

Academe she argues for academic freedom—within limits—through the predicament of Henry Mulcahy, who is fired by his university's president for being a Communist sympathizer, while satirizing the resultant protests from his liberal colleagues.

During and after the Vietnam War, McCarthy continued her satirical political analyses; however, her later novels suggest what Abrams calls "a romantic longing for a pre-industrial, pastoral past as idealized in the rural, folk culture of North Vietnam" (xi). *Birds of America* (1971) "exposes the conflict between liberal values and social reality" by setting Peter, a nineteen-year-old American, in Paris during the late 1960s antiwar protests, where he tries to pursue an egalitarian agenda in the midst of crass consumerism and the "mass consumption of art" (Abrams 93).

Perhaps because of McCarthy's conservative shift and immersion into American politics, *Birds of America* and later political novels did not fare well. By telling the story from the point of view of a nineteen-year-old protagonist, sometimes *Birds of America* sounds like the angry ranting of a university freshman; at other points it sounds more like its middle-aged author (Abrams 95). Compare, for example, Peter's outburst to Mr. Small—"You saw that mob scene [in the museum] this morning. They don't even listen to their stupid guides" (296)—to his reflections on their conversation: "Mr. Small's personal plexiglass bell evidently caused a kind of itchiness or inflammation that kept him irritable and peevish" (301). Such vacillations in style and voice tend to obscure the novel's political arguments.

Despite a promising plot, *Cannibals and Missionaries* (1979) suffers a similar fate. The novel's message presciently ponders the "conflict between liberal, egalitarian principles and aesthetic values"—a terrorist hijacking of a plane bound for the Middle East jump starts a plot involving a hostage situation in Iran with the hoary philosophical conundrum of "the value of art versus life" as the underlying theme (Abrams 93). In this novel McCarthy tried (in vain) to avoid her usual satirical bent (Abrams 102). Because of her desire to convey opposition to mass consumerism, however, the plot becomes mired in what Abrams terms "a lengthy disquisition on the relative value of art, life, and liberty" (103), as well as interminable wrangling among the hostages. After the hostages are finally released, the novel winds down with yet another rambling disquisition supposedly taken from a hostage's journal: "Frescoes, monumental sculpture, bas-reliefs, altar panels, town-hall paintings are stable, cemented into place & time. Celebrations, *vide* triumphal arches. Lots carted off in war. . . pillage. But that felt as desecration, contrary to original intention. Whereas church vessels & easel paintings almost 'made' to be stolen" (366). After stumbling through eight pages of this small-font diatribe, the journal readers settle down to watch an in-flight movie—an ironic and inauspicious conclusion.

Like her political novels, McCarthy's writings on the subject of Vietnam remain relatively unknown and unsuccessful. As its title suggests, one of the few reviews of *Cannibals and Missionaries*, "The Blinders She Wears," published by James Fallows in the *Washington Monthly*, criticized McCarthy for a "lack of objectivity so profound as to make even sympathizers wary" (qtd. in Brightman, *Writing Dangerously* 554). But readers and reviewers may not have rejected McCarthy as much as her message. Brightman notes that during this period, over two hundred books were written on Vietnam. Moreover, McCarthy's collection of essays, *The Writing on the Wall* (1970), was published at the same time and fared well, leaving her to conclude: "So it could not be just me that nobody wanted to hear from. . . . Perhaps me on Vietnam—the combination" (Brightman, *Writing Dangerously* 555). Whatever the reason, Brightman concludes that the public's response (or lack thereof) "has relegated McCarthy's wartime writing, unfairly, to a limbo in American letters" (*Writing Dangerously* 555).

Satire

In her essay "The Fact in Fiction," McCarthy declared, "There must be no indulgence, no false note." The fate of her political novels suggests she did not follow her own advice. But not all of McCarthy's novels were overtly political, nor was all of her satire dismissed. Indeed, Maureen Howard recalls that "For a woman coming of age in the 1950s, to read Mary McCarthy was a jolt in the right direction. That direction is the arrow (a bright, pulsing neon) pointing upstairs. Upstairs is the head bone, gray matter" (195). Over the course of her career, McCarthy's intellect was evident in her style and intensity. Howard declared McCarthy's early criticism "sharp, savvy, urbane" and her later essays "energetic, as always, and independent of fashion" (196–97). As McCarthy herself once said, "It is difficult not to write satire" (qtd. in Grumbach 146).

Throughout her writing career, McCarthy pulled no punches. When William Carlos Williams reviewed *The Company She Keeps* for Simon and Schuster in 1942, he commented that "Mary McCarthy, as Mary Mc-

Carthy, is something to be surmounted—and a man had better be feeling fit when he takes her on." Her fiction, he continued, "is written principally for those it attacks. . . . The men are pretty foul, but she really likes them, they complement her" (qtd. in Brightman, *Writing Dangerously* 207). This characterization is directed at what may be McCarthy's most infamous short story, "The Man in the Brooks Brothers Shirt."

As the man (in real life, George Black, although the description also fits McCarthy's husband, Edmund Wilson) enters the club car in which Mary's alter ego, Meg, sits, she observes that "The greater part of his head appeared to be pink, also, though actually toward the back there was a good deal of closely cropped pale-grey hair that harmonized with his trousers. He looked, she decided, like a middle-aged baby, like a young pig, like something in a seed catalogue" (81). Later, after spending the day drinking with him, Meg decides: "*She liked him.* Why, it was impossible to say. The attraction was not sexual, for, as the whisky went down in the bottle, his face took on a more and more porcine look that became so distasteful to her that she could hardly meet his gaze" (95). Unfortunately, after spending the night together, the porcine resemblance resurfaces: "He looked very fat and the short hair on his chest was gray" (108).

What some critics fail to note is McCarthy's honest treatment of her female characters, not to mention the sophisticated style in which the story is told. "The Man in the Brooks Brothers Shirt" is relayed by an omniscient third-person narrator attuned to Meg's inner thoughts. Thus, while readers learn only that her male seducer is an unattractive, overly sentimental, adulterous, occasionally acute businessman, we are privy to Meg's ongoing critical self-evaluations. Consequently, we understand that rather than complementing this "pig," she sees herself pretty clearly. Reacting to a political slur, Meg thinks, "The man's vulgarity was undeniable. For some time now she had been attempting (for her own sake) to whitewash him, but the crude raw material would shine through in spite of her." After a few whiskeys, she wonders if this man is the one, "the one she kept looking for, the one who could tell her what she was really like" (94).

In the following reflection, visions of the young Mary McCarthy emerge as Meg admits "when as a homely high-school girl, she had rejected the Church's filing system, together with her aunt's illiterate morality, she had given away her sense of herself" (101). The next morning, caught trying to escape their Pullman compartment before the man awakes, "[Meg's] own squeamishness and sick distaste, which a moment before had seemed virtuous in her, now appeared heartless, even frivolous, in the face of his emotion" (109). Such insights suggest that rather than dismissing McCarthy's female personae and her male characters as birds of a feather, her seducers come across as one dimensional, whereas the female characters are multifaceted. Maureen Howard is right on target when she comments that McCarthy's prose contains an "arrow (a bright, pulsing neon) pointing upstairs" (195).

Ironically, McCarthy seemed unaware of how her writing might be perceived. Although she admitted she would like to humiliate her enemies by writing "punitive satire," she claimed she decided not to because she lacked the talent. Those feelings were belied with the publication of *The Group*.

In this novel McCarthy undertook what Brightman (and Fanning before her) calls a "linguistic experiment": she attempted to mimic "that bird chorus of voices from [her] Vassar dormitory thirty years before" (*Writing Dangerously* 480). To illustrate the vapidity of the rich, McCarthy makes practically their every pronouncement an indictment. When Dick tells Dottie to buy herself a pessary, or diaphragm, her reply underscores the speaker's naiveté: "'Yes, Dick,' Dottie whispered, her hand twisting the doorknob, while she let her eyes tell him softly what a deep reverent moment this was, a sort of pledge between them" (61). McCarthy mocks herself in the character of Kay Petersen by describing her as "The girl who went east and made good. . . . by marrying Harald. It all sounds so glamorous" (421). Priss Hartshorn makes all of the characters look bad when she expounds on the difficulty of great wealth—"a frightful handicap; it insulated you from living." Such "linguistic subversion" should come as no surprise from the poor girl among the Vassar elite who tried hard to fit into their social circle even as she abhorred their snobbery. Recall Krause's definition of satire: "In the oral and written Irish tradition, language itself, the power of words, is a great offensive weapon, a potent and public act of comic aggression that fortifies one against one's enemies" (34). Yet *The Group* does much more than criticize the rich.

"Social satire was [McCarthy's] vehicle for social observation and the kind of sexual comedy that meant so much to my generation," Morris Dickstein writes, "the generation that came of age just before the Pill, just before the sexual and behavioral revolutions and the 1960s took hold" (25). Rather than viewing McCarthy as malicious or "bitchy," he views her as a "highbrow scold" who, like most satirists, used language as a "defense against feeling" (24–25). It is unfortunate that few serious reviewers recognized this quality. Beverly Gross offers a likely explanation. McCarthy was a powerful intellectual, "a woman who had a mind and spoke it." While such traits are praiseworthy in a man, "A woman with the same traits is domineering, threatening, castrating—in a word, a bitch" (28). In sum, McCarthy was damned because she was a woman. Alfred Kazin described her as having "a wholly destructive critical mind" (155). William Barrett suggests "She rather struck terror into some male bosoms" (67). Even her friend Dwight McDonald likened her smile to a shark's: "When most pretty girls smile at you," he wrote, "you feel terrific. When Mary smiles at you, you look to see if your fly is open" (qtd. in Gelderman 184).

Clearly, McCarthy's gender affected her critics' judgment. She was a satirist; consequently, like others of her ilk, she did not discriminate in her targets. "Catholics and Stalinists, Trotskyites and Freudians, all felt the sting of her rejections," writes Margaret Scanlan (35). Yet McCarthy's critics probably retracted their claws when she turned her eyes on Joe McCarthy and the victims of his blacklist, and again when she attacked the Hanoi government in the late 1960s and Watergate in the 1970s. Throughout much of her life, McCarthy's writing stemmed from her "liberal intellectual convictions about the moral worth of art and education and about the need for a progressive politics" (Scanlan 35). In sum, it was not so much her style as her gender that bothered her critics. Given the era in which she wrote, such attitudes are not surprising. What makes McCarthy unique is not that she continued the stylistic approach honed by her Irish forebears, but that she is the first notable Irish American *female* satirist.

The Search for Identity through Memoir

In *The Irish Voice in America* Charles Fanning suggests that Charles Driscoll's 1943 memoir, *Kansas Irish*, is the model for the Irish American genre. This model is characterized by tempering harsh reality with compassion, developing fully rounded characters, and providing explicit details of the characters' life and times (Fanning 301–2). Mary McCarthy's three memoirs—*Memories of a Catholic Girlhood*, *How I Grew*, and the posthumous *Intellectual Memoirs*—to some extent follow this pattern. With each succeeding volume, however, the characters become less rounded even as the details surrounding their lives grow gradually more explicit.

Memories of a Catholic Girlhood contrasts the McCarthy children's idyllic life in Seattle, where the children reveled in presents, parties, and treats, with the unhappy times following their parents' death from influenza, when Mary and her brothers are taken in by her cruel and penurious Aunt Margaret and Uncle Myers Shrivers. Oblique passages describing the couple suggest McCarthy's early compassion muffled her resentment: "One of the great shocks connected with the loss of my parents was an aesthetic one; even if my guardians had been nice I should probably not have liked them because they were so unpleasing to look at and their grammar and accents were so lacking in correctness" (17). Similarly, McCarthy concludes her first chapter with the comment, "Read poor for *orphan* throughout and you get a kind of allegory or broad social satire on the theme of wealth and poverty," suggesting her disdain for pity (49).

McCarthy devotes the first three chapters to these relatives, conveying the physical and psychological abuse she and her brothers suffered at their hands. Simultaneously, these chapters establish McCarthy's ambivalence toward her faith, for what appeared beautiful and pure when taught by her mother appears cruel and hypocritical when practiced by the Minneapolis McCarthys. After being miraculously "rescued" by her maternal grandparents, the Prestons, from Seattle, Mary's life changes (even as she ponders why they abandoned her brothers). Attending Sacred Heart Academy, her faith is initially renewed as evidenced by her desire to convert her Protestant grandfather, if not save his soul. McCarthy's account of her friendships and conversations with the nuns who taught at the convent show how her faith was briefly restored, while her debates with priests regarding her loss of faith (feigned to attract attention) reveal how, for McCarthy, intellect tops faith. These debates, coupled with a vignette describing a nun's inability to listen or believe Mary has only cut herself (as opposed to menstruating), provide strong allegories suggesting that the church is removed from reality. Yet running throughout the remaining chapters, which focus on McCarthy's social life and attempts to escape her grandparents' vigilance, her early training repeatedly surfaces as she reflects on her deceptions.

Brightman asserts that *Memories of a Catholic Girlhood* "marked a breakthrough for McCarthy," for in writing it she came to understand herself (54). This may explain why her second memoir, *How I Grew*, does not extend much beyond the time period covered in *Memories*. Instead, *How I Grew* revisits the same ground with a more mature, if not jaundiced, eye.

"I had the choice of forgiving those incredible relatives of mine or pity-ing myself on their account," McCarthy writes (17). Forgiveness did not seem feasible. Instead, McCarthy leavens self-pity with humor. "Laughter is the great antidote for self-pity," she continues. "Yet probably it does tend to dry one's feelings out a little, as if by exposing them to a vigorous wind, so that something must be subtracted from the compensation I seem to have received for injuries sustained" (17). But other elements were sub-tracted as well.

Whereas the first memoir focuses on Mary's innocence—what Bright-man refers to as a "bundle of overexcited scruples"—the second suggests that Mary (like most people) was sometimes less than scrupulous. Many of the same themes and stories from Memories are revisited in more depth: religion, lying to her grandparents, the impact of reading, education at boarding school, her friends, and her budding intellect. However, McCar-thy also describes losing her virginity at age fourteen to Forest Cosby (a man of twenty-seven), thus identifying one of the men her grandfather scared off at Lake Crescent in an episode recalled in Memories. After describing the seduction in detail, she then reflects on her fear ("I was scared silly"), her subsequent disillusion ("I felt as if I had died"), his rejection (with an unsigned letter), and her revenge (she refused to date him when she was older).

Interwoven with the themes of religion, education, and seduction, McCarthy discloses two or three other minor affairs. Importantly, she also discusses the resultant guilt and how she dealt with it. "When you have committed an action that you cannot bear to think about, that causes you to writhe in retrospect, do not seek to evade the memory: make yourself relive it, confront it repeatedly over and over, till finally, you will discover, through sheer repetition it loses its power to pain you." True to form, she then reflects on this process: "It works, but I am not sure it is a good thing. Perhaps I did something to my immortal soul," she ponders. "As I forced revolting memories to surge up before my closed eyes, almost burning the closed lids with fiery self-disgust, did I kill a moral nerve? . . . Is it right to overcome self-disgust?" Analyzing these feelings, McCarthy admits, "So I was a true girl of my generation, bent on taking the last trace of sin out of sex. . . . All I knew at the time was that I had devised a method that let me live with myself. . . . I was getting myself in training for my adult 'career of crime'" (How I Grew 156–57). What apparently saved McCarthy from a full-blown sexual "crime spree" was her literary taste, for after reading letters from various suitors, her critical, intellectual sense overrode any budding infatuation. The men she had relationships with, she notes, had all "written a good letter" (160). Among these men was Harold Johnsrud, McCarthy's first husband in life and Kay's in *The Group*. Johnsrud and McCarthy's friends and professors at Vassar are discussed in the memoir's last three chapters, which in many ways serve as precursors to the early chapters in *The Group*.

Unlike *Memories of a Catholic Girlhood*, in which the key episodes are capsulated in individual chapters, *How I Grew* is less organized and more expansive. Although it does not venture far beyond the ground covered earlier, the additional details convey a more mature, less self-absorbed McCarthy while providing the background for characters and themes that appear in her subsequent works.

When comparing *How I Grew* to McCarthy's final memoir, *Intellectual Memoirs*, Carol Brightman maintains that the energy, feeling, and compassion of the previous volumes has dissipated (*Writing Dangerously* 633). But it could also be argued that McCarthy moved from flowery narration to a straightforward rendering of her life; moreover, rather than retelling the earlier events of her life, this volume begins in 1936 when she is married to Harold "John" Johnsrud and "at the high point of the slight attraction [she] felt toward Communism" (3)—the same period covered by *The Group*. In writing this volume, McCarthy seems to be following her own dictum: "My standards were high—higher for fiction than for biography—which could justify itself by instructiveness" (*Intellectual Memoirs* 28).

McCarthy names names, such as the parties involved in the walkout supporting the waiters' strike at the Waldorf (Dorothy Parker and Haywood Broun, among others); models for characters in novels (Harold Loeb, the inspiration for Robert Cohn in *The Sun Also Rises*, and Gerald Murphy, cast as Dick Diver in *Tender Is the Night*); and the first of her intellectual circle to quit the Marxist party, James T. Farrell. She discusses her progressive friendships with bourgeois blacks (Nella Larsen, author of *Passing*, and Dorothy Peterson, the actress) and describes her various literary enemies (for example, Malcolm Cowley). She admits to numerous affairs, touching only briefly on her reasons while noting that a psychoanalyst told her she "felt compelled to leave the [first] man she loved because [her] parents had left [her]," to which she responds: "Possibly. What I sensed myself was inexorability, the *moerae* at work, independently of my will, of my likes or dislikes." She attributes her breakup with John Porter, the man who led her to leave Johnsrud, in part to her affair with "the man in the Brooks Brothers shirt" (43). She acknowledges her guilt for not admitting her feelings had changed, which more or less led to Porter's death in Mexico—"a rather shaking thought," she admits (45).

At another point McCarthy discusses a conversation with Vassar professor Miss Sandison, who advised her "not to depend on having love." While this wisdom impressed her, McCarthy reveals, "I am sure it is true but, unlike Miss Sandison, I am not up to it. I have seldom been capable of living without love, not for more than a month or so" (52). This fact becomes evident toward the middle of *Intellectual Memoirs* when McCarthy begins describing the brief affairs she undertook after her divorce from Johnsrud, moving from Bob Misch to Leo Huberman (author of *Man's Worldly Gifts*), to Bill Mangold, Harold Rome, and nameless others. "It was getting rather alarming," she declares. "I realized one day that in twenty-four hours I had slept with three different men" (62). Unfortunately, she then briefly compares their "sexual equipment." Such details may explain why Brightman deemed the memoir "unlovable" (*Writing Dangerously* 620).

Yet McCarthy devotes considerable space—almost half of the volume—to her love affair with Philip Rahv. Indeed, even as she begins recounting her relationship with Edmund Wilson, she notes, "Philip had an open heart and a childish, somewhat docile nature with those he had opened it to, few as they were. That he could accept my penitence— and not from any weakness—must have meant that he understood that I loved him. I did, and still do, vividly, as I write these words" (*Intellectual Memoirs* 95–97). McCarthy concludes the three-chapter, unfinished memoir by explaining her reasons for marrying Wilson despite her love for Rahv, revealing shame at her deception and ruing her decision.

Morris Dickstein, who interviewed McCarthy toward the end of her life, declared *Memories of a Catholic Girlhood* "the last book in which McCarthy was fully able to strike this balance between tenderness and intelligence, between 'the facts' and the feelings" (24). The pages devoted to Rahv suggest otherwise. Although McCarthy credits marriage to Wilson for her publishing success, she paid a high price for fame.

Sexuality, Feminism, Culture, and Critique

When Mary McCarthy's short story "The Man in the Brooks Brothers Shirt" was published, William Barrett, one of her colleagues at the *Partisan Review*, wrote, "We did not know it then, but she was in fact firing the first salvo in the feminist war that now rages within our society" (67). McCarthy biographer Carol Brightman disagreed, arguing that this story was no more a salvo "than William Burrough's *Naked Lunch* is a blow against drug addiction" (*Writing Dangerously* 206). But Brightman's denial seems more a reflection of McCarthy's feelings than an accurate assessment of her fiction. "Each generation of American intellectuals," writes Norman Podhoretz, "has had a slot for a female writer, preferably a 'dark-haired one with supreme intellectual self-confidence and a keen desire for prominence'" (qtd. in Bernstein). "Among the New York intellectuals, the Dark Lady was Mary McCarthy. McCarthy's combination of elegant style and macho bravado," Elaine Showalter explains, "not only made her the first of the New York Dark Ladies, but also the most feared," for she was the darkest of the dark— a feminist intellectual (179).

In those days the term *feminist intellectual* was not bandied about. Even so, McCarthy embodied it. Showalter continues, "without a feminist movement to offer an alternative intellectual community, or a group like Heterodoxy to unite them, women intellectuals in New York internalized many of the values of the *Partisan Review,* competed for its recognition, and measured themselves against its moral and political standards" (180).

McCarthy's motto was taken from Chaucer's Criseyde—"I am myn owene woman, wel at ease" (*Company She Keeps* 104)—yet she was a rabid antifeminist. She has often been quoted as saying that feminism "just does not say hello to me at all" (Brightman, *Writing Dangerously* 342). "Feminism," she declared, "is bad for women. . . . [I]t induces a very bad emotional state," fomenting emotions such as "self-pity, covetousness, and greed" by indicting "self-dependency" and emphasizing "male privilege" (342). Clearly, McCarthy's definition of feminism was limited. "I've always liked being a woman," she declared. "I like the domestic arts, cooking and gardening. I like clothes very, very much," as well as women's ability to "get their way without direct confrontation" (Brightman, *Writing Dangerously* 343). Nevertheless, McCarthy admitted she was "sort of an Uncle Tom from this point of view," since she made her living in the male-dominated world of publishing (Brightman, *Writing Dangerously* 95).

Betty Freidan attributes this duality to McCarthy's age: "The first wave of feminism stopped not long after the winning of the vote in 1920 and the second wave began in the sixties. Mary McCarthy was in the generation in between" (qtd. in Kiernan 711). Maureen Howard adds that like

Doris Lessing and Lillian Hellman, McCarthy "backed away from the feminist movement" because "having performed so well on their own, they did
not want to be associated with the disenfranchised" (qtd. in Kiernan 712).

Feminist themes are most obvious in two of McCarthy's works: her
first publication, *The Company She Keeps*, a collection of six short stories
published in 1942, and *The Group*, published two decades later. An early
version of *The Group*, *The Company She Keeps* is a thinly veiled semi-
autobiographical account of McCarthy's life after graduating from Vassar,
during which she marries, moves to New York, has an affair, divorces, and
works for a publisher. Running throughout this collection is a prominent
feminist theme: the search for identity. In the first story, "Cruel and Bar-
barous Treatment," Meg explores the reasons behind her divorce, focusing
primarily on her own selfish need for attention and excitement. Rather
than berate herself, she feels "gratitude toward the Young Man [with
whom she had the affair] for having unwillingly effected her transit into a
new life" (20). McCarthy admits in *Intellectual Memoirs* that in this story
(the first she published) she was "trying to give some form to what had
happened between John [her husband], John Porter [the Young Man],
and [herself]." However, she continues, "I do not see that I was really like
the nameless heroine" (35–36)—an admission that does not reflect well
on her.

The collection's third story, "The Man in the Brooks Brothers Shirt"—
perhaps McCarthy's best known story—recounts Meg Sergant's seduction
by/of an unattractive traveling salesman, Mr. Breen, during their cross-
country train trip to the West Coast. Meg, divorced and engaged to a new
man, coolly analyzes the seduction and her alternating feelings of pleasure
and disgust for both herself and Breen. In her analysis of this story, Willene Hardy notes that Meg emerges a slightly better person (42). Inter-
mittently self-aware, at one point she realizes "Dear Jesus . . . I'm really as
hard as nails." Vowing to redeem herself, she goes to bed with Breen again,
thinking, "This . . . is going to be the only real act of charity I have ever
performed in my life; it will be the only time I have ever given anything
when it honestly hurt me to do so" (114). But these feelings are not permanent. After the affair has ended and Meg's father has died, Breen sends
a telegram saying, "YOU HAVE LOST THE BEST FRIEND YOU WILL
EVER HAVE." Meg quickly tears it up, thinking, "It would be dreadful if
anyone had seen it" (134). Such feelings once again mirror McCarthy's
life. As she says in *Intellectual Memoirs*, "George Black's ardor was an

embarrassment to me—a deserved punishment. Hard up as I was for male company, I kept him out of sight" (50).

The other standout in this collection, "Portrait of the Intellectual as a Yale Man," once again features Margaret, who once again commits adultery with a married man. Because of the story's focus, the reader learns little about Margaret; McCarthy depicts her persona only as "our gay divorcee" speaking "in a rather breathless voice" about her divorce in Reno (188). This ironic self-awareness does not change. As the final story in the collection, "Ghostly Father, I Confess," concludes, Margaret "for the first time . . . saw her own extremity, saw that it was some failure in self-love that obliged her to snatch blindly at the love of others, hoping to love herself through them . . . And yet, walking on, she could still detect her own frauds" (303).

In scenes more graphic than the 1950s readers of women's novels were accustomed to, McCarthy's works explicitly address sex. A Charmed Life— yet another thinly veiled autobiographical tome, this time (in parts) satirizing McCarthy's relationship with Edmund Wilson (Brightman, Writing Dangerously 243)—is perhaps most notable for the sex scene between Miles/Wilson and Martha/Mary after both have remarried:

> She had struggled at first, quite violently, when he flung himself on top of her on the sofa. But he had her pinioned beneath him with the whole weight of his body. . . . She wanted it, obviously, or she would not have asked him in. The angry squirming of her body, the twisting and turning of her head, filled him with amused tolerance and quickened his excitement as he crushed his member against her reluctant pelvis. . . . "Don't," she cried sharply. . . . She sat up in indignation, and his hand slipped in and held her breast cupped. . . . "Please don't," she begged, with tears in her eyes, while he squeezed her nipples between his fingertips; they were hard before he touched them; her breath was coming quickly. . . . Compunction smote him; he ought not to have done this, he said to himself tenderly. Tenderness inflamed his member. Clasping her fragile body brusquely to him, he thrust himself into her with short, quick strokes. A gasp of pain came from her, and it was over. (199–203)

Carol Brightman dismisses critics such as Eleanor Widmer who declared that such passages "anticipated the sexual revolution of the '60s"; however,

Brightman's assertion that McCarthy is "the doyenne of pre-revolutionary sex" with "no fear of flying in her bedrooms, only of getting caught" (246), seems, rather, to confirm Widmer, for participants in the sexual revolution were generally no less afraid. Moreover, Brightman's rebuttal seems to overlook the fact that, at the time, such passages were revolutionary for women authors.

Although McCarthy's first two memoirs were surprisingly less frank, *The Group* (1963), published between them, graduates to coverage of the female orgasm, not yet a feminist literary staple. In this novel McCarthy explores the aspirations of seven female graduates of the Vassar class of 1931, juxtaposing what Janet Kalven terms "pre-feminist" desires for a meaningful career and a happy marriage with the mores and realities of American society in the 1930s. In the process, McCarthy introduces the reader not only to women's sexual pleasure but also to birth control, adultery, impotence, mental illness, homosexuality, spousal abuse, and the double standard.

The main character of *The Group*, Kay (generally accepted as McCarthy's alter ego), openly lives with her fiancé, Harald, and shares details of her sex life with the young women in the group. In a time when birth control had only recently been legalized, the characters discuss it openly. One of the males suggests birth control is used only by "adulteresses, mistresses, prostitutes, and the like," as opposed to respectable married women. Although Kay contradicts him, she is no better, declaring that "Birth control . . . was for those who know how to use it and value it—the educated classes" (75). When McCarthy's antagonist, Norinne, visits a doctor to seek advice about her husband's impotence, she reports that the doctor asked "whether I wanted to have children. . . . When I said no, I didn't, he practically booted me out of the office. He told me I should consider myself lucky that my husband didn't want intercourse. Sex wasn't necessary for a woman, he said" (165). Another character, Lakey, has a lesbian lover, although their sex scenes are not recounted.

Most notable is Dottie's first sexual encounter, which she openly pursues. The graphic foreplay and seduction cover several pages, culminating in the following passage:

[W]hile she was praying for it to be over, surprise of surprises, she started to like it a little. She got the idea, and her body began to move too in answer, as he pressed *that* home in her slowly, over and over, and slowly drew it back. . . . Her breath came quicker. Each lingering stroke, like a violin bow, made her palpitate for the next. Then all of a sudden, she seemed to explode in a series of long, uncontrollable contractions that embarrassed her, like the hiccups, the moment they were over, for it was as if she had forgotten Dick as a person. (41)

McCarthy uses *The Group* to remind readers of the unfortunate disparity between the characters' liberal theories and the reality of their marriages, for once they marry independence disappears. At the beginning of the novel Kay is a strong-willed, independent woman, but as the story progresses she becomes increasingly helpless and miserable. Soon the reader finds Kay tiptoeing around her husband Harald, eager to please and dreadfully afraid of upsetting him. Priss, another group member, is introduced as a political activist, but after she marries and gives birth she becomes so weak-willed that she lets her newborn cry for hours rather than disobey her husband and nurse the baby before he is "scheduled" to be fed.

Such dichotomies tend to confuse twenty-first-century readers. Although Mary McCarthy might be considered an early feminist for writing such a daring novel, her characters did not achieve a similar level of self-confidence. As one of my students wrote, "they showed small threads of feminism in them . . . The problem is that they think one thing and do another. When it comes down to it, they seem to feel that they live in a man's world and that they should follow his rules without much question" (qtd. in S. Ebest 267). Nevertheless, McCarthy's characters represent the seeds of change, for "most of them still had to struggle with the patriarchal control that tried to suppress them" (qtd. in S. Ebest 267). Arthur Schlesinger Jr., a longtime friend of McCarthy, nicely captures this dichotomy, writing, "She was a feminist by example, not by exhortation" (203).

Although possessed of a rather hefty ego, McCarthy attributed her literary successes to the men in her life: she argued that because of her relationship with Philip Rahv, she was hired to write for the *Partisan Review*; because of her marriage to Edmund Wilson, she started writing fiction; and because her third husband, Bowden Broadwater, took care of her personal life, she was able to continue writing (Brightman, "Writing Dangerously" 142). In this realm McCarthy was uncharacteristically modest. Elaine Showalter points out that "Acceptance by the *Partisan Review* was the crucial initiation rite for aspiring New York intellectuals." It was an old boys club that, despite its avant-garde views, "excluded women. . . . Over a fifty-year period, only 12 percent of the essays in the *Partisan Review* were by women" (179). Yet these men hired McCarthy to write for, and with, them.

Despite a liberated lifestyle that included four husbands, numerous lovers, and financial independence, McCarthy never accepted feminism; in a 1979 interview with Miriam Gross, she said, "As for Women's Lib, it bores me. Of course I believe in equal pay and equality before the law and so on, but this whole myth about how different the world would have been if it had been female dominated. . . . I've never noticed that women were less warlike than men. And in marriage—an equal division of tasks is impossible—it's a judgment of Solomon" (qtd. in Donohue 95). Yet McCarthy never took her husbands' names. No wonder her nickname was "Contrary Mary."

Indeed, Contrary Mary was known to attack antifeminists. In 1947 she reviewed Ferdinand Lundberg and Marynia Farnham's *Modern Women, the Lost Sex*, which argues that "the industrial revolution eventually led women . . . to despise their own reproductive capabilities . . . and ultimately to agitate for gender equality" (qtd. in Perkins 121). In analyzing the review, McCarthy's "discomfort with [the authors'] anti-feminism is palpable" (Perkins 123). She begins by skewering their contentions that "women should avoid higher education in favor of childbearing," noting that this holds true only if the woman is not, like one of the authors, a doctor. She argues against the notion that "normative psychology dictates appropriate gender roles for both women and men," suggesting that the problem is not a matter of "women versus machines" but rather "women *as* machines" (qtd. in Perkins 125). Most notably, she refutes the authors' contention that "the female orgasm is the 'natural' reward to those women who obey the biological imperative to reproduce and nurture children within . . . a heterosexual marriage" (125).

Regardless of her protestations, McCarthy's work certainly fits the definition of the feminist novel laid out by Patrocinio Schweikert. Feminist novels reflect political struggle—a theme evident not only in Kay and Norinne's (*The Group*) participation in socialist strikes but also in their attempts to outwit their husbands' dominance. Connection to a community and the "struggle against patriarchy" are often prominent themes. On this subject, Donohue notes that "although her heroines do not achieve [McCarthy's] success in life they are painfully, humorously aware of their positions, and that is still a very feminist awareness" (96). In these novels, female experiences and value systems are examined and more likely to be reified, leading women readers to identify more easily with the characters and plots. Martha Duffy concurs, writing that McCarthy "inspired generations of women because she wrote about 'a woman's domestic strategies, her finances, her female friendships, her minute biological concerns. Every syllabus on feminist literature is indebted to her" (qtd. in Donohue 95–96). In feminist novels the story is viewed as a manifestation of the author's voice. Anyone who has read McCarthy's novels and biographies recognizes the constant interweaving of fiction with reality.

Although McCarthy's life, like her work, appears contradictory, she stands not only as a role model for women but also as arguably the first contemporary Irish American feminist writer. John Crowley refers to *The Group* as "a pioneering work of feminist fiction" (qtd. in Donohue 95). While discussing her leftist affiliations, Alan Wald notes that McCarthy "naturally attracts the interests of feminists" (70). Alison Lurie agrees:

> From the appearance of her first stories, she has altered the public idea of what a women of letters can be. In spite of her declared disinterest in feminism, she has surely changed the lives of generations of intelligent young women. . . . Her achievement was to invent herself as a totally new type of woman who stood for both sense and sensibility; who was both coolly and professionally intellectual, and frankly passionate. When we learned that she had also managed to combine a lively and varied erotic life with marriage and motherhood, we were amazed. Maybe, as the editor of *Cosmopolitan* was to put it much later, we could have it all. (19)

Given her views on feminism, McCarthy would likely prefer to be remembered for her intellect, and upon her death Elizabeth Hardwick gave McCarthy her due: "If there were any real ancestor among American women for Mary McCarthy, it might be Margaret Fuller. . . . Both women have will power, confidence, and a subversive soul sustained by exceptional energy" (qtd. in Kakutani B10).

Mary McCarthy served as a role model for generations of feminists, from Susan Sontag and Germaine Greer to, of all people, Camille Paglia (Showalter 303). More importantly, McCarthy opened the door for Irish American feminist writers. Although she may not have said "hello" to feminism, I think Mary McCarthy would have welcomed these writers and their multifaceted characters.

Notes

1. Ron Ebest notes that Clara Laughlin and Kathleen Norris's novels imply this, although divorce is never an option. Instead, the image of the "contented widow is a staple of pre-Depression Irish-American writing" explored by males and females alike (32).

2. In the early twentieth century Anne O'Hagan, Ruth McKenney, and Barbara Mullen were also known for their light satire. O'Hagan's was concentrated in her nonliterary essays (see R. Ebest 114 ff); McKenney's in her plays, most notably *My Sister Eileen* and *The McKenneys Carry On* (see Fanning 301); and Mullen's in her memoir *Life Is My Adventure* (R. Ebest 245).

3. As note 2 makes evident, McCarthy was not the first Irish American woman to write a memoir; she was, however, the first to produce a stylistically significant work of this genre.

4. Like McCarthy, neither Kathleen Norris nor Anne O'Hagan considered themselves feminists, even though their best-known nonliterary publications — Norris's *Hands Full of Living* and O'Hagan's essays in *Harper's Bazaar* and *Vanity Fair* — decried the Irish American woman's lot (see R. Ebest 34, 114–15).

Works Cited

Abrams, Sabrina Fuchs. *Mary McCarthy: Gender, Politics, and the Postwar Intellectual*. New York: Lang, 2004.

Barrett, William. *The Truants: Adventures Among the Intellectuals*. New York: Anchor/Doubleday, 1982.

Bernstein, Richard. "Susan Sontag, as Image and as Herself." *New York Times* 26 Jan. 1989: 26.

Brightman, Carol, ed. *Between Friends: The Correspondence of Hannah Arendt and Mary McCarthy, 1949–1975*. New York: Harcourt Brace, 1995.

———. *Writing Dangerously: Mary McCarthy and Her World*. New York: Clarkson Potter, 1992.

———. "Writing Dangerously." *Mirabella* Aug. 1992: 133–34.

Conroy, Frank. *Stop Time*. New York: Viking, 1967.

Dickstein, Morris. "A Glint of Malice." *Twenty-Four Ways of Looking at Mary McCarthy*. Ed. Eve Stwertka and Margo Viscusi. Westport, CT: Greenwood Press, 1996. 17–27.

Donohue, Stacy Lee. "The Reluctant Radical: The Irish-Catholic Element." *Twenty-Four Ways of Looking at Mary McCarthy*. Ed. Eve Stwertka and Margo Viscusi. Westport, CT: Greenwood Press, 1996. 87–99.

Dunne, John Gregory. *Harp*. New York: Simon and Schuster, 1989.

Ebest, Sally. "Evolving Feminisms." *Reconciling Catholicism and Feminism?* Ed. Sally Barr Ebest and Ron Ebest. Notre Dame, IN: University of Notre Dame Press, 2003. 263–79.

Ebest, Ron. *Private Histories: The Writing of Irish Americans, 1900–1935.* Notre Dame, IN: University of Notre Dame Press, 2005.

Fanning, Charles. *The Irish Voice in America.* 2nd ed. Lexington: University of Kentucky Press, 2000.

Field Day Anthology of Irish Women's Writing and Traditions. Ed. Angela Bourke, Siobhan Kilfeather, Maria Luddy, Margaret Mac Curtain, Geraldine Meaney, Mairin Ni Dhonnchadha, Mary O'Dowd, and Clair Wills. Volumes 4 and 5. New York: New York University Press, 2001.

Gelderman, Doris. *Mary McCarthy: A Life.* New York: St. Martins, 1988.

Gross, Beverly. "Bitch." *Salmagundi* 103 (Summer 1994): 146–56.

Grumbach, Doris. *The Company She Kept.* New York: Coward-McCann, 1967.

Hardy, Willene Schaefer. *Mary McCarthy.* New York: Ungar, 1981.

Howard, Maureen. *Facts of Life.* Boston: Little Brown, 1986.

Kakutani, Michiko. "Mary McCarthy, 77, Is Dead; Novelist, Memoirist, and Critic." *New York Times* 26 Oct. 1989: B10.

Kalven, Janet. "Feminism and Catholicism." *Reconciling Catholicism and Feminism?* Ed. Sally Barr Ebest and Ron Ebest. Notre Dame, IN: University of Notre Dame Press, 2003. 32–46.

Kazin, Alfred. *Starting Out in the Thirties.* Boston: Little, Brown, 1965.

Kiernan, Frances. *Seeing Mary Plain.* New York: W. W. Norton, 2000.

Krause, David. *The Profane Book of Irish Comedy.* Ithaca, NY: Cornell University Press, 1982.

Lurie, Alison. "True Confessions." Rev. of *How I Grew,* by Mary McCarthy. *New York Review of Books* 11 June 1987: 19–20.

McCarthy, Mary. *Birds of America.* New York: Harcourt Brace Jovanovich, 1971.

———. *Cannibals and Missionaries.* New York: Harcourt Brace Jovanovich, 1979.

———. *Cast a Cold Eye.* New York: Harcourt Brace, 1950.

———. *A Charmed Life.* New York: Harcourt Brace, 1955.

———. *The Company She Keeps.* New York: Dell, 1942.

———. "The Fact in Fiction." *On the Contrary.* New York: Farrar, 1961.

———. *The Group.* San Diego, CA: Harcourt Brace, 1963.

———. *The Groves of Academe.* London: Weidenfield and Nicolson, 1952.

———. *Hanoi.* New York: Harcourt Brace and World, 1968.

———. *How I Grew.* New York: Harcourt Brace Jovanovich, 1986.

———. *The Hounds of Summer and Other Stories.* New York: Avon, 1981.

———. *Ideas and the Novel.* New York: Harcourt Brace Jovanovich, 1980.

———. *Intellectual Memoirs: New York 1936–38.* New York: Harcourt Brace Jovanovich, 1993.

———. *Mary McCarthy's Theatre Chronicles, 1937–1962.* New York: Farrar, Straus, 1963.

————. *The Mask of State: Watergate Portraits*. New York: Harcourt Brace Jovanovich, 1974.

————. *Medina*. New York: Harcourt Brace Jovanovich, 1971.

————. *Memories of a Catholic Girlhood*. New York: Harcourt, Brace and World, 1957.

————. *The Oasis*. New York: Avon, 1949.

————. *The Seventeenth Degree*. New York: Harcourt Brace Jovanovich, 1974.

————. *Sights and Spectacles: Theatre Chronicles, 1937–56*. New York: Meridian, 1957.

————. *The Stones of Florence*. New York: Harcourt Brace, 1957.

————. *Venice Observed*. Paris: G. and R. Bernier, 1956.

————. *Vietnam*. New York: Harcourt, Brace and World, 1967.

McKenzie, Barbara. *Mary McCarthy*. New York: Twayne, 1967.

Perkins, Priscilla. "Frigid Women, Frozen Dinners: The Bio-Politics of 'Tyranny of the Orgasm.'" *Twenty-Four Ways of Looking at Mary McCarthy*. Ed. Eve Stwertka and Margo Viscusi. Westport, CT: Greenwood Press, 1996. 121–28.

Scanlan, Margaret. "Terrorists, Artists, and Intellectuals." *Twenty-Four Ways of Looking at Mary McCarthy*. Ed. Eve Stwertka and Margo Viscusi. Westport, CT: Greenwood Press, 1996. 35–42.

Schlesinger, Arthur, Jr. "Remembrances of an Old Friend." *Twenty-Four Ways of Looking at Mary McCarthy*. Ed. Eve Stwertka and Margo Viscusi. Westport, CT: Greenwood Press, 1996. 201–4.

Schweikert, Patrocinio. "Reading Ourselves: Toward a Feminist Theory of Reading." *Feminisms*. Ed. Robyn R. Warhol and Diane Price Herndl. New Brunswick, NJ: Rutgers University Press, 1991. 525–50.

Showalter, Elaine. *Inventing Herself: Claiming a Feminist Intellectual Heritage*. New York: Scribner's, 2001.

Stwertka, Eve, and Margo Viscusi, eds. *Twenty-Four Ways of Looking at Mary McCarthy*. Westport, CT: Greenwood Press, 1996.

Wald, Alan. "The Left Reconsidered." *Twenty-Four Ways of Looking at Mary McCarthy*. Ed. Eve Stwertka and Margo Viscusi. Westport, CT: Greenwood Press, 1996. 69–76.

Wilford, Hugh. *The New York Intellectuals: From Vanguard to Institution*. Manchester: Manchester University Press, 1995.

CHAPTER 2

Maureen Howard's
"Landscapes of Memory"

PATRICIA KEEFE DURSO

As I walked up the steps of the New York Public Library to meet Maureen Howard, the sky was slowly darkening, even though it was only 11:00 in the morning. Hurricane Isabel was on the way, so the darkness seemed oddly appropriate. Already I imagined I saw Howard's characters around every corner. As I stood on Fifth Avenue in front of the library, I could see Mary Agnes Keely in her red silk dress fresh off the *Bridgeport Bus*, passing by in a taxi looking at the "Library lions (obviously old friends)" (24). Peering around back, I could see *Before My Time*'s Jim Cogan racing to stop Shelley Waltz as she stood with her religious sect preparing to blow up the library (231). Now, with the hurricane approaching, I thought of the powerful presence of nature in Howard's fiction: Hurricane Alma, which effectively redirects Elizabeth's life in *Grace Abounding* as she drives into the "eye of the storm" (114); the "year of the gypsy moth" (77) that marks the death and desertion precipitating Maude's coming of age at forty-three; and the "Biblical storm" (13) that ushers in the millennium and casts its young lovers out of their Edenic garden in *A Lover's Almanac*. These storms, however, are but barometers of the shifting climate in Howard's "landscape[s] of memory,"[1] their passage uprooting not just old maple trees but, more significantly, deep-seated memories.

Ultimately, the force and power of memory in Howard's works is equal to if not greater than any storm, Biblical or otherwise, for it is the transformative journey through "landscapes of memory," through the past, that ultimately enables Howard's characters to move forward in the present. The "responsibility of the present to the past"[2] is a recurring concern in Howard's fiction, as all her characters struggle with the same basic questions Howard posed in an interview: "[A]re we really going to find the past a burden, or are we going to find out something about ourselves from what is given to us? Are we going to be able to go forward with the history we discover? Personal history, family history or, in a larger sense, public history?"[3] Howard's fiction focuses largely on the Irish American experience as she seeks to answer these questions and explore the role of the past—of personal, family, and public history—in the formation of the self. The answer that resurfaces throughout her works is clear: If the past is left unexamined or distorted by a sentimental outlook or one that otherwise obscures the truth, it will become a burden and arrest growth. If, however, the past is honestly examined and historical truths are confronted and acknowledged, the past will become usable and growth will be possible.

The force of memories of family, home, and Ireland is evocatively referred to in one of Howard's more recent works as "the stirring of roots and blood" (*Big as Life* 99), and it is this stirring of the past—stripped of sentimentality, bare, and honest—that distinguishes Howard's focus on the themes of home and family. These themes, as Charles Fanning notes in *The Irish Voice in America* (2000), have been a "major part of the Irish-American literary tradition all the way back to the start" (328), but Howard's novels also travel well beyond what she calls the "family core" (personal interview). Her work intertwines issues such as art, politics, nature, science, and literature with personal history, exposing the tangled roots that reach deep, down, and around the homes, through the soil, through the cities, and across the ocean to "the Other Side" (*Natural History* 42) and back again. Regarding the blood that stirs with these roots, Howard said, "there's violence underneath—of emotions—not necessarily physical violence, but emotional violence and tragedy and displacement" (personal interview).

Howard's unconventional and challenging narrative style reinforces this displacement as her "landscapes of memory" move like shifting tectonic plates that come together, rub against each other, split open, and shift and move again, reconnect with another plate, and finally all come together to form a world "big as life" that is uniquely Howard's. That this fictional world is also distinctly Irish American cannot go unnoticed, particularly in Howard's thematic focus on home and family and her structural emphasis on displacement and departures.

Howard's family history, conveyed in sharp yet loving prose in her memoir *Facts of Life*—a work that Fanning points out is part of the "significant sub-genre of late-twentieth-century Irish-American autobiography" (301)—provides a ready backdrop for her fictional explorations of the tensions in Irish American life. Maureen Kearns Howard was born to William Kearns and Loretta Burns Kearns on June 28, 1930, in Bridgeport, Connecticut, a town with a strong Irish community and an enduring pull on Howard's literary imagination. While both of Howard's parents hailed from Bridgeport's Irish community, her father was from the town's poorer Irish "East Side," while her mother came from Bridgeport's Irish nobility. Howard was particularly attached to her maternal grandparents, who were "gods" in her mind (*Facts* 95). Her maternal grandfather, a "handsome Irishman" (*Facts* 92), lived the quintessential Irish success story: he built a carting and hauling business into a small paving empire, married a "sprightly redhead[ed]" (*Facts* 94) Irish girl from New York City, and eventually built a palatial home on property he purchased from "the faded Yankee gentility for whom his mother had served as the Irish maid" (*Facts* 97). The marriage of this ostensible "Diamond Jim Brady" of Bridgeport's Smith-educated daughter, Loretta, to William Kearns—of the "poor Kearnses on the East Side" of Bridgeport—was a disappointment to Howard's grandfather (*Facts* 102, 106).

As Fanning notes, at this point in time (the early twentieth century), "Irish America remained an ambivalent culture in transition, still busy shoring up its hard-won incursions into the middle-class" (239); this ambivalence can be heard in Howard's mother's voice as she "patronized her own" with a simple turn of phrase: "Oh, the Irish" (*Facts* 11). "We were taught," Howard notes, "to take the Irish lightly," to mock "the world we came from—the tap routines and accordion music on Saint Patrick's night, the Catholic Messenger with its simpering parables of sacrifice" (*Facts* 11, 12). But Howard realizes that "[i]n laughing at them we laughed at ourselves, didn't we, Catholics in good standing, pure potato-Irish famine, gone fine with our cut glass and linens from McCutcheon's" (*Facts* 13). Howard's personal experience calls attention to issues of class and assimilation and the ambiguities surrounding both; in mocking "the Irish" Howard's family not only mocked themselves but also displaced themselves—unwilling to identify fully with the Irish ethnic community but unable to fit seamlessly into "white" America. As George O'Brien observes, *Facts of Life* "functions as a meditation on the mercuriality of an identity trained in, but not conditioned by, a strong awareness of ethnicity. The roots of the tension between training and self-awareness that pervade Howard's novels are explored in a way that reveals the limitations of identity conceived of solely in terms of its ethnic origins and the problematic shapelessness of identity conceived of without an adequate negotiation of those origins" (95). It is precisely a "negotiation of those origins" that Howard's novels demand as a prerequisite to growth and self-definition.

When I met with Howard, she was finishing *The Silver Screen* (2004) and beginning a fellowship at the New York Public Library's Center for Scholars and Writers to work on a series of essays on the illustrated novel in English.[4] Howard began her writing career in 1960 with the publication of her first novel, *Not a Word About Nightingales* (which she has put behind her as an exercise, a "small academic novel").[5] It was her second novel, *Bridgeport Bus* (1965)—driven by the unforgettable Irish American protagonist Mary Agnes Keely and characterized by a sharp wit and defiance of convention (narrative and otherwise)—that commanded the attention of critics and readers. Howard followed that novel with *Before My Time* (1974), which focuses on two strands of an Irish American family, and soon after that she published her memoir *Facts of Life*. *Facts of Life* was awarded the National Book Critics Circle Award for Nonfiction and the PEN Kaufman Award; hailed by the *New York Times Book Review* as a "portrait of the artist as a young woman" (Rev. of *Facts of Life*) (one of many comparisons to James Joyce that Howard's work has invoked throughout the years); and decreed by Fanning's landmark study *The Irish Voice in America* as "a significant document in Irish-American cultural self-definition" (345). Following the tremendous success of her memoir, Howard published three novels: *Grace Abounding* (1982), *Expensive Habits* (1986), and *Natural History* (1992). All three were finalists for the PEN/Faulkner Award and continued to expand and establish her reputation as an innovative and challenging writer with a "highly developed technical skill and . . . alert heart"

(Casey 46). Howard's current project, a quartet of books about the seasons, thus far includes *A Lover's Almanac* (1998), *Big as Life: Three Tales for Spring* (2001), and *The Silver Screen* (2004), works shaped around winter, spring, and summer, respectively (the "fall" book is yet to come). Howard's work has been supported by fellowships from the Bellagio, Ingram Merrill, and Guggenheim Foundations, among others, and she has received awards from the National Endowment for the Arts, the American Academy of Arts and Letters, and the Radcliffe Institute.

In addition to producing an award-winning body of fiction, Howard has also found time for what she modestly refers to as "respectable piece-work" ("Before I Go" 7): literary criticism, most notably on Virginia Woolf and Edith Wharton; numerous essays and book reviews; a play, "Songs at Twilight"; and poems and various short pieces.[6] Howard's accomplishments as a writer, critic, and teacher (currently at Columbia)[7] do indeed "give us pause," as she has said of Edith Wharton's productivity (in "On *The House of Mirth*"). Like Virginia Woolf, Howard has taken on "overwhelming literary commitments" and yet has certainly managed to do, as she has said of Woolf, "a lot of fine writing . . . on the side" ("Before I Go" 7).

Aside from book reviews and the occasional critical essay, however, Kerry Ahearn's 1984 observation that there has been "scarce commentary" (171) on Howard's books still holds true, although Fanning's discussion of her work in *The Irish Voice in America* (first in 1990 and then in the expanded second edition in 2000) has brought her — like many other Irish American writers he discusses — wider attention. In that groundbreaking study, Fanning identifies "light" and "dark" strains of "contemporary Irish-American stylized fiction" and holds up Howard as the strongest example of the light, or "positive side" (344). The "light strain," as Fanning defines it, "appears in the service of fruitful iconoclasm and growth, in novels where linguistic exuberance is a comic, vital, and ultimately creative force. . . . Here impatience with narrative conventions is part and parcel of healthy contempt for strictures on behavior that stifle the soul groping toward change for the better" (342–43). Indeed, Howard's style is anything but conventional, her voice anything but reverential, and her "contempt for strictures on behavior" evident on every page of her books. Staples of her writing include nonlinear fragmented narratives, frequent shifts in point of view and narrative voice, stories embedded within stories, and fact merged with fiction (most evident from *Natural History* forward). As Fanning observes, Howard's experimental style suggests that "experience is too tricky and fascinating, too full, for straightforward narrative. Life means too much, not too little, to be rendered in logical, linear form" (344).

Howard's unconventional and highly performative narratives, which call upon the language and techniques of theater, movie, sideshow, and docudrama[8] and are written with an "unusual blend of wit, impeccable style and humanity" (Levin 28), take on a wide variety of themes. The "major Irish-American concerns of politics, religion, and family" (Fanning 317) are all present to one degree or another in Howard's work, but religion and family dominate her thematic landscape (though they by no means limit that landscape, for Howard's reach—indeed, her grasp—is truly "big as life"). Irish Catholic culture, for example, is an integral part of the set upon which Howard's stories play out, but it is there more for mood and dramatic effect than anything else. "My religious periods," Howard writes in *Facts of Life*, "have been genuine only as dramatic exercises" (35), a point well illustrated by her childhood suicide attempt with a grapefruit knife after she unintentionally broke her fast on the morning of her First Holy Communion (34). That same sense of drama—of the connection between religious ritual and dramatic performance—infuses many of her novels. For example, the small theater of the confessional booth becomes the site of the "next show," the sinners waiting in line as if for a movie (*Grace Abounding* 13). When we come out of that theater, our eyes blinking in the sudden sunlight, we find the sun hanging "like a distant Eucharist in the sky" (*Facts* 153). It is this figuratively transubstantiated sun that sheds perpetual light on the "landscapes of memory" in Howard's novels—a landscape in which the marks of Howard's distinctly Irish American "Catholic training" (*Facts* 33) are ever present yet distanced, where reverence for the natural world displaces reverence for the ecclesiastical world, where parents try "to make Catholics" out of their children (*Before My Time* 109), where children try to deal with the "shredded ends" of their Catholicism as adults (*Grace Abounding* 32), and where, ultimately, literature and art become the new religion. Literature, for example, becomes Mary Agnes Keely's religion in *Bridgeport Bus* as she makes her "devotions" to "the *Daily News* for conversational tidbits, a Jane Austen novel to bring marriage into focus, and *My Antonia* for the *sine qua non* of the immigrant scene" (192). Likewise, Catherine's pious "peasant faith" (8) as a child in *Natural History* is inevitably displaced as books become her "daily bread," the public library "her holy place," and the Dewey Decimal System one of many "new rituals" (241). In the end, she finds salvation in the art of weaving: "Tell of your conversion to sanity and loom," she intones, "Tedious, possessed of that newfound religion, tell" (358–59).

As evocative and weighty as they are, however, religious imagery and metaphors are but shadows in Howard's fiction; the main subjects, which cast those shadows by the light of that "distant Eucharist in the sky," are the family and home. Howard's "landscapes of memory," however, are anything but cozy and domestic; in fact, they are characterized by a flight from home—a simultaneous desire for and rejection of that primordial place. In an autobiographical section in Big as Life, for example, Howard situates her "landscape of memory" in a place that is at once "happy" and "stifling"— "the happy, stifling embrace of two city lots on North Avenue in Bridgeport" (224–25). Howard's fictional homes are likewise characterized by a palpable tension, a simultaneous push and pull, an embrace both "happy" and "stifling." Like Howard, Louise Moffet in A Lover's Almanac, for instance, bases her art on her own "landscape[s] of memory" (7), working specifically within a "landscape of home" that is "at once yearning and rejecting" (88). Louise's—and by extension Howard's—tension-filled, deeply shaded "landscape[s] of home," however, are most definitely not nostalgic or sentimental. In fact, I would say sentimentalism is the eighth deadly sin in Howard's fiction. As Marc Robinson wrote in a review of Natural History, Howard "writes about her abiding subject, the family, with fierce rigor. . . . Not for her the cozy domestic zones where passions are labeled and personal histories are smugly untangled."

Indeed, at times the tensions and tangles of family figuratively and literally draw blood in Howard's work. In Bridgeport Bus Lydia's white gloves turn a "shocking crimson" (80) from a child's book that "bleed[s]" (62) in her hands; in Big as Life Nuala's "removal from Ireland" by her family is marked by that "stirring of roots and blood" each spring (99); also in Big as Life, John James Audubon figuratively sacrifices his wife and family while he literally "killed for his art" (143); in Before My Time Laura kisses a young Jimmy Cogan with "violence" (219)—that same Jimmy whose blood is "drawn to the surface with silk cord" by his father (45); and in Bridgeport Bus Mary Agnes and her mother "play a cannibal game," "eat[ing] each other over the years, tender morsel by morsel until there is nothing left but dry bone and wig" (4). While some blood is spilled in her pages, the wounds in Howard's fiction are primarily psychological, stemming, for instance, from a desire for gentility and conformity on the part of an older (immigrant or first) generation of Irish Americans and a need for self-definition and self-assertion on the part of a younger (second or third) generation, who feel trapped by conformity and "cursed with gentility" (*Bridgeport Bus* 6).

It is not surprising, then, that the focus throughout much of Howard's work is on *leaving*—leaving home, leaving that place that restricts, curses, draws blood to the point where there is nothing left but "dry bone and wig." "You start," Howard explained, "from home, an idea of place, a place that is central, shaping," a place "that creates almost an imagery of home" but "which need not be, and is not always, totally nurturing at all" (personal interview). Thinking back to "poor old Mary Agnes's" flight from her suffocating home in *Bridgeport Bus*, in our interview Howard stressed that "leaving is very important" and tellingly connected this idea to Chekhov (a writer to whom we find allusions throughout Howard's fiction)[9]: "I often think," she said, "about Chekhov's plays—the three biggies—all they're about, you know, to be extraordinarily reductive, is the people who stay and the people who go away. That's all they're about. Of course, lives hang on that line. The whole drama of life hangs on the fact that some people go and some cannot go." Likewise, Howard's "landscapes of memory" are crowded with comings and goings (mostly the latter), as her novels continually impress upon us the fact that lives do indeed "hang on" the decision to leave or stay. The import of staying versus leaving is conveyed, for example, even through minor characters such as Muriel Mueller in *Big as Life* (who we never even meet but only hear about): "well, you do know," an "ancient Librarian" confides to the reader, "she stayed" (202). Staying makes all the difference; Muriel looks "oddly out of place" in family snapshots (175) and paints landscapes that suggest "some grief or loss" (176). Howard's novels continually underscore that staying—in that place of comfort, on the path that offers emotional safety (yet paralysis on so many other levels)—is a choice that results in a loss, narrowing and restricting possibility, while leaving is a choice that allows for growth, possibility, and change.

A focus on "the people who stay and the people who go" is, of course, particularly significant and historically resonant in terms of the Irish American experience. As Hasia R. Diner notes in *Erin's Daughters in America* (1983), "[b]eginning in the early nineteenth century, the exodus from Ireland to the United States amounted to a virtual tidal wave of human beings leaving one home and seeking another" (30). While lives have literally hung on the fact that some people could leave and some could not—that is, that some left Ireland and some did not—lives have also figuratively hung on the fact that some were able to leave Irish immigrant ghettos in America and some could not, that some went beyond the "limited geography of work, church, home" (*Natural History* 42) and some did not, that some escaped those "bonds of correctness" (*Before My Time* 99) and some did not. In Howard's work the trajectory of comings and goings is a wide one, her characters taking their place among what she has called elsewhere "the many departures, the emotional and imaginative departures echoing the great emigration from Ireland" ("Foreword" xii). Howard's memoir demonstrates at every turn her own insistence on leaving and escaping those "bonds." Indeed, in "Assimilation Blues: Maureen Howard's *Facts of Life*," George O'Brien suggests that the "persistent sense of breaking off, breaking out, breaking away" in *Facts of Life* is partly a result of Howard's Irish origins, their colonial roots, and the associated "difficulty in establishing a place to be" (97). "[W]hat emerges most convincing," he continues, "is the writer's position between . . . home and world" (98).

As Joanna Scott observes, Howard is one of the "independent voices, the indefinable writers, the writers who won't stay put in any category, who take on big subjects and little subjects, who write both lyrically and crisply, and who keep expanding the field."[10] Nevertheless, it is clear that the Irish American experience has shaped and informed her writing in significant ways. Whether we see Howard's work as a negotiation of the ambiguities of ethnicity and identity, a cautionary tale about the perils of ignoring the past, a study of those who left versus those who stayed behind, a meditation on the force of memory, an indictment of sentimentality, or—perhaps most succinctly—a thematic and formal articulation of the "yearn[ing] to cross boundaries" ("Foreword" xii) that restrict and confine, we cannot help but see that Howard returns again and again to the particular experience of Irish Americans and uses that experience to speak to the universal, to the immigrant soul in everyone, to the "soul groping toward change for the better" (Fanning 343). As Howard observes about the writers in *Cabbage and Bones: An Anthology of Irish-American Women's Fiction* (1997), although they are "more or less Irish, more or less American, they write, as all fair writers do, of an experience that is at once universal and particular" ("Foreword" xiv). The same is true of Howard herself, as the following discussion of her novels will illustrate.

WHEN WE MEET ALBERT SEDGELY, the protagonist of Howard's first novel, *Not a Word About Nightingales*, he has already "taken life, an immeasurable, rich fabric and snipped it away, cut it down to his size" (61). While this only gives us a glimpse of Howard's scope and virtuosity, it does introduce a central thread in Howard's work: the sin of cutting life "down to . . . size." Although Albert initially summons the courage to leave his safe, predictable life—rejecting the tight-fitting "dull garment of his past" (61)—in the end he returns, his courage and conviction in the journey gone as he willingly puts that "dull garment" back on.

In her second novel, *Bridgeport Bus*, Howard gives us a protagonist, Mary Agnes Keely ("Ag"), who is more successful in leaving a constricted life and redefining herself. Indeed, Ag is determined to cast off that "dull garment" of her past and roll wildly in her "red silk dress" (16), in what Doris Grumbach has called "one of the most astutely funny novels of our time" ("Maureen Howard's Understated Elegance"). As Fanning observes, in this second novel Howard "explores the thematic roots of her own Irish Catholic upbringing in Bridgeport" and "stylistically burst[s] out to what from now on becomes her method—a mélange of styles and forms that expresses her impatience with conventional narrative modes" (344). From the opening paragraph of *Bridgeport Bus* we see that Ag's life literally "hangs on" whether she stays in Bridgeport or leaves. In her childhood home "stuffed with darkness," filled with furniture "all colorless as time, all under a layer of antediluvian silt" (5), Ag plays that "cannibal game" (4) with her mother—"a big Irish woman 'fulla life' with eyes ready to cry" (5), always "looking for crosses to bear" (141)—and her mother is winning the game. When we meet Ag she is "gaunt," tall and thin with a "shamefully concave chest" (6), and her "nerves are raw" from "meaningless day[s] at work" (3). While Ag dramatically likens her flight to Rimbaud's—" 'The hour of flight will be the hour of death for me' " (16)—we know that it is the figurative death of a "thirty-five-year-old virgin" (7), an obedient daughter, an "early-to-bed soul" (13) that Ag welcomes and accepts. Ag leaves home, significantly, in the spring (at the end of Lent, just before Easter, and the end of the first chapter), a time of rebirth and renewal.[11] And just as Joyce's Stephen Dedalus (with whom the literary, writerly Ag has inevitably been compared) takes flight from Ireland with "silence, exile, and cunning" as his tools, Ag takes flight from Bridgeport with just the "bare necessities: one suitcase, the beginning of this story" (16).

Read in the context of the great emigration from Ireland to America, Ag's journey from Bridgeport to New York City is, in many ways, an immigrant's tale. Her apartment in New York City becomes "the first place on earth, a Paradise without Adam or as yet a snake" (58)—it is a prelapsarian (indeed, pre-male) place that provides infinite possibilities for Ag's new life (and eventual "fall"). What Ag finds and demands in New York City is her "cut of life" (36), which she goes after with a voracious appetite, literally and figuratively gorging her gaunt self on the "smorgasbord of New York" (37). Ag's thin and "gaunt" frame, punctuated by her "concave chest," evokes images of starving Irish immigrants fleeing the Great Hunger. While Ag's hunger is not literal but figurative, not physical but emotional, it is nonetheless acutely felt and must be satiated in order for her to survive. Likewise, her desire to escape a dismal "brown and gray" landscape (akin to Joyce's landscape in *Dubliners*, particularly in stories such as "Araby"), as well as familial and religious constrictions and a mind-numbing job, call to mind images of later waves of Irish immigrants to America who were seeking freedom, a new world, and a land of promise and plenty.

In this new world Ag sets a "modest plan" for herself: "record life around you, Mary Agnes. Chart your painful journey to freedom" (83). Ag's journal makes up the majority of the novel's narrative, documenting her journey outward and "fall" into knowledge about sex, men, and life. Through it all, however, the "dark rooms" of her "mother's dingy flat" in Bridgeport still "imprison" (38) Ag, dominating her "landscape of memory" while her mother's "endless keening, ancient, racially remembered" (13) seems to echo through the New York streets. At the end of the novel, Ag is pregnant, alone, and in a home for unwed mothers, yet she has "triumphed" nevertheless: she recognizes that it is "no great sin to be, at last, alone" (309). Like many of Howard's other characters and waves of Irish immigrants before them, Ag claims New York City as her new home: "The City: It is my home" (305). While Ag may die in childbirth at the end of the novel (critics are divided on this question), it is clear that her decision to leave Bridgeport—to emigrate, as it were, to New York City—was her only route to life.

Like New York City, Boston attracted a huge number of Irish immigrants. In her third novel, *Before My Time*, Howard explores the different modes of Irish assimilation by juxtaposing the lives of the descendants of two sisters who emigrated from Ireland and settled in Boston and Brooklyn respectively. While both sisters initially lived in Brooklyn's Irish community, one sister left after marrying into a blue-blood Boston family while the other stayed behind.

Laura Quinn is the daughter of the sister who fled to Boston; her story documents the centrality of ethnicity to a sense of self and the loss of self that can result from assimilation into "white" America. Laura lives in the

Boston suburbs, is the wife of a lawyer and mother of two children, and writes nonfiction (her current project is about women in politics). From the start of the novel it is clear that Laura is figuratively homeless: she grew up in a home in Boston that was "not home" but a place where her father's people tried to "make a lady" out of her, "peel off the Irish or the New York," she says, "I'd picked up from my mother, one as bad as the other to them" (90). Laura's identity as an adult is similarly circumscribed and defined by others; when we meet her she is living in a "terribly dishonest house" (6) and has "lost the sense" of her world; she is no longer able to "justify the tidy vision" she was to "pass on" to her children (239). As Doris Grumbach observes in a review of *Before My Time*, we see here the "theme of an un-eventful, deeply felt, nonprogress, of captivity in the sacrament and ritual of marriage, of life as a series of inconsequential events, poignant and terrible, signifying little" ("Things Happen"). Laura's is a life in quiet, re-pressed crisis.

Mill Cogan is the daughter of the sister who stayed in Brooklyn in the immigrant Irish Catholic community in which her parents settled. Her story documents a crisis engendered not by the loss of ethnicity but by the trappings of Irish ethnicity: martyrdom, drink, and poverty. Living in a third-floor apartment on Bruckner Boulevard in Brooklyn where even the plants cannot stay alive, she is married to an Irish salesman who con-tinually "fails" her and their three children by gambling away his earnings. Mill drinks (gin) to temper the disappointment of her current life and to deal with the "desire that still rose in her to run away. But she didn't leave. Mill stayed with what was set before her" (149). When her teenage son Jim, with his "unmistakably Irish" features (10), is sent to live with Laura and her family for a few weeks, the novel explores this coming together of very different worlds—Boston and Brooklyn, age and youth, female and male, leaving and staying—in terms of what it means for Laura, whose undefined fears (perhaps of aging, or of "dwindling expectations" [3]) are strongly felt from the first paragraph of the novel.

Laura's journey in *Before My Time* is not literal like Ag's in *Bridge-port Bus*; rather, it is a figurative journey into the past, a journey away from an unexamined life, away from a "dishonest" home in which she plays a predefined role instead of living a self-defined life. It is a journey toward the freedom that comes with letting go of disabling expectations, of con-formity, of being a "good girl" (240). While Laura never physically leaves her home, she does leave psychologically—this we known from the first page when we are told "she's not altogether there" (3). And in the end, "[l]ike so many American heroes" (though Howard's is refreshingly female), Laura "fixes on the one flickering light on the horizon, her doubt like new knowledge in her heart" (241). What Laura has found, to borrow Howard's words from *Facts of Life*, is the sense that she "could make a choice, if not now, one day" (76). Ultimately, Laura's figurative escape from her "dishonest house" results in a "painful but affirmative release into possibility" (Fanning 343). It is just this sort of narrative resolution that makes Howard one of the strongest examples of the "positive side" of contemporary Irish American fiction (Fanning 344).

Both *Bridgeport Bus* and *Before My Time* emphasize the "movement outward, beyond constriction to openness and freedom" that is a hallmark of much recent Irish American fiction (Fanning 329). Howard's fourth novel, *Grace Abounding*, similarly documents a move from a narrow, restricted life into one of possibility as it structurally and thematically dramatizes the journey to and from home. Organized in three parts ("Sin," "Sorrow," and "Minor Chalzion"), *Grace Abounding* traces the life of a young widow, Maude Dowd-Lesser, and her journey into sight, as well as her daughter's journey into voice. "Sin" is framed by Maude's trips to visit her aging mother. While she drives to her mother's apartment on the highway—a "dull drive" where her focus on her filial "duty" eclipses imagination (45)—she drives home from her mother's apartment on the back roads—a "grandiose adventure" where she briefly leaves, literally and figuratively, the predictable, safe road. She rides on these backroads with a "familiar slow leak," "the gas tank nearly empty," "begging for a blowout," "[a]ny small accident" (4–6) that might open the door to one of her many sexual fantasies (for example, "[s]cene[s] of crude lust" with a state trooper or teenage hitchhikers [4]). When she arrives at the "dead reality of home" she is yet another person—"the proper widow"—although here she is child-like, with a "matronly" fourteen-year-old daughter, Elizabeth, who is "methodical and mournful" (11) and does all the cooking and cleaning. Maude's road trips in this first section emphasize both the cyclical nature of her journeys and the space between coming and going, the space that feeds the imagination. Maude is ultimately caught in a loop, however, going from one home to another, from one prescribed identity (dutiful daughter) to another (proper widow). She is in stasis, her journey getting her nowhere, her "sin" a wasted life.

Various events finally drive Maude to leave the home in which both she and Elizabeth have been trapped. They move to New York City, that eternal place of growth and possibility in Howard's fiction. In New York Maude and Elizabeth essentially become different people; Maude remarries and becomes a child therapist, and Elizabeth pursues a promising singing career but too quickly gives it up for marriage and family in the suburbs. By the end of the novel, however, Elizabeth reclaims her voice as she sings a requiem for the dead (159), a song that the reader recognizes as not only for those characters who have died (Elizabeth's father; a young patient of Maude's) but also for those selves that Maude and Elizabeth have left behind. While the characters in *Grace Abounding* do not undergo the type of spiritual conversion the novel's title suggests (if we read it as an allusion to John Bunyan's 1666 *Grace Abounding to the Chief of Sinners*), they do recognize the sin of cutting life "down to size" and the grace of being given another chance.

Howard's fifth novel, *Expensive Habits*—heralded by Jonathan Yardley as a "book rich in integrity and elegance, by a writer who matters"—once again sets us down in New York City, a place, as Howard has said, that "has become an overlay" (over Bridgeport), giving her "another sense of place" (Swaim). Like Maude and Elizabeth in *Grace Abounding,* Maggie Flood (nee Lynch), the Irish American protagonist in *Expensive Habits,* is also blessed with another chance at life. It is New Year's Eve 1976, and forty-five-year-old Maggie has been told she has a heart problem that will kill her within the year; however, by the end of the novel she has "faked out death" (296). Like so many of Howard's characters, Maggie leaves, fleeing the "simple people" she came from—"[p]rovincial people with narrow views," "[c]atholic all around" (49). A celebrated fiction writer in New York literary circles, her success is marred by the feeling that she sold out, set "the bars down" and leapt "the easy hurdles" (35), particularly because she rewrote her first novel (*Child's Play,* the story of an Irish American family and categorized as a "woman's book" [55]) to please her editor and popular, sentimental tastes. Maggie's success is also marred, as Jonathan Yardley puts it, by the "conviction that her books, which are the story of her life, have told that story wrong—that they are riddled with self-serving falsehoods that have damaged others" (2). Howard has acknowledged her "mistrust" of "confessions"—"[t]hey seem from the vantage point of my Catholic training to suggest an easy road to redemption" (*Facts of Life* 33). Thus, it is safe to say that her character Maggie—who compares the confessional to a "puppet theater," the line of penitents to a "movie line" at the Rialto, and the sinner to the one who runs "the show" (13)—possesses the same cynicism, but that does not temper her need to confess (at least on paper), to rewrite the past and "undo the harm" (44) she has done through her novels. Indeed, *Expensive Habit*'s first words, "Go and sin no more" (13), immediately introduce the theme of atonement and announce the "sin" of distorting the past.

Like much of Howard's fiction, *Expensive Habits* sets us down in a "landscape of memory" that spins ever deeper into the past; her prose is "dense, complex, disturbing, authoritative" (Johnson), and the narrative is driven by memories and punctuated by stories within stories. As Maggie attempts to tell the "true and annotated version" (81), the "unforgivable truth" (82) of her life, she feels her heart failing, her time dwindling, so she "work[s] with a frenzy to set the record straight, as though she were ripping out the seams of her life" (116). *Expensive Habits* is, for the most part, a narrative propelled forward by the past, by Maggie's "unraveling" (81), but that movement is brought to an abrupt stop by a tragedy in the present. At the end, we leave Maggie defiantly standing out in the cold and the rain, leaning back into the past, into memories, as a source of strength for moving forward—or, at the very least, for staying in place: "They could never call her in. Her mother who was sickly would come to the screen door or call from her bed, her voice filtered through starched white curtains, distant and fearful, calling, 'Margaret—come in, come in.' She would not go, defiant, then dreaming on in the dangerous night air" (298). At the novel's conclusion Margaret remains figuratively gone, refusing to return to a life behind those stiffly "starched white curtains."

As the narrator reminds us at the end of *Expensive Habits*, as a child Maggie dreamed of becoming "Madame Lulu, the human meteor" at the circus (297). It is this love of risks and tricks, this strong sense of performance, that fuels her writing: "Ladies and Gentlemen, step right up," she says at the start of her story, "Margaret Flood knows how to warm up the audience" (16). That is exactly what *Expensive Habits* and all of Howard's previous novels do: they warm us up for the "big show": Howard's sixth novel, *Natural History*. Many reviewers have commented upon the various Joycean aspects of *Natural History*. The *New York Review of Books*, for example, compares the "cinematic episodes" in one section of Howard's novel to the "Nighttown section of Ulysses" (Edwards), but it is the strong sense of performance in Howard's novel, akin to what Howard calls Joyce's "performance with words," that most invites the comparison (fostered, of course, by the Irishness of Howard, her characters, and her themes).[12]

When we spoke, Howard observed that Joyce "was enormously conscious" that "writing is a performing art." She clearly shares this conviction: "the idea of voice and performance," she said, "is enormously important to me." While this belief in writing's performative nature is evident in both the content and form of all of her novels since *Bridgeport Bus*, the language of theater and film, sideshow and circus, show tunes and performance, tricks and magic is nowhere more apparent and more central to the narrative than in *Natural History*, where performative effects are achieved not with a sleight of hand but with a sleight of words, not with death-defying acts but with convention-defying narratives. As Marc Robinson states: "Linguistically acrobatic, imaginatively daring, Howard herself is the most debonair performer in *Natural History*. Her attraction to theater animates many of her previous books; here, however, she gives herself full rein to ponder the form explicitly—in screenplay fragments, in monologues, in musings on the daily circuses at and away from home." In *Natural History* Howard's penchant for performance and defiance of conventions (whether narrative, religious, gendered, or otherwise) come together to create a book that is, as Fanning writes, a "dazzling, full realization of Howard's trademark and identifiably Irish-American literary concerns with the presence of the past, the spirit of urban place, and Joycean technical wizardry, all in the service of emotional truth" (364).

A "sense of place," which Howard has emphasized is "one of the most important things to a writer," takes center stage in *Natural History* as Howard turns the spotlight back on the city of Bridgeport (Swaim). While *Bridgeport Bus* introduced us to Howard's hometown, we left it so quickly we may as well have been looking at it from the rear window of that bus. In *Natural History*, however, we return and embrace "this rich and generous place" (391). Indeed, more than one reviewer has suggested that Bridgeport is the "central character" in *Natural History*; Pearl K. Bell even refers to the city as the "hero" of the book, calling Bridgeport "Howard's Dublin."[13]

A pair of maps (or rather, a narrative describing them) of Bridgeport frame *Natural History*, structurally emphasizing both the sense of place so integral to this novel and the search for home so central to the immigrant experience. The first map is Howard's, circa 1944; the second, circa 1688, belongs to another Irish artist, Braddock Mead. *Natural History* begins with a cartographer drawing an elaborately detailed, lovingly rendered map of Bridgeport. The reader is immediately pulled in, becoming one with the cartographer, as Howard directs the "art-shop pen" (1). Of course, Howard's is not going to be an ordinary map but rather a map that "marr[ies]" "natural history" and "human history"; it plots not only geographical but also emotional, psychological, and familial sites. Such a map cannot, of course, be drawn from a "[b]ird's-eye view" (1) or from the ceiling of that "glorious cathedral." Indeed, Howard's Bridgeport has a magnetic, almost primordial pull: the cartographer ("you") is pulled further and further in, eventually leaving off "scientific" mapping altogether to record "a storied topography" complete with buildings, people, sounds, and vignettes until, finally, you are "[d]riven to words" and you "topple off your stool as though North Wind with puffed cheeks on a very old map blows you down. . . . Down to earth, in a windowless place you set the uncertain boundaries of recall" (3).[14] And down on the ground we are, in the next narrative moment, with a boy and his bike as the story begins.

It is a testimony to the richness and complexity of *Natural History* that it is difficult (if not impossible) to provide a neat plot summary. John Casey compares reading it to watching "a display of the aurora borealis"; Carol Anshaw calls it an "exponential explosion of all our complacent ideas of what a story is"; Pearl K. Bell observes that "any attempt to convey what passes for plot in *Natural History* is doomed." This is exactly what Howard was aiming for. When I met with Howard, I made the mistake of asking her what her upcoming novel, *The Silver Screen*, was about. Her response was telling: "if you can say what your novel is about, in a capsule, it's probably a lousy novel." While it is difficult to encapsulate what many of Howard's novels are "about" in their defiance of traditional conventions of plot, this is nowhere more true than in *Natural History*. The novel consists of three sections: "Natural History: I," "Museum Pieces," and "Natural History: II." The main focus throughout is on Catherine ("Cath") and James Bray, a sister and brother in an Irish American family that mirrors Howard's own in a variety of ways (indeed, a parallel reading of *Natural History* and Howard's memoir, *Facts of Life*, calls attention to many similarities between the Irish American Bray family and her own). The events of one Saturday in March (circa 1944),[15] narrated in "Natural History: I," set the stage for the novel, as Cath and James struggle to reconcile their past—the events of that day, including a murder case their detective father is involved in—with their present. Are they "going to find the past a burden," or are they "going to find out something about [them]selves from what is given to [them]"?[16] That is one of the main questions *Natural History* asks as it documents not the flight from, but the return to, home.

The childhood events and relationships dominating Cath and James's "landscape of memories" are established in "Natural History: I." Howard meticulously metes out the information about each character here, for the

Bray family and their home are indeed the center of the map we started with, a point spelled out for us in case we've missed it: "X marked the Dev-lin [Bray] house in their detailed inset, the stucco house at Parrott and North Avenue" (42). This "X" is the point to which the novel continually returns; even after the physical house has been demolished, paved over for I-95, we see that the emotional imprint the house has left in the minds of Cath and James is indestructible. Significantly, the parting shots of each of the main characters in "Natural History: I" emphasize how close they have stayed to—or strayed from (again, the emphasis on who stays and who leaves)—that "X" on the map. James and Cath's mother, Nell Bray (nee Devlin), has "driven crosstown, up and downhill in a zigzag of missed con-nections" but is relieved to arrive "home at last" (41). She is most com-fortable staying within the "limited geography of work, church, home" that she inherited from her Irish parents (42). Their father, Billy Bray, the only detective in the State's Attorney's Office, has spent the day investigat-ing a murder; he has "looped far up to the Merritt in pursuit of the homi-cide, then made the day business-as-usual" (42). James "has barely left the neighborhood" (42)—his way out is through shows, movies, and magic—specifically the dark, curtained, theater-like home of Mr. De Martino and the Rialto double feature. Cath, on the other hand, "has traveled far be-yond her prescribed course: home, church, school, library" and has "sailed forth unmetaphorically" (though in quite a Joycean fashion) "to the hea-then shore of St. John's Episcopal hall and the eerie isle of the damned in Howland's basement" (44).

While "Natural History: I" provides us with a map of the landscape—physical, emotional, spiritual, familial, and sexual—of Cath and James's childhood, "Natural History: II" provides us with a similarly nuanced land-scape of their adult selves, showing us the contours of "the afterlife" (390) that they have been granted (bringing them forward for their final curtain call, if you will). Between these two sections is "Museum Pieces," which Fanning has referred to as the "heart of the novel" (364). In this section the map we started with acquires the most depth, shading, and complexity. By the time the curtain opens in "Museum Pieces," years have passed since that March day in 1944 on which we began. Both Cath and James have physically left Bridgeport, although it is clear that they have not really trav-eled very far: James, an unheralded actor, is trapped in a "Closet Drama," and Cath, an aging "spinster," is living out her own drama in "The Lives of the Saints" (two of the eight sections of "Museum Pieces"). Both have inherited a flair for the dramatic, with James applying it to the stage and Cath applying it to a life lived in the wake of saints and sinners.

Significantly, in "Double Entry," the most visually and structurally arresting section in "Museum Pieces," Cath and James (who have become estranged as adults) make the journey back home. James returns to Bridgeport to scout it for a movie he plans to make (and star in as his detective father) about the murder that occurred when they were children; Cath goes back to stop James from making that movie and exposing what she believes to be her father's role in letting the murderer go free. The narrative detailing this story in "Double Entry" is confined to the recto (right-hand) pages, while another text appears on the verso (left-hand) pages. As its name implies, this "Double Entry" section is presented in the style of a bookkeeping ledger, with two separate texts running side-by-side. As Howard has pointed out, the text on the verso pages was designed to have the "quality of an album."[17] In this album we visit Bridgeport's parks and statues, the P. T. Barnum Museum, and the shopping arcade; we read newspaper clippings, quotes, poems, letters, excerpts from Howard's own journals, and occasional asides from the narrator/Howard; and we see photographs—including one childhood photo of the author herself—plus sketches of statues, posters, birds, advertisements, and more. The album on the verso pages is Howard's source material; in the language of "double entry" accounting, it is the "credit" side. The text on the recto pages—which continues the story of Cath and James in the present time of the novel—is the "debit" side, where the equity built up from the past is "spent" on the present. What this narrative form (and content) ultimately suggest is that without a full accounting of our past, we can never fully balance our present.

Natural History suggests that the journey home—as represented by Cath and James's journey in "Double Entry"—can (like the journey away from home) be transformative; in fact, it is necessary for continued growth and balance. In "The Enduring Commitment of a Faithful Storyteller," Howard writes that the "reward of looking back must be the ability to move on," and Cath and James do indeed emerge stronger from their journey back to Bridgeport. By the end of the novel, James (formerly an inadequate father, distant husband, and unsatisfied actor "on the brink of middle-aged despair" [383]) has settled into a successful television series and fathered a new baby. Cath has literally and symbolically "Raise[d] the Roof" on her ranch house (381). Just as she has broken through that "one-story house" (353), she has freed herself from a life-long obsession with

that one story from her childhood, an "Old Phantom of a primary narrative myth" (382) that controlled and narrowed her life.

But what of those who cannot return home, who cannot cross over
(even if, of course, the eventual goal is to leave again)? What of those
who cannot confront their pasts, whether to mine the riches or exorcise
the ghosts? The "inability to return," as Howard has suggested, is the "fate
of some people who can never go back," a fate that may be as crippling as
the inability to leave in the first place (personal interview). The narrator
of the "Double Entry" section (ostensibly Howard herself) tellingly refers
to the "album" portion of it as "the other side" (222) of the novel. Thus,
Howard is borrowing a trope that has long been used by Irish immigrants
to refer to Ireland, just as Nell Bray's parents always referred to Ireland as
"the Other Side," "too distant for names" (42). The novel's textual "other
side," like Ireland, is a distant, almost foreign place, a haunting place of
memories and myth, history and stories. Significantly, the narrator is "unable to cross over" (244) from this "other side": she is "confined" to "the
left-hand side of the page" (240), she "[s]kulk[s] on the other side . . . as
marginalia, diddling with apocrypha" (240). It is clear, she later confesses,
that she "yearn[s] to leave, to cross over" (284), but she cannot, thereby
providing the reader with a complex fictional representation of the yearning to leave, to cross, to transgress boundaries between Ireland and America,
past and present, fact and fiction, public and private. If, as Howard writes
in the foreword to *Cabbage and Bones*, "cross[ing] over" is "a route to escape" (xii), then the inability to cross over is a route to stagnation, stasis,
and paralysis.

This is the lesson Nuala ("Nell") Boyle teaches us in *Big as Life: Three
Tales for Spring*, the second installment in Howard's seasons quartet. As the
subtitle suggests, this novel is broken into three loosely interrelated "tales"
for April, May, and June.[18] All of the tales invoke legends, myths, or fairy
tales; at the same time, they freely cross back and forth between fact and
fiction (moving, for instance, from a would-be fairy tale princess in her
tower, to a fictionalized John James Audubon in his forest, to a sixteen-
year-old Maureen Howard in the Bridgeport Library). Nell's tale, "The
Magdalene," is set partly in Ireland and has been called the "most powerful of the three stories" (Filbin 503). Love, sex, and religion collide in this
tale, where provincial villagers conspire to have Nell banished from her
home and family in the small Irish town of Inishmurray, accusing her of
being a "harlot," a "strumpet" (111), the "very Magdalene" herself (112). It

is Easter 1938, a "bitter season" (99), when Nell, an eighteen-year-old "black Sligo beauty" (90), is sent from Ireland to live with her uncle Frank Boyle and his family in America. Barely a year after her arrival she is raped by her young cousin, and she is blamed (123) as "the hoor from the other side" (92). She goes on to study nursing and serve as a "Home Sister" in the war, her hard work a "poultice on the injuries of [her] past" (98) as she remains "determinedly unmarried" (120). As such, Nell remains, like the statue of Mary Magdalene she sees in Florence, a "'saint, sorry all her long life'" (104), trapped (despite her derision of penitence) in the role of "The Magdalene." She cannot go home to Ireland. This inability to confront her past, Howard suggests, results in a retreat "into a world in which she distorts her whole life" (Interview, *Talking Volumes*).

In the first installment of the seasons quartet, *A Lover's Almanac*, we met Nell's cousin Mae O'Connor (nee Boyle), the only member of the Boyle family to befriend Nell. Though Mae is already grown and deceased by the present time of *A Lover's Almanac*, she plays a role — as the past always does — in Howard's novels. *A Lover's Almanac* is Howard's winter's tale.[19] Set in January, February, and March of 2000 in New York City, it is structured like the Old Farmer's Almanac[20] — that is, as a compendium of quotes, dates, facts, and fiction. While Nell's life was distorted by an inability to return home to Ireland, by a conviction that she must "live up to [her] legend," Mae's life is distorted by an inability to leave what Nell calls "the neutrality of Park Avenue" (*Big as Life* 105). A "woman who's had no adventures," May has married and lives on Fifth Avenue "not far from where she was born" (*Big as Life* 100, 112). An "innocent victim of a sheltered life," Mae lives a "life of acceptance," while her daughter Fiona, a refugee "from their commonplace life on Fifth Avenue," lives a life of rebellion (*Big as Life* 112–13, 114). Louise Moffett, another character who appears in both *A Lover's Almanac* and *Big as Life* (works that are clearly not traditional "sequels," although some characters do reappear and walk across a shared "landscape of memory"), emphatically leaves her Wisconsin farmhouse for intellectually and culturally greener pastures in New York City, yet she spends her time painting "landscape[s] of home" that are both "yearning and rejecting" (*Lover's Almanac* 88). Hailed as "a brilliant and convincing urban mindscape," Howard's "lover's" almanac clearly sets us down in a "landscape of desire" (Skow 159), but it is shaped more by a desire for a usable past, a home, and a meaningful life than by a desire for romantic love.

Both *A Lover's Almanac* and *Big as Life* call particular attention to the ways in which fairy tales and myths—stories deeply intertwined within our collective "landscape of memories"—can distort, sentimentalize, and inhibit our ability to leave, to break out of predefined roles.[21] The crippling temptation for Nell and Mae (as it is for Louise and Artie, both unprepared for the weight of a heavily symbolic "fallen" apple tree in *A Lover's Almanac*) is not borne of a desire for knowledge but rather a desire to live in a myth, to sentimentalize the past. This is explicitly illustrated in *Big as Life* when Nell fears not the man (her uncle) who makes unwanted advances toward her but the danger of the sentimental stories that might weaken her resolve against him: "There were nights so lonely I might have welcomed him, my fear not of Frank Boyle, fear of the stories I could tell myself to make him a hero—working his way to America on a freighter, a penniless boarding-house mick marrying in a romantic fit before he went off to the war" (94). Nell's "sin," if she gave in, would not be embracing sexuality but rather sentimentality.

This emphasis on the need to "force observation, destroy nostalgia" (*Lover's Almanac* 11) is felt throughout Howard's works. *Facts of Life*, for example, suggests that nostalgia can "contaminate" you (83), while *Expensive Habits* suggests that fairy tales "garbl[e] the truth, conceal . . . the necessary detail" (226). The need to escape not only suffocating or "dishonest" homes but also myth, nostalgia, fairy tales, and sentimentalized half-truths—all of which tighten the "bonds of correctness," deepen the siren's song to stay, leave us stranded on the "other side" of life—is, in Howard's works, an imperative, an act that the "whole drama of life" does indeed "hang on."

AT THE END OF A REVIEW of *Grace Abounding*, Ada Long acknowledges that her review has made Maude, the main character, "seem much simpler than she is, for she does indeed exist in many versions." Likewise, I am concerned that I have made Howard's novels seem simpler than they are; her casts of characters are so large, her themes so all-encompassing, her voices so varied, her novels so rich that it would take far more space than I have here to do justice to them. Howard's stories send her readers spiraling back into the depths of the page, into the past, into our own memories, co-mingling with the narrative like the May/December lovers Marie Claude and Hans in *Big as Life*—amazed, thankful, needy. "[T]here is the world," Howard writes "like a great dry sponge waiting for a flow of words"

("Before I Go"). As she opens the tap with each book, that flow rushes so fast, so strong, that it is almost impossible to soak it all up at once. We must go back, and back again, to read and reread in order to absorb fully what flows over us, quenching our thirst yet at the same time whetting our appetite for more.

One of the last things Howard and I discussed in our interview was her upcoming novel, *The Silver Screen*. It takes place, Howard said, around 1928–29, when the motion pictures were converting "from silence to sound." In it, she is primarily concerned with "the idea of who has voice and who doesn't," as well as "the idea of choices" in this context. "My woman," Howard says of one of the main characters, "*could* have made it had she *chosen* to. Perfectly beautiful voice, but she chose not to. She made another choice." Howard is quick to emphasize, however, that "that's only *part* of the story."[22]

Why am I not surprised? I am wondering what those other parts might be as I leave the library, the sky darker now, the wind oddly still. It is the calm, I know, before the storm. I imagine I can hear "the stirring of roots and blood." I listen carefully, wondering what Maureen Kearns Howard, an "American original with Irish connections" (Fanning 368), will conjure up next.

Notes

1. See, for example, the autobiographical section "Myself" in *Big as Life*, where Howard situates her "landscape of memory" firmly in "the happy, stifling embrace of two city lots on North Avenue in Bridgeport" (225). Also see *A Lover's Almanac*, where Howard describes Louise's painting as a "landscape of memory" (7).

2. Howard, "Lillian Hellman Remembers."

3. Interview on MPR's "Midmorning," May 24, 2000.

4. Howard's interest in the illustrated novel is evident in her own work from *Natural History* forward. One section of *Natural History* ("Double Entry"), modeled on an album, includes drawings, photos, ads, and other illustrations. In *A Lover's Almanac* and *Big as Life* Howard continues to use illustrations. In *A Lover's Almanac*, for example, we find illustrations modeled on pages from the Old Farmer's Almanacs, and in *Big as Life* we find illustrations at the start of each section (and at times elsewhere) to complement the text—to add, as Howard suggested when we spoke, a "kind of delight in the page when you look at it." Howard carefully selects all illustrations in her novels and tales herself. For example, for the "Children with Matches" section in *Big as Life*, Howard wanted a "house with a tower" but was unable to find

exactly what she wanted after perusing various design and architectural books. She eventually decided to use a picture hanging on her pantry wall that was "taken from a pattern book of houses of that era" and that "was actually a house in Bridgeport, Connecticut," despite the fact that this tale is not set in Bridgeport. Indeed, Howard's hometown of Bridgeport maintains a presence in a variety of ways throughout her works. (All quotes from my interview with Howard).

5. Personal interview. Also see Howard's comments about *Not a Word About Nightingales* in *Facts of Life*: "I wrote a mannered academic novel, actually a parody of that genre and so at a further remove from life. If there is any strength there (I will never look back to see) it can only be in what I wanted that book to reflect: a sense of order as I knew it in the late fifties and early sixties with all the forms that I accepted and even enjoyed: that was the enormous joke about life—that our passion must be contained if we were not to be fools" (80). *Not a Word About Nightingales* did garner substantial praise from more than one reviewer for its "extraordinary skill and control" (*New Yorker*).

6. Howard's criticism, essays, and other writings have been published widely in places such as the *New York Times Book Review*, the *New Republic*, the *New Yorker*, the *Hudson Review*, the *Yale Review*, *Vogue*, *Vanity Fair*, the *Nation*, and *Conjunctions*. She has also written introductions for the work of writers such as Virginia Woolf and Willa Cather; see, for example, Woolf's *Mrs. Dalloway* (Harvest Books, 1990) and Cather's *Three Novels: O Pioneers!, The Song of the Lark, and My Antonia* (Carroll & Graf, 1998). In addition, Howard collected, edited, and wrote introductions for *Seven American Women Writers of the Twentieth Century: An Introduction* (University of Minnesota Press, 1977) and *The Penguin Book of Contemporary American Essays* (Viking, 1984). Most recently, Howard has put together a two-volume collection of Edith Wharton's stories, *Edith Wharton: Collected Stories 1891–1910* and *Edith Wharton: Collected Stories 1911–1937* (Library of America, 2001).

Howard's play, "Songs at Twilight: A Play with Songs," was produced March 8, 1977, at the La MaMa Experimental Theatre Club in New York City. It was directed by Michael Montel, with music composed by George Kent. I have been unable to locate the script for the play, and Howard said she did not think she had a copy of it. An interesting aside here is that Howard also tried her hand at acting on stage, but, as she said in our interview, "[t]here are times when blessed things happen to certain people who are singers or actresses or maybe painters or whatever—when they understand *I'm not really good enough at this.*"

I specifically say "short pieces" here rather than short stories. When we spoke, Howard noted that she does not "really write short stories." This is supported also by her comments in "The Enduring Commitment of a Faithful Storyteller," as she reflects on her choice of genre: "Not long ago I came upon a copy of the first and only story I ever published. It did not appear to be absolutely dreadful, but then I read only the first page. I have not written a story since. The novel became my game." That said, Howard's "Bridgeport Bus" (published in the *Hudson Review*, Winter 1960–61) and

"Sherry" (published in the *Hudson Review*, Autumn 1964) both received O. Henry Award prizes for excellence in the short story genre.

7. Howard has taught at numerous other universities, including Yale, Rutgers, Princeton, the University of Houston, the City College of New York, and Amherst.

8. See Howard's essay on docudrama, "You Are There," for details on her views about this genre and an interesting discussion that points, on many levels, to the differences and similarities between docudrama and Howard's fiction.

9. While there are countless literary (and other) allusions in Howard's novels, Chekhov's presence is one of the more memorable: for example, the small "Chekhovian garden" that sustains Mary Agnes in *Bridgeport Bus* (39) and the production of Chekhov's play "The Seagull" that James stars in (and is transformed by) in *Natural History*.

10. Scott also places the following writers in this group, along with Howard: Ellen Akins, Andrea Barrett, Kathryn Davis, Rebecca Goldstein, Toni Morrison, Cynthia Ozick, and Susan Sontag.

11. Spring—a time marked both by the natural world and the Catholic Church as a time of rebirth and renewal—is the starting point for many of Howard's other novels as well (for example, *Not a Word About Nightingales*, *Before My Time*, *Grace Abounding*, *Natural History*, and *Big as Life*), and those that do not begin in spring begin precisely at the turn of the New Year (*Expensive Habits* and *A Lover's Almanac*), another traditional site of new beginnings (beginnings that are almost always made possible by the act of leaving).

12. Personal interview. Reviewers who pointed to Joycean qualities in *Natural History* include, for example, Marc Robinson (*New Republic*), Carol Anshaw (*Chicago Tribune*), and Thomas R. Edwards (*New York Review of Books*).

13. See Pearl K. Bell's review of *Natural History* in the *Partisan Review*; see also John Casey's review in the *New York Times*, which suggests that Bridgeport "is really the central character" (46).

14. The map drawn in these opening pages, with its "[b]ird's eye view" (2), "North Wind with puffed cheeks" (3), and lavish details, is evocative of the children's story Nell reads to Catherine in *Natural History*'s first section: *East o' the Sun and West o' the Moon* (49), a classic Norwegian fairy tale about a young girl who sets out to rescue her prince. As noted by *Publishers Weekly*, the most well-known translation of this tale, by Sir George Webbe Dasent (1859), is lavishly illustrated and includes a "dizzying bird's-eye view," "the North Wind, rising from the mists like a bearded Old Testament patriarch," and "lavish endpapers, in the style of an Old World cartographer" (from a review of *East o' the Sun and West o' the Moon*).

15. There are a number of indicators in that first section regarding the year in which it is set, although ultimately the exact time is unclear—we are, after all, operating within those "uncertain boundaries of recall." That it is early spring (March) we know right away (3–4), and based on the newspaper Nell glances through, which reports the "continuing struggle at Monte Cassino" (42), it appears to be 1944 (Monte Casino was a five-month battle in World War II in the winter of 1944, so we

could assume it is March 1944). That said, the narrative resists being pinpointed in a specific date or time. Later, for example, in "The Spinster's Tale," Catherine tells herself stories of her childhood that take place in 1945 (349) (the war is over in Europe, so we know it is past May 1945 [351]) when she is eleven years old (352, 355); however, she also marks herself at eleven years of age when Isabelle Poole murdered the soldier (355), an event that the opening passage places in March 1944.

16. Interview on MPR's "Midmorning." Howard was speaking about characters in *Big as Life*, although her words may be applied to many of her characters.

17. "Salvaging the Family Junk," a brief interview with Howard, explains her aims for the album and provides notes on the contents (for example, Howard points to a photo of her childhood self with friends).

18. As Howard stated in an interview: "I decided to call them tales because I don't think they are novellas, but they're not stories in the sense of American short stories. They really are tales, and each one in a way connects to a sense of fairy tales or the more mythic world of tale telling" (interview on MPR's "Talking Volumes," June 14, 2000).

19. Shakespeare's *A Winter's Tale* is, of course, a source here. As Howard explains: "I went back to that harsh late comedy of Shakespeare's, 'A Winter's Tale,' which has both old and young lovers, and ends with a bittersweet reconciliation. That glorious work was only a touchstone, for I've bent the Bard's lovers quite out of shape, though Cyril and Sylvie—my golden oldies—have lived middling fair lives without each other for fifty years. And my young lovers—urban, savvy, cynical— are children who have not tested the depths of love as the novel opens" (Interview, "Penguin Reading Guide"). In his review of the novel in the *New York Review of Books*, Michael Wood points out one of the ways in which Howard calls upon Shakespeare's *Winter's Tale*: Howard quotes lines from Shakespeare's play ("I turn my glasse, and give my Scene such growing / As you had slept between") in order to "signal a narrative elision, a time beyond what seems to be the end of the tale."

20. Howard says the form of the Old Farmer's Almanac "appealed to [her] as a perfect system to display the little stories by which we mark our days along with the almost operatic accomplishments of technology and the never ending tragedies of our society as we come to the end of this era" (Interview, "Penguin Reading Guide").

21. Fairy tales and myths appear throughout Howard's previous novels like the trail of "soft white crumbs of Wonder Bread" (165) that James imagines dropping in the woods in *Natural History* (a trail, of course, designed to lead the way back "home"). *A Lover's Almanac* and *Big as Life* respond, in many ways, to questions raised about fairy tales in these previous works: Do fairy tales, as *Bridgeport Bus* suggests, make us "bleed" (62)? Do fairy tales, as *Expensive Habits* claims, "garbl[e] the truth, conceal . . . the necessary detail" (226)? Is there violence in the space between fairy tales and reality? Do fairy tales set us up for a fall? In *Bridgeport Bus*, for instance, we find Ag's friend Lydia living in a cottage with an "Alice-in-Wonderland door" (72) with a deranged, abusive husband (Wonderland, after all, is a place in which nothing is quite what it seems). After she leaves her husband, Lydia returns to a job

in children's books in which she "emasculat[es] our fairy tales" (220) to make sure that "nowadays," as Lydia says, "children's books [do] not bleed" (62). In *Natural History* the language of fairy tales invites us into one section with "Once in a pleasant land," but at the same time the narrator warns us not to "expect the baggage of kingdoms" (349). Cath and James's mother in *Natural History* also acknowledges her attempt to "*bind them to me . . . with pie and fairy tales so the world could not feed them its thin story, so they would . . . never outgrow East of the Moon . . . The Golden Key*" (325; emphasis in the original).

22. According to Howard, the original title for *The Silver Screen* was *Pilgrims*.

Works Cited

Ahearn, Kerry. "Pursuing the Self: Maureen Howard's *Facts of Life* and *Before My Time*." *Critique* 25.4 (1984): 171–79.

Anshaw, Carol. "Circling Back to Bridgeport: Maureen Howard's Unconventional Saga of a Family and a City." Rev. of *Natural History*, by Maureen Howard. *Chicago Tribune Books* 25 Oct. 1992: 1.

Bell, Pearl. Rev. of *Natural History*, by Maureen Howard. *Partisan Review* 60.1 (1993): 68–70.

Casey, John. "The Promise of American Life." Rev. of *Natural History*, by Maureen Howard. *New York Times Book Review* 18 Oct. 1992: 1, 46.

Diner, Hasia R. *Erin's Daughters in America: Irish Immigrant Women in the Nineteenth Century*. Baltimore, MD: Johns Hopkins University Press, 1983.

Edwards, Thomas R. "Design for Living." Rev. of *Natural History*, by Maureen Howard. *New York Review of Books* 3 Dec. 1992: 30–32.

Fanning, Charles. *The Irish Voice in America: 250 Years of Irish-American Fiction*. 2nd ed. Lexington: University Press of Kentucky, 2000.

Filbin, Thomas. "The Law of Desire." *Hudson Review* 54.3 (2001): 498–504.

Grumbach, Doris. "Maureen Howard's Understated Elegance." Rev. of *Grace Abounding*, by Maureen Howard. *Washington Post* 10 Oct. 1982.

———. "Things Happen, Seem to Mean Something, Then Disappear into Memory." Rev. of *Before My Time*, by Maureen Howard. *New York Times*, 19 Jan. 1975.

Howard, Maureen. *A Lover's Almanac*. New York: Penguin, 1999.

———. "Before I Go I Have Something to Say." *New York Times Book Review* 25 April 1982: 7.

———. *Before My Time*. New York: Penguin, 1974.

———. *Big as Life: Three Tales for Spring*. New York: Penguin, 2001.

———. *Bridgeport Bus*. New York: Penguin, 1965.

———. "The Enduring Commitment of a Faithful Storyteller." *New York Times* 14 Feb. 2000. 1 April 2007 <http://partners.nytimes.com/library/books/021400writing-toward.html>.

————. *Expensive Habits*. New York: Summit Books, 1986.

————. *Facts of Life*. New York: Penguin, 1978.

————. Foreword. *Cabbage and Bones: An Anthology of Irish-American Women's Fiction*. Edited by Caledonia Kearns. New York: Henry Holt and Company, 1997. xi–xiv.

————. *Grace Abounding*. Boston: Little, Brown and Company, 1982.

————. Interview. *Midmorning*. Minnesota Public Radio. 24 May 2000. 1 Sept. 2003 <http://www.mpr.org/www/books/titles/howard_bigaslife.shtml>.

————. Interview. "Penguin Reading Guide for *A Lover's Almanac*." 1999. 21 April 2007 <http://us.penguingroup.com/static/rguides/us/lovers_almanac.html>.

————. Interview. *Talking Volumes*. Minnesota Public Radio.14 June 2000. 1 Sept. 2003 <http://www.mpr.org/www/books/titles/howard_bigaslife.shtml>.

————. "Lillian Hellman Remembers." *Washington Post* 8 June 1980: 3.

————. *Natural History*. New York: Harper Perennial, 1992.

————. *Not a Word About Nightingales*. New York: Penguin, 1960.

————. "On *The House of Mirth*." *Raritan* 15.3 (1996): 1–23.

————. Personal Interview. 18 Sept. 2003.

————. "Salvaging the Family Junk." *New York Times Book Review* 18 Oct. 1992: 46.

————. "You Are There." *Beyond Document: Essays on Nonfiction Film*. Ed. Charles Warren. Hanover: Wesleyan University Press, 1996. 181–204.

Johnson, Nora. Rev. of *Expensive Habits*, by Maureen Howard. *Los Angeles Times Book Review* 18 May 1986: 1.

Levin, Martin. "A Reader's Report." Rev. of *Bridgeport Bus*, by Maureen Howard. *New York Times Book Review* 29 Aug. 1965: 28.

Long, Ada. "Surprises." Rev. of *Grace Abounding*, by Maureen Howard. *New York Review of Books* 2 Dec. 1982.

O'Brien, George. "Assimilation Blues: Maureen Howard's *Facts of Life*." *MELUS* 18.1 (1993): 95–102.

Rev. of *East o' the Sun and West o' the Moon*, by Peter Christen Asbjornsen (illustrated by Jorgen Engebretsen Moe and George Webbe Dasent). *Publishers Weekly*. 21 April 2007 <http://www.amazon.com/East-West-Moon-Works-Translation/dp/1564020495>.

Rev. of *Facts of Life* (excerpt), by Maureen Howard. *Books of the Century: A Hundred Years of Authors, Ideas and Literature*. Edited by Charles McGrath et al. New York: Random House, 1998. 512.

Rev. of *Not a Word About Nightingales*, by Maureen Howard. *New Yorker* 31 March 1962: 140–41.

Rev. of *A Lover's Almanac*, by Maureen Howard. *Publishers Weekly* 13 Oct. 1997: 54.

Robinson, Marc. Rev. of *Natural History*, by Maureen Howard. *New Republic* 9 Nov. 1992: 46–49.

Scott, Joanna. "Male Writers vs. Female Writers: Beyond the Preconceptions." *Salon* 2 July 1998. 8 Aug. 2003 <http://www.salon.com/media/1998/07/02media.html>.

Skow, John. "As the Millennium Turns." Rev. of *A Lover's Almanac*, by Maureen Howard. *Time* 151.5 (1998).

Swaim, Don. "Audio Interview with Maureen Howard." *Wired for Books*. Ohio University, 1982. 20 Aug. 2003 <http://wiredforbooks.org/maureenhoward/>.

Wood, Michael. "On the Love Boat." Rev. of *A Lover's Almanac*, by Maureen Howard. *New York Review of Books* 16 July 1998.

Yardley, Jonathan. Rev. of *Expensive Habits*, by Maureen Howard. *Washington Post Book World* 11 May 1986: 3.

CHAPTER 3

Moments of Kindness, Moments of Recognition

The Achievement of Maeve Brennan

JOHN M. MENAGHAN

Somebody said, "We are real only in moments of kindness." Moments of kindness, moments of recognition—if there is a difference it is a faint one.
—Maeve Brennan, The Long-Winded Lady, 3

Maeve Brennan was born in Ireland in 1917 and spent her formative years in Ranelagh, a residential neighborhood in Dublin. In 1934, at age seventeen, she left Ireland and moved with her family to Washington, D.C., where her father Robert Brennan took a diplomatic post in the service of the recently formed Irish Free State. When the family moved back to Ireland, Brennan chose to remain in America. Settling in New York, she worked as a copywriter for *Harper's Bazaar* and then, in 1949, joined the staff of the *New Yorker*. For three decades she contributed book reviews, fashion pieces, and—for "The Talk of the Town"—a series of short sketches concerning daily life in Manhattan. These last were brought together under the title *The Long-Winded Lady* (1969), her "Talk of the Town" persona. But Brennan's major achievement consists of her fiction, most of which also appeared in the *New Yorker* and in two collections published during her lifetime: *In and Out of Never Never Land* (1969) and *Christmas Eve* (1974). In 1993, at the age of seventy-six, she died at a nursing home in upstate New York.

Brennan's last years were marked by mental illness. By the time of her death, her work had been largely forgotten. Then in 1997 *The Springs of Affection*, a posthumous collection of her best Dublin stories, appeared, simultaneously bringing new attention to this neglected figure and conveying the impression that Brennan, like James Joyce before her, had turned her back on her native Ireland only to spend the rest of her life writing about the world she left behind. In 1998 a new, expanded edition of *The Long-Winded Lady* served to draw attention to Brennan's extensive nonfiction writings about her adopted, rather than her native, land. In 1999 a second posthumous collection, *The Rose Garden*, restored the remainder of Brennan's short stories to print. This collection further undermined any posthumous portrayal of her as a female James Joyce, for only a handful of its stories are set in Dublin while the majority unfold, like her "Talk of the Town" pieces, in and around New York. Finally, the year 2000 brought a last, unexpected development: the publication of *The Visitor*, a newly discovered, unpublished novella written in the 1940s concerning the return of a young woman to Dublin after six years spent not in New York but in Paris.

Brennan, who made a number of visits to Ireland over the years, set the majority of her fiction not only in Ireland but in her native Dublin. This fact helps to explain why *The Springs of Affection* invites comparison with Joyce's *Dubliners*. Yet *The Rose Garden*, with its mix of Irish and American characters and its frequent New York area settings, and *The Long-Winded Lady*'s fifty-plus New York–based pieces, make a strong case for Brennan as an Irish American writer. Although *The Visitor*, with its Dublin-Paris axis, gives Brennan the appearance of being both thoroughly Irish and a bit more "European" than in the rest of her work, Paris may simply be a fictional stand-in here for New York, a device by which she could simultaneously explore and disguise her own conflicted sense of both belonging to and having become a "visitor" to her native land. Finally, Brennan's decision to spend her entire adult life living and working in America provides a clear basis for regarding her as an Irish American writer.

In her later years Brennan clearly saw herself as *both* a New Yorker and an exile. In her "Author's Note" to the first edition of *The Long-Winded Lady*, she said of herself (or rather, her persona): "Even after more than twenty-five years the long-winded lady cannot think of herself as a 'real' New Yorker. If she has a title, it is one held by many others, that of a traveler in residence" (1–2). It seems Brennan would have both understood and appreciated the advice of a more recent émigré to America, Romanian writer Andrei Codrescu, that one ought to live in a place where one feels like a tourist and vacation where one feels at home. The question in Brennan's case, though, is whether there was in the end any place, anywhere at all, she felt truly at home.

The other difficulty is exactly how best to describe Brennan's life and work: A traveler in residence. An émigré who wrote best—but not exclusively—about the world she had left behind. A woman who in her youth had endured perhaps the most turbulent period in Irish history, who in her late adolescence lived the life of a diplomat's daughter in Washington, who in her young womanhood was noted for her beauty as well as her fierce intelligence and sharp wit, who spent the majority of her adult life writing for the most celebrated magazine in America if not the world, yet who in her last years suffered a series of mental breakdowns (and, it appears, at least one period of homelessness) before dying in a nursing home, twelve years after her last *New Yorker* contribution. A woman whose work is, as the biographical note to one of her posthumous volumes suggests, suffused with "a feeling of irresolution"—and, I would add, of profound restlessness. A woman at home, perhaps, neither in Ireland nor America, neither in Dublin nor New York. A writer who brought her fierce intelligence, sharp eye, and stunning command of language to bear on the two worlds she knew best—Ireland and America—and who in the process became a writer both quintessentially Irish and at the same time international in her vision, scope, and impact on writers and readers around the world.

To explore in any meaningful way the question of Brennan's relation not only to Joyce but also to other key figures in the Irish short story tradition—Frank O'Connor, Sean O'Faolain, Liam O'Flaherty, Elizabeth Bowen, Mary Lavin, and Kate O'Brien—would require another essay, if not a book.[1] Judging by the fact that at the July 2005 International Association for the Study of Irish Literature conference in Prague Brennan figured prominently in two separate panels, such studies may be imminent.[2] Meanwhile, as Angela Bourke observes, the most direct influence on

Brennan's development as a writer was her editor and fellow writer at the *New Yorker,* William Maxwell (who also worked with O'Connor and many other *New Yorker* writers). As Bourke puts it, Maxwell "edited [Brennan's] short stories, and soon became the person for whom she wrote" (192). In terms of Brennan's own influence on a younger generation of writers, the decades of obscurity prior to her recent rediscovery suggest that such influence may only be beginning. Bourke intriguingly reports, however, that Brennan took the young Elizabeth Cullinan, who joined the *New Yorker* in 1955 at the age of twenty-two, under her wing: "Maeve encouraged her in her writing" and enthusiastically reviewed Cullinan's novel, *House of Gold,* when it appeared in 1970, near the end of Brennan's own career at the magazine (209, 255).

If it is difficult to fix the exact degree to which Brennan is an Irish American writer, it is perhaps equally difficult to know how to describe her key works. Are they the two volumes Brennan herself published during her lifetime, with stories set in both Irish and American locales — that is to say Dublin and New York and environs? Or are they the posthumous volumes? Because the three books that put Brennan's fiction back before the reading public — *The Springs of Affection, The Rose Garden,* and *The Visitor* — have all appeared within the past few years, and because these are the most likely points of entry into her work for most readers, I shall give a brief account of each, along with some passing reference to *The Long-Winded Lady.* As these volumes make clear, despite her lifelong restlessness and later "troubles," Brennan's achievement is substantial and, in its best moments, absolutely stunning.

As several reviewers have noted, whatever the power of the individual stories, the clearly related ones (sharing characters and settings) gain impact by being grouped together. *The Springs of Affection,* the first posthumous volume to appear, is divided into three sections. The first seven stories are among Brennan's most autobiographical, focusing on a Dublin family closely resembling her own and chronicling events that appear to have taken place during her childhood. Though there are certainly conflicts and tensions in these stories, they paint a mostly affectionate portrait of childhood and family life. The second set of stories is a different affair entirely. These six devastatingly sad stories chronicle the mostly happy courtship and unhappy marriage of Rose and Hubert Derdon, who live not only on the same street but in the same house in Ranelagh as Brennan and her family — one of fifty-two red-brick houses on a dead-end street, with small back gardens divided by low stone walls (Bourke 172). The third and final group of eight stories also anatomizes a Dublin marriage, this one between Delia and Martin Bagot; their relationship is, as William Maxwell puts it, "a marriage . . . again unsatisfactory and in some ways similar" to the Derdons' unhappy union. All but one of the stories in this section are "gentler" than the Derdon stories. The exception, "The Springs of Affection," which Maxwell describes as "in form, if not quite in length, a novella," is regarded by most reviewers as her finest (*Springs of Affection* 9–10).

Like Joyce's first three *Dubliners* stories, the first seven stories in *The Springs of Affection* are told from the first-person perspective of a child— or an adult character recounting childhood experiences. Unlike Joyce's youthful protagonist, this narrator is female, and unlike his unnamed boy she is not an only child living with an aunt and uncle but has a name, a father, a mother, and several siblings living in what appears, at its best moments, to be a fairly happy family—at least by comparison to the paralyzed and mostly miserable figures populating *Dubliners*. These stories seem clearly autobiographical: the little girl is even called Maeve, and the first of the stories, "The Morning after the Big Fire," gives some hint of the author's early interest in storytelling. When a nearby parking garage catches fire one night, the eight-year-old narrator regards it not as a tragedy or even a misfortune but as a very exciting development and "a really satisfactory fire" (16). She derives even greater satisfaction from being the first to tell those neighbors unaware of the blaze: "McRory's was burnt down last night!" (17). Having been forbidden, however, to investigate on her own, Maeve has had to rely on her father's report, so when one of the newly informed neighbors goes to take a look, she is "enraged" by the impending loss of her "authority" as teller of the tale (17–18).

In "The Barrel of Rumors" and elsewhere we learn of the mother's charitable impulses: "In Dublin, my mother used to take parcels of food to a community of Poor Clare nuns" (30). On this occasion she charges the now twelve-year-old Maeve with taking her infant brother along to the convent so that the nuns, normally cut off from all contact with the outside world, can have a look at him. Once again, as in the opening story, Maeve finds herself frustrated, this time by her brother's direct experience of a place to which she is forbidden access. In "The Day We Got Our Own Back," the new Irish government is hunting Maeve's father because he is among those who, having rejected the treaty with Britain, are waging a civil war against their former comrades. We also learn that the mother's married life has been dominated by "trouble and anxiety" from the time of the Easter Rising until the Civil War: her husband, now on the run, had earlier been "captured and condemned to death and then to penal servitude for life" in England, only to be released a year later (38).

In "The Lie" the narrator kills off a little joke she has shared with her mother concerning the standard penance she received each time she went to confession: "I saw the little joke die, and I knew that I had killed it" (43). Jealous of her younger sister, she destroys a toy sewing machine the sister loves and then lies about it. After confessing to the priest and receiving a much harsher penance than usual, she foolishly reveals the penance to her family, and her mother knows immediately that she has lied. The little girl hardly knows what to say or think when, instead of being angry, the mother says: "Oh, Maeve, . . . my poor child, why couldn't you have kept your mouth shut?" (46). Meanwhile, "The Devil in Us" shows the more vicious side of an Irish Catholic upbringing when Maeve and other girls are unfairly singled out by the nuns at her boarding school as being lazy troublemakers and given to understand that God is not on their side, while "The Clever One" makes clear that Ireland is no place for a young woman with "notions" in her head (60).

Compared to Brennan's more substantial achievements, these stories are rather slight, but taken together they have a charm and evocativeness that reveal a good deal about her childhood in Ireland. At the same time, they hint at certain less savory aspects of twentieth-century Irish life that may have been the driving force behind Brennan's decision to remain in America when her family returned, in Joyce's famous phrase, to "dear dirty Dublin."

The succeeding two groups of stories suggest still other reasons for a young woman with "notions" to seek her fortune outside Ireland. The second group charts the courtship and marriage of Rose and Hubert Derdon. "A Young Girl Can Spoil Her Chances" begins on the forty-third anniversary of the day Rose's father died, two days before her tenth birthday. It quickly becomes evident that Rose has never recovered from this loss and that her marriage to Hubert is excruciatingly unhappy. We also learn that the couple has a son, whom Rose has smothered with affection even as Hubert kept his distance. The son, John, has escaped the family dynamic by becoming a priest. That dynamic consists now of deadening habits of distance and misunderstanding between the couple, yet the story also takes us back to the beginning of their relationship, when the future seemed to promise at least a chance of happiness. As Hubert tellingly remarks at the end of the story, "it was hard to form a good habit when you were older, and just as hard to break a bad habit once it had taken hold of you" (98).

In "A Free Choice" young Rose attends a dance at the house of her dead father's former employer. Amid both sad and happy memories and impressions of her father's role in the decoration of this house, she wonders why Hubert, also in attendance, has not come to ask her for a dance. Hubert, meanwhile, finds himself fearing he has lost Rose to some other man. In the end they come together in something like harmony, but this missing of each other even as they long for one another is a motif that will resonate throughout the remainder of the stories and the rest of their lives together. In "The Poor Men and Women" we learn more about the tortured relations between Hubert and Rose, whose very acts of kindness to one another end in acrimony and hurt feelings because Rose is afraid of Hubert and he has given up trying to "reach" her. Further, we see that the once close relationship between Rose and John, the son turned priest, has its own tensions and difficulties, including Rose's desire for physical contact and John's concern that she not touch his "consecrated hands" (138).

"An Attack of Hunger" reveals that Hubert is ashamed of his wife but feels there is nothing to be done and that Rose secretly wishes Hubert had died, believing it would have kept John with her. In John's absence she has two dreams: the first that he has come back, and the second that he, rather than Hubert, has died. In the end, however, after a bitter fight, Rose returns to the idea of Hubert dying, with the new twist that she would then be able to attend to John in his parish once he is given one, as she convinces herself he will be. "Family Walls" reveals the true depths of each partner's misery and at the same time takes us back to the time when they were happy—at least as happy as they would ever be—before circling back to the present with Hubert watching Rose in her garden, her only refuge from misery. At that moment, we are told, "[t]he evening light spoke, and what it said was, 'There is nothing more to be said.' There is nothing more to be said because what remains to be said must not be said. It is too late for Rose" (192).

In "The Drowned Man," the last story in the group, it is Rose who has died, and Hubert feels nothing so much as an overwhelming desire to get inside her room and have a look around. Devoid of grief, he cannot quite bring himself to reveal this fact to anyone. When he is at last left alone long enough to explore the room, he feels not a sense of Rose's presence or even her absence but only an emptiness: "nothing he could pit himself against" (202). Remembering the moment when he asked Rose to marry him, he reflects, not for the first time, that "he had fallen in love with her for the exact qualities that were not hers at all" (209). Weeping at last yet still unable to feel a specific grief for the loss of his wife, he longs to confess to his sister, who is crying in sympathy at what she takes to be grief, "that it was all only a masquerade and that he was only a sham of a man" (211). He does not tell her or anyone else, however, what he is really feeling—or not feeling. At the close of the story, we understand just how isolated in their unhappiness each partner has been and know that what remains to Hubert of life will be little more than a living death, with not even grief and longing to fill his last lonely nights and days.

Delia and Martin Bagot, the couple at the heart of the third set of stories, have their own problems. If their marriage is not quite as excruciating as the Derdons', it has its fair share of pain and regret mixed with kinder, gentler moments of a family life that includes two young daughters and several animals. "The Twelfth Wedding Anniversary" reveals that a third child has died and that Martin sleeps not with his wife but in the small extra room, leaving Delia to reflect that if they had bought a smaller house they might have been happier because Martin would never have gotten such a notion in his head. We also learn that Martin hates the animals loved by his wife and children, and that everyone—the animals included—is happier when he is not at home. Martin has remembered the anniversary but has "wanted no sentimental reminders." What he wants, in fact, is simply "to be left alone" (225).

In "The Eldest Child" Delia meditates upon a loss from which, it slowly becomes clear, she has hardly even begun to recover. Her response has been to turn her house into "a kingdom, significant, private, and safe" (266). Wondering if she is perhaps a bit unbalanced, she nevertheless takes comfort in a song only she hears and in the "small shape" of her dead son, a shape she sees "drift[ing] uncomplainingly from distant horizon to still more distant horizon" (268). In the end Delia finds a kind of comfort in the thought that she will never lose sight of this shape and in the knowledge of what she herself must do: "He was traveling a long way, but she would watch him. She was his mother, and it was all she could do for him now" (272).

In "Stories of Africa" we learn more about Delia's past when an aging bishop who had been her father's friend comes for a visit; at the same time we receive some insight into how this family and its little world look to the children. Like Rose Derdon, Delia lost her father when she was young, in this case at the age of two. While the grand lady who has brought the bishop to their little house takes the children for a ride in her "big black car," the bishop tells her of his own boyhood and the time he spent on her family's farm in Wexford. Prompted to talk about herself, Delia finds herself feeling that "although she had walked the path without assurance, she had kept to her appointed direction, and she had not trespassed, and she had made no undue demands, and she had not spoiled anything along the way," a conviction that gives her a strange sense of comfort (290).

In "Christmas Eve" we learn that Martin "never knew for sure whether Delia and the children were his anchor or his burden, [but] at the moment he didn't care" (304). Delia, meanwhile, "couldn't see any connection at all between herself as she used to be and herself as she was now, and she couldn't understand how with a husband and two children in the house she was lonely and afraid" (306). Yet in the end the story offers a surprisingly reassuring set of assertions: that "whether . . . love finds daily, hourly expression in warm embraces and in the instinctive kind of attentiveness animals give to their young or whether it is largely unexpressed, as it was among the Bagots, does not really matter very much in the very long run" and that "the child grown old and in the dark knows only that what is under his hand is a rock that will never give way" (307).

Such a spirit of tenderness and forgiveness provides a stark contrast to the final story in both this group and the collection. "The Springs of Affection," in Maxwell's view, "belongs with the great short stories of the century," and his own impressive summary bears repeating here.

> Both Delia and Martin are dead and the whole sweep of their lives is dealt with in a masterly fashion by moving in and out of the mind of Martin's sister, Min, who kept house for him after Delia died and who is now a very old woman. She hated Delia. She wear's Martin's wedding ring on her finger. She has brought back to Wexford as much of the Bagots' books and furniture as she can crowd into her small flat and sits in happy possession of it. What in the earlier stories was an at times almost unbearable sadness is now an unflattering irony. Dominated by false pride, ungenerous, unreachable, unkind, the old woman is the embodiment of that side of the Irish temperament that delights in mockery and rejoices in the downfall of those whom life has smiled on. (*Springs of Affection* 10)

This brilliant story's power is made even greater by its placement at the end of the sequence. Indeed, the earlier stories both add to its power and make the flawed family dynamics of the Bagot household look better through comparison to Min's "happy possession" of the leavings from lives that were, with all their failings, fears, and pain, far richer and more fulfilling than her own.

Whereas *The Springs of Affection* brought Brennan's most impressive stories back to the public's attention, *The Rose Garden* collects her remaining stories, and the results, while still impressive, are decidedly more mixed. The opening stories, inspired by her marriage to fellow *New Yorker* writer St. Clair McKelway and their time together in Sneden's Landing, are set in the exclusive community of Herbert's Retreat, thirty miles north of New York City and populated, sometimes prominently and sometimes peripherally, by Irish émigrés, mostly in the form of live-in housemaids. These satirical stories alternately adopt the perspectives of the exclusive community's privileged residents and their mostly scornful Irish maids. As such, they are perhaps the most Irish American of Brennan's stories.[3]

In "The View from the Kitchen" the maids watch in amusement as George and Leona Harkey entertain "Charles Runyon, the critic," or rather, Leona and Charles entertain themselves at George's expense while one maid gossips to another that Leona married George in order to be able to tear down his house and improve her own view of the river (13). In "The Divine Fireplace" the Tillbrights' maid Stasia cannot wait to board the bus that will take her and her fellow Irish maids to Sunday mass so she can regale them with the wild behavior that took place in the house the previous night. It seems that when Harry Tillbright's second wife learned there was a closed-off fireplace in the kitchen, she drunkenly insisted that the equally intoxicated Harry open it immediately. As a result, the dinner was ruined, the house made a mess, the electricity shorted out, and all the reindeer meat in the deep-freeze spoiled. The maids, ardent converts to central heating, find this tale thoroughly diverting, but Stasia is distressed to discover the bus stopping at the church before she has managed to tell the whole story. Like the little girl in "The Morning after the Big Fire" she laments that this will mean the loss of her "authority," since on the way back they will all "be crowding around and chattering and interrupting her, getting the story all wrong" (110).

The last of these stories, "The Servant's Dance," brings the worlds of maids and masters together at an annual dance to which the maids invite

men from the city—mostly Irish policemen and firemen—and, more reluc-
tantly, their employers. Bridie, the eldest maid, has the bright idea to hatch
a revenge-driven conspiracy among the servants and their friends. While
being thoroughly affable to the employers, they plan at the same time, contrary to the usual practice, to decline to ask any of them to dance. Just when
this subtle humiliation of the employers would seem to have been achieved,
however, it turns out the men from the city have bugged the event and have
on tape all sorts of remarks neither Bridie nor the employers had intended
for general consumption. These men, who make the secret tapes in order
to have a good laugh back in the city at their hosts' expense, serve as a kind
of substitute for Brennan herself as the outside observer. Neatly bringing
together the two worlds of servant and master, Irish and American, to share
a common fate, Brennan shows that her sympathies are not all on one side,
if indeed they are on any side at all.

The stories in the second group are, with one exception, set in Dublin.
The exception, "The Bride," again bridges the two worlds of Ireland and
America by focusing on Margaret Casey, an Irish maid in Scarsdale about
to marry a man she does not love. Margaret finds herself ruefully reflecting
on the life in Ireland she once had and the way her sister usurped her rightful place in their parents' home. "The Rose Garden" shows how Mary Lam-
bert, "an Irish shopkeeper, left a widow at the age of thirty-nine" and with
two children to raise, finds her only solace in the garden opened to the public once a year, on the Feast of the Sacred Heart, by the nuns of the Holy
Passion (184). In "The Beginning of a Long Story" we appear to be back
on the same street as in The Springs of Affection, this time in the house of "a
government clerk with a wife and three small daughters" (205). Like that
earlier volume, this one provides yet another instance of Tolstoy's dictum
that each unhappy family is unhappy in its own way.

The next three stories are set in Manhattan. In "The Daughters" a
forty-year-old woman, "one of the hotel's permanent guests," waits in a
fancy hotel lobby for her father to take her to lunch (225). "A Snowy Night
on West Forty-ninth Street," set mostly in a Broadway restaurant, ends with
the narrator alone at home, staring out at the snow, and "I See You, Bianca"
concerns a small white cat that has disappeared and that her owner, not
knowing her fate, cannot forget.

The final stories, all but one set in East Hampton, again seem autobiographical, treating Brennan's own adult and (compared with the Irish
maids) considerably more privileged American adventure. In "A Large Bee"

Mary Ann Whitty, a thin mask for Brennan herself, rescues a bee in distress. Later, hearing an inner voice say all her work has been futile, she seems undaunted, content with having done a good deed. By contrast, "In and Out of Never-Never Land" involves a small child showing Mary Ann matches she is forbidden to have. Failing to lecture the child or seize the matches, Mary Ann frets about it afterwards, but when later that night the child, ironically, saves her own house from burning down, Mary Ann finds herself oddly glad that she herself had earlier failed to do "the right thing" (301).

The Visitor, Brennan's recently discovered novella, tells the tale of an embittered old woman bent on punishing her granddaughter for the sins of the girl's mother, who presumed first to marry the old woman's beloved son and then to escape the marriage by fleeing to Paris, compounding the offence by convincing her daughter Anastasia to join her there. When her mother dies, Anastasia, whose father meanwhile has also passed away, returns to the house where she was born, expecting to find a home. Instead, she finds a grandmother who wishes she had not come and who persists in regarding her stay as a visit rather than a homecoming. Like Min in "The Springs of Affection," the grandmother has long ago chosen spite over love, and in the end Anastasia has no real choice but to end her "visit" and depart. Forced out of the only real home she has ever known, Anastasia achieves a small revenge by standing in the square outside the house and embarrassing her grandmother before all the neighbors and passersby: "She stepped back barefooted into the street with her eyes turned expectantly up to the open window. Full of derision and fright, . . . she stared up and began to sing" a schoolgirl song about "a happy land" far away (80). "The rowdy errand boys," we are told, "became instantly silent, and so did all the place around, and a passing motorist came to a halt, for a look" (80). Finally, when the faces of her grandmother and Katherine the housemaid at last appear in the window, Anastasia calls out to them: "Goodbye, Grandmother. Goodbye, Katharine. You see, I haven't gone yet . . ." (81).

In these reissued stories and newly discovered novella, the reader is offered a view of both Ireland and America that is, as one reviewer puts it, "clear, unsentimental, and occasionally heartbreaking" (Allen 75). In The Long-Winded Lady, too, Brennan works her magic with words, preserving a part of New York, and by extension America, that even as she wrote was rapidly passing away, an act of literary preservation that takes on a still deeper resonance in the wake of 9/11. Having watched her native land change in the aftermath of independence in ways she could not have imagined, Brennan may have been particularly well-suited and well-positioned to chronicle the somewhat subtler but in their own way equally distressing changes she saw taking place in the city and country that had become her adopted home.

As a writer and a woman moving restlessly between her Irish and American places, characters, and selves, Brennan displays in her fiction a startlingly acute insight into the fates of women caught up in loveless marriages, lonely spinsterhood, and a set of social expectations they can try either to conform to or defy but that take a toll either way on their lives and their desire for happiness, safety, and fulfillment. Yet she shows almost as clearly how men, despite their clear social advantages and greater freedom, are left frustrated and unfulfilled by their work and their family life in a world where their own roles, though different, are almost as strictly prescribed as those of the women in their lives. Briefly married and childless, Brennan also displays a deep insight into childhood and, without ever yielding to sentimentality, a deep affection for both children and animals.

In the end, however, it is not Brennan's attitudes or insights that most distinguish her fiction but rather the sheer quality of her writing. She is not merely an interesting writer or a talented one. At her best, she is simply magnificent. And while she could be scathing in her satire, Brennan is perhaps most impressive in her own "moments of kindness"—a kind of finely tuned and unsentimental compassion for those who have, as she herself so sadly would, simply (or complexly) lost their way in the world. Mixed in with those moments, too, are her "moments of recognition," when a sense of our shared fate blunts her satire and she shows just how easy it is to pave the road to hell not just with good intentions but missed chances, unfortunate silences, and words and gestures that injure even when they are meant to heal.

In her final years fate was not kind to Maeve Brennan, but a decade after her death her work has been, as it were, resurrected and placed before us like an unexpected gift. She is, as John Updike puts it, "constantly alert, sharp-eyed as a sparrow for the crumbs of human event" (124–25). And so, when reading her, must we be. Brennan's literary resurrection, like her decline into obscurity, is itself a very human event—one it would be a terrible mistake to miss. Read her. With some exceptions, she will not cheer you up, but she will thrill you with the recognition not merely of how difficult life—family life in particular—can be but of what it truly means, and what it is really like, to be alive.

Notes

1. On top of all that, there is the dearth of criticism with which to contend. In part because Brennan is a writer hard to place, in part because she essentially disappeared off the literary map and has only recently been brought back to prominence (if that is not too strong a word), in part perhaps because she wrote short stories and a single novella rather than novels, there is as yet no body of criticism devoted to her work. The recent critical biography by Angela Bourke, *Maeve Brennan: Homesick at the* New Yorker, provides a great deal of information on the relation between Brennan's life and work and some insightful critical commentary on the work itself, but beyond this valuable resource there is as yet little to go on beyond book reviews.

2. At that conference I presented a version of the present chapter. At the 2006 conference at the University of New South Wales in Sydney, I presented a paper entitled "The Female James Joyce," which examines the question of Joyce's influence on Brennan in greater detail.

3. Bourke, who calls these stories "rich with coded messages about what the maids see and how they understand it," goes on to suggest that if Brennan had been "describing African-American domestics" and had "come to *The New Yorker* from Antigua, say, as Jamaica Kincaid did some years later, rather than from Ireland, readers might have had a different understanding of the relationships she portrayed between the homeowners of Herbert's Retreat and their maids" (182). Although such cross-racial comparisons are always tricky, another writer that might come to mind in this context is Langston Hughes and his volume of short stories *The Ways of White Folks*.

Works Cited

Allen, Brooke. "Clear, Affecting, Subtle." Review of *The Visitor,* by Maeve Brennan. *New Criterion* 18 (2000): 75.

Bourke, Angela. *Maeve Brennan, Homesick at the* New Yorker. New York: Counterpoint, 2004.

Brennan, Maeve. *The Long-Winded Lady.* New York: Houghton Mifflin, 1998.

———. *The Rose Garden.* Washington, DC: Counterpoint, 2000.

———. *The Springs of Affection.* Introduction by William Maxwell. New York: Houghton Mifflin, 1997.

———. *The Visitor.* London: Atlantic Books, 2002.

Updike, John. "Talk of a Sad Town." *Atlantic Monthly* 224 (1969): 124–25.

RELIGION AND ETHICS

CHAPTER 4

"Forget about Being Irish"

Family, Transgression, and Identity in the Fiction of Elizabeth Cullinan

KATHLEEN McINERNEY

Louise Gallagher, a young woman having lunch with her married lover, fusses over her omelet—it is meatless Friday—in a Manhattan restaurant. Speaking of the menu, Louise says, "Fish will always mean Catholic to me, and . . . Catholic meant Irish and Irish meant lower class." Her lover admonishes, "Forget about being Irish," but she cannot (Cullinan, "An Accident," in *Yellow Roses* 83).

The *oeuvre* of novelist and short story writer Elizabeth Cullinan offers an acutely detailed portrait of the domestic life and identity of Irish Americans in the latter half of the twentieth century; it explores the challenge of defining the self within and against cultural categories, principally within the context of Catholicism and the emotional weight of family life. Limning the tensions between the inherited preoccupations of an immigrant family and the desires of a young female narrator as she seeks her own way, Cullinan describes the multivalent legacy of the diaspora for Irish

97

Americans. In particular, Cullinan represents the tensions of identity as they are experienced by the "dutiful daughters" of Irish America. Of Irish American women writers Maureen Howard has written: "These women of the Irish Diaspora were all fated to be dutiful daughters . . . the duty that many of these writers take on is to discover what is wayward in their souls, where transgression in thought or deed may lead to a finer, sometimes more generous understanding of a limiting world or to self-discovery" (xi).

In *House of Gold* and many of her short stories, Cullinan creates narratives of constriction and containment: the voices of generations of daughters, bound by familial duty and a discourse of Catholic doctrine, are heard as they struggle to identify and escape this architecture of containment that is their inheritance. In the tradition of other diaspora fiction by women— for example, Maxine Hong Kingston's *Memoirs of a Woman Warrior*, Toni Morrison's *Beloved*, Laura Esquivel's *Like Water for Chocolate*, and Jamaica Kincaid's "Girl,"—women's struggle for identity is often mediated and inscribed by a maternal legacy of constriction, cultural conservatism, and pathological protectiveness. While many of the narratives reveal a pattern of resistance to the mother and eventual reconciliation and healing, Cullinan's fiction suggests the impossibility of reconciling the primary mother-daughter relationship and the psychic necessity of inventing an identity not contaminated by a maternal tyranny born of immigrant anxiety.

Elizabeth Cullinan's publications to date include the novels *House of Gold* (1969) and *A Change of Scene* (1982); two collections of short stories, *In the Time of Adam* (1971) and *Yellow Roses* (1977); and numerous short stories appearing in the *New Yorker* and the *Irish Literary Supplement*. Cullinan's stories have also been published in a variety of anthologies, including *Cabbages and Bones: An Anthology of Irish American Women's Fiction* (1997), *Best Irish Short Stories, Number 3* (1978), *Best American Short Stories* (1978), and *Cutting the Night in Two: Short Stories by Irish Women Writers* (2001). Maureen Murphy notes that Cullinan's fiction has been associated with that of Chekhov, Joyce, J. F. Powers, Maeve Brennan, and Edwin O'Connor (139, 143). Murphy also argues that Cullinan established her own particular narrative voice through the persona and perspective of her young female characters (14). Describing Cullinan's attention to craft, Joyce Carol Oates commented in a 1971 review of *House of Gold* that Cullinan's writing is distinguished by its "precision, gravity and grace—the small happenings of a day, the arc of a life, the demands of temperament, background and necessity" (6).

Born in 1933 to Cornelius and Irene (O'Connell) Cullinan in New York City, Elizabeth Cullinan grew up in the Bronx. She graduated from Marymount College in 1954. Following graduation, she was hired to be William Maxwell's secretary at the *New Yorker* and worked there from 1955 to 1959. Cullinan lived in Ireland during 1960 and 1963. After returning home, Cullinan worked as a freelance writer and published *House of Gold*. In 1977 she was invited to teach at the University of Iowa Writer's Workshop and then in the English Department at the University of Massachusetts–Amherst in the following year. In 1979 Cullinan was appointed to the English faculty at Fordham University. She now lives in Manhattan and currently is writing a novel about her years at the *New Yorker*.

Manifestly autobiographical, Cullinan's fiction is set in New York and the surrounding areas or in Ireland. A mapping of the journey between these places structures her fiction; indeed, many of the works open with a character in motion, traveling to the next place by bus, boat, or car, crossing continents and traversing interior territories. Transit and movement surface as thematic elements of her protagonists' lives, underscoring their inability to call a single place home: both *home* and *homeland* are, for these children and grandchildren of immigrants, fraught with multiple meanings, many of which are not particularly generous. While her childhood was closely prescribed, as a young woman Cullinan found ethnic identity more elusive and complicated. Of her family's sense of heritage, Cullinan says, "Mother hated the Irish. We were supposed to be above all of that" (personal interview). Yet in the world beyond home, identity seemed an inescapable fact. Indeed, according to Cullinan she was defined as Irish in her years at the *New Yorker*, and this construction was the impetus for her travel to Ireland; she says, "One of the ways I was recognized at the *New Yorker* was as an Irish Catholic. It adhered to me" (personal interview). This identification, complicated by her mother's repudiation of her heritage, also isolated and stigmatized Cullinan in the then Anglo-Protestant culture at the *New Yorker*: "My loyalty to it is terribly bound up. Irishness has quite a lot to do with the *New Yorker*. I was really quite a freak there" (personal interview). In her autobiographical narratives Cullinan probes the emotional valences and constrictions of the psychic complications associated with marginalization.

Cullinan's first novel, *House of Gold*, is an acute examination of the Devlin family—particularly two female characters, Elizabeth Carroll and her adolescent daughter Winnie—within the highly textured tensions and challenges of family life. Many of Cullinan's short stories, particularly those set in New York, also deal with coming of age within a psychologically destructive family, including "The Voices of the Dead," "Sum and Substance," "The Power of Prayer," and "Only Human." The young Irish American woman from New York attempting to navigate Dublin culture recurs in some of Cullinan's other works, including the novel A *Change of Scene* and several short stories from the collections *In the Time of Adam* and *Yellow Roses*. These narratives render the interior life of a young woman subjected to or practicing a series of displacements and/or placements in her attempt to locate psychic citizenship. The adolescent version of the character Winnie in Cullinan's first novel, *House of Gold*, reappears as the young woman Ann Clarke in A *Change of Scene* and, alternatively, as Louise Gallagher, Ellen MacGuire, and Marjorie Cunningham in Cullinan's short stories. Gathering up these kindred female characters, it is possible to weave together the subjectivities at various points in life and see one life narrated through each. In establishing the fictional metapersona, we can read across a number of Cullinan's works to discern the internal and social constraints within and on this narrator and map her efforts toward defining an obscure and fragile identity, a project explicitly defined by ethnicity, gender, and religiosity.

Cullinan's debut with *House of Gold* revealed her to be a young writer with superior talent. Cullinan's attention to precision of detail, the inner lives of her characters, and sophisticated narrative structures places her as an American writer meticulously attendant to craft. Charles Fanning lauds her *House of Gold*, observing that it "exemplifies contemporary Irish American domestic fiction at its best . . . a definitive portrait of crippling psychic damage that can occur within Irish families" (335). The novel spans thirty hours and describes the Devlin family as they gather for the imminent death of their mother, the tyrannical Julia Devlin, in the family home. While Julia is no longer conscious, her formidable legacy is revealed in the adult children's insecurities and anxieties as well as their collective defensive maneuvers to maintain the family mythology. The counter-narratives contesting the pathological family dynamic emerge here as well.

The inherited narrative, created by Mrs. Devlin, is shaped by immigrant anxiety and zealous Catholicism. Much of Mrs. Devlin's life was devoted to proving wrong her sister's prediction that if she married Mr. Devlin she would be eating "snowballs for dinner" (167). Mrs. Devlin is driven to achieve respectability in middle-class America. Her achievements braid together consumption and religion in an Irish American arrival story, including the sacrament of homeownership and the organization of a rigorously pious family. All of this is reified though the projected family narrative, but its preservation has a price. Maeve Brennan observes that Julia Devlin "has always seen herself as Our Lord's intermediary, and as His intermediary, she has been able to enjoy eating her children and having them too" (130). Several of her children are "given to God" as members of the clergy, two die young, and the others, particularly Elizabeth, live in the service of their mother's emotional and day-to-day needs. All are required to maintain the myth of secure and happy childhoods gathered around the holy mother: "'There'd never be any other times like those at home with the family. There's just so much happiness to remember,'" insists Mother Mary James, one of the Devlin children. "'Such a wealth of it! A wealth of it!'" (193). Yet it is at Julia Devlin's deathbed that the family narrative is disrupted and the toxic emotional oppressiveness, not a wealth of happiness, of the house of gold begins to be revealed. The house of gold, a reference to the litany of the Blessed Virgin, is not golden but stained and constraining, and Julia Devlin is a parodic stand-in for the Holy Mother.

The novel opens with the waking of Elizabeth Devlin Carroll, the youngest adult child of Julia. While Elizabeth is a mother herself with her own teenage daughters, she is a blurry character, incomplete in self-definition. She remains "so much a daughter, a daughter more than anything else" (14), and she is trapped in a life of pathological obligation to her mother, a trap created by Julia. Elizabeth is wounded, with a "rope around her heart" (192). Yet, as we see in the unfolding of events, she is waking to a keener awareness of the damaging conditions she has endured in her family life.

Throughout the day, more Devlins arrive: Elizabeth's husband Edwin, an unreliable and passive man with a gambling problem, and their daughters, Winnie and Julie. The members of the family who are clergy, privileged in the Devlin family, also appear, including Sisters Mary James and Helen Marie. Father Phil's arrival warrants much announcement; he is the eldest as well as a priest. Father Phil also controls the family interactions and discourse as arbiter of what is to be spoken or silenced. The next living son, Tom, along with his wife Claire and their two young sons, soon arrive.

Justin, the black sheep of the family and youngest son, has been living with Mama Devlin and tending bar. As scapegoat, Justin offers a lens onto the family that resists the agreed-upon narrative. In counterpoint to

Mother Mary James's rapture about the family's congregation, Justin thinks, "they [will] all be home again—all of them" (24) and vomits. Justin also perceives the façade of the house of gold. The home itself, mirroring the church across the street, is full of holy statues, but they are gaudy and "pitiful," notes Brennan, "a shanty-Irish dream come true and gilded—where a lithograph of the flaming, engorged Heart of Jesus is more real than any words Christ ever uttered . . . the house is a tabernacle for the rabidly devout motherhood of Julia Devlin" (130). Through Justin's eyes we see the statuary: the Infant of Prague, Our Lady of the Miraculous Medal, and Saint Joseph. Justin knows where to find the two delicate cracks showing where the Infant's head has been cemented repeatedly. Justin recalls the night when he had come home late and knocked the Infant to the floor: "His head rolled under the dresser, His gilt globe went under the bed" (221). Justin's recollection is interrupted when he observes Sister Sebastian, the hired nursing sister at Mrs. Devlin's bedside, put her hand up to rub her own head. He thinks, "She had been here all day when usually at this hour, she'd be arriving. She worked at night. She was at people's service. That made her different from the other nuns, different from the two downstairs . . . he'd also found out she was a good sport: she never minded if he smoked or had a couple of cans of beer" (221). In contrast to Julia and her obsession with propriety and the appearance of virtuousness, Sister Sebastian, a Spanish immigrant who speaks broken English, is the authentically sacred figure—spiritual and compassionate. It is her head that hurts at the moment Justin thinks of the broken Infant's head.

Elizabeth's experience of her family and identity as defined by the family's needs reveals her profound obligation to her mother and her ambivalence to that duty. As the youngest daughter, Elizabeth has occupied the traditional role as primary caretaker of her mother. She, Edwin, and their daughters have lived, until recently, in rooms at the top of the house, and it is their departure that causes Elizabeth to believe she has figuratively and literally broken her mother's heart, causing her fatal illness. As the story unfolds, however, it is revealed that Mrs. Devlin has been misdiagnosed; it is not her heart that is failing but, in fact, cancer that could have been treated with surgery. The family members have been made aware, through another doctor, of the misdiagnosis, but some choose to continue to believe—and, ironically, cause their mother's death in doing so—the family doctor, Dr. Hyland, thereby weaving the religiously symbolic, damaged heart into the family narrative. Also, to challenge Dr. Hyland—the voice of authority—represents transgression for these anxious children of immigrants. Thus, Elizabeth's guilt is symbolically transformed into an element of the public family narrative, and her emergent resistance serves to indemnify her, in her siblings' eyes, even further.

At Julia's wake Edwin Carroll comments on the public Devlin story: "The Devlins were drawing together to present a front to the world outside their world, and it would be a good front, perfect in every detail. People would believe it" (296). Elizabeth, however, attempts to challenge this when she nearly discloses her ambivalence about her obligations to her mother. Later Mrs. Hyland, the doctor's wife, points out Elizabeth's culpability in her own mother's death: "I said to Harold then, Mama Devlin's heart is broken. Elizabeth was her whole life. She'll never be able to live without her" (307). These words, provoking inexorable guilt in Elizabeth, eclipse any nascent resistance she had possessed. It is Winnie, witness to these events, who is able to challenge the narrative and confront Mrs. Hyland with her husband's misdiagnosis. As the mother is seen in her child, so is Elizabeth seen in Winnie—a generation away from Julia and the family's neuroses. It is Elizabeth's waking from the deep sleep of obedience that is realized in Winnie's defiance of the family codes and her agency in the revealing and dissolving of the destructive family narrative. These female characters are central to the collaborative resolution of truth telling and reinvention of identity in House of Gold.

The later novel, A Change of Scene, portrays a young woman who leaves her family and a failed affair and travels to Ireland seeking refuge and a relationship, but instead she accumulates a set of less certain understandings of her place within the world. If House of Gold, as Charles Fanning writes, represents exemplary Irish American domestic fiction, A Change of Scene and many of Cullinan's short stories may be seen as Irish American escape stories. The question that follows the female protagonists of Cullinan's fiction, however, is Escape to what?

To chronicle these narratives of departure, we can look first at three short stories in the Yellow Roses collection: "An Accident," "Yellow Roses," and "A Forgone Conclusion." In these stories Cullinan focuses on the conclusion of Louise Gallagher's affair with a married man. Evident in the stories are the conflicting influences of Catholicity and ethnicity. The narrator describes an ethical world oddly skewed by the secular culture of the second half of the twentieth century—including expanded definitions of acceptable, or at least less censured, romantic arrangements as well as the redefinition of women's roles and opportunities in the sphere outside of the home. The Catholic Church, however, while it has turned the altar around, still clings to rigid notions of divorce and remarriage, leaving Cullinan's narrator, Louise, to invent her own hybrid ethos by piecing together conflicting cultural mores to fashion an understandable but illogical resolution. While Louise has been able to sustain an affair with a married man, she also says it is an "inconclusive affair. That they should go on indefinitely the way they were seemed unlikely, but that they should part seemed unnecessary, and anything else seemed out of the question since Louise was Catholic" (90). In a restaurant Louise reflects on the incongruities she has set up for herself: out of loyalty she still honors meatless Fridays: "Habit or virtue, she thinks, it surely made no sense to be digging around into an omelette on Friday with a married man . . . she was genuinely distracted now" (93). Aware of the generations of mothers and daughters around her and imagining their judging of her predicament, Louise begins to detach from Charlie and, at the story's end, she says good-bye to him.

Louise transforms into Ann Clarke in *A Change of Scene*, and Ann also remains preoccupied with Catholicism and uncertainty about her ethnic heritage and identity. At the outset of the novel, Ann is preparing to leave for an extended stay in Ireland. Picking up and continuing the strand of the affair from the short stories, Ann tells us: "I was in love but the man was already married unsatisfactorily but firmly it seemed to me for I am Catholic, though this man made me question what I had previously taken for granted about religion and everything else—leaving me emotionally stranded in the process." Suffering from a malaise and uncertainty brought on by the end of the affair, she imagines a spiritual renewal, perhaps even pilgrimage, in her journey: "At the back of my mind there was also the idea that living in a chronically Catholic country would automatically sort out my feelings on the whole subject" (10).

Ann travels, ostensibly, to study Irish language and literature, but one of the draws of Ireland to her is to "know people who were at my stage of life and seemed to be going in my direction" (12). In discussing her study plans with a friend in New York—in truth, the Irish writer Frank O'Connor—Ann is chided for not applying to University College Dublin rather than Trinity, where she would be "among her own kind" (personal interview). Yet Ann's relationship to her ethnic identity is defined by both shame and absence; she writes: "My reasons for going in the first place had something to do with getting away from them and their troubles, none of it original . . . my parents' dreams resulted in lives of bitterness for them and a heritage of insecurity for me and my sister" (13). While Cullinan's *House of Gold* and a number of her short stories address the intersections of ethnicity and damaging familial relationships, *A Change of Scene,* as an escape narrative, includes little of Ann's family aside from a brief and unwelcome visit to Dublin from her sister. Ann has no family that she knows of in Ireland, and it seems that that sort of information would be rejected by Ann's family: in a recent interview, Cullinan said of her family, "We looked down on any sort of attention paid to being Irish. We were really outsiders in our own lives" (personal interview).

To be an outsider in one's own life, particularly as defined by an ethnic identity, plays outs powerfully in Ann Clarke's time in Ireland in *A Change of Scene,* and the instability of this cultural identity is clear. Part of Ann's journey to Ireland, then, is to test the ethnic identity that is both a source of shame in her family as well as — as Cullinan discovered in her time at the *New Yorker*—something that endured within a larger social context. In *A Change of Scene* Ann is searching, but this search is shaped by her ambivalent understandings and enactment of identities. The title of the novel itself, as well as frequent references to drama and masking throughout the novel, suggest the performative nature of Irish-ness and Irish American-ness. Cullinan's description of this young New Yorker in Dublin is subject to various readings: Ann, the ingénue abroad, the anxious exile, the female narcissist, and a liminal character on a pilgrimage, hoping to resolve the internal argument as to just who and what she is. Cullinan describes her own time in Ireland as "a puzzle. I found out that Irish was not a category I belonged to in Ireland" (personal interview). In fact, Ann's attempt to pin down her identity may be defined as a journey not toward hybridity but toward indeterminacy and absence: not belonging and not anything.

In Ireland Ann does not spend much time studying—little of the novel discloses her intellectual life. While she imagines that learning Irish would be a "matchless souvenir" (34), she gets a cold a few weeks into the term and essentially drops out of school: "Trinity came to be little more than an alibi. When anyone asked me what I was doing in Dublin, I'd say 'I'm a student.'" The story highlights the interior life of Ann and the social relationships she develops in Dublin, many of them through her friends in the United States. Elizabeth Cullinan herself had met many writers associated with the *New Yorker* and, notably, developed a friendship with Mary Lavin, seen as Oona Ross in *A Change of Scene.* In Ireland Ann is drawn to Oona and her daughters, and she thinks: "Oona struck me as someone who could make a success of any uncompromising circumstances. Hadn't she more than retrieved her widowhood, making that condition as interesting and as full of possibility as any other? At least that was how life at the Mews looked to me" (65). Young Ann, while avowing no interest in family life or relationships, finds some of her happiest moments at the Mews with Oona and the girls. Ann also spends a good deal of time in pubs, making friends with Tomas O'Domhnaill and his crowd, attempting to fit in but never really managing to. Ann falls prey to naïve generalizations as she studies the Irish and romanticizes: "The attached house gave a heartening impression of poverty and security, deprivation and comfort" (15) Ann says, and "Their faces, or rather one face—the Irish face with its depth of expression that spoke to me of native wit and intelligence, of an extraordinary grasp of life and a keener appreciation of it" (56). Yet the narrator is aware of this romanticizing. One of Oona's teenage daughters explodes at Ann during a conversation: "You're always going on about Ireland. It's no bloody Eden you know" (170). Ann also realizes, at the end of a long romantic affair with Tomas, that his relationship with her would never be serious: "He'll marry an Irish girl," she says (165). Jim Larkin, a minor character who is suggestive of the Irish novelist John McGaghern (personal interview), is quite in love with Ann, but she does not love him. Nonetheless, when he later announces to her that he has fallen in love, and Ann, mistakenly imagining it still to be with her, says, "My being foreign is all that attracts you," Jim says, "The girl's Irish" (176). Jim underscores the new girl's kinship with him: "She's from Carlow, only a couple of villages from my own. . . . Her hair is pitch black and her eyes the color of gentians." Ann is again reminded of what she is not: "A real Irish beauty, Ann thinks, the original" (176).

The end of another relationship upon her, and echoing Elizabeth Cullinan's own remark that, for her, "Living in Ireland was confusing . . . a puzzle," Ann prepares to leave. It is not an ethnic identity she can resolve here, she decides, but the familiarity of the rituals of mass and the church offer a solace, double-edged though it may be. Embedded throughout the narrative are Ann's gestures toward her faith and religious practice, but the final scenes of the novel are most imbricated in what turns out to be a particularly complicated set of meanings associated with the Catholic Church. Looking around at her fellow churchgoers, Ann finds comfort in their affinity for each other: "They were a quarrelsome people, always at odds with each other," but "[n]othing they did or said changed the fact that they belonged together" (186). Ann romanticizes to the very end and invokes a nearly parodic image, representing the Irish in this church as rustic, even coarse: "Pious old women, men with hangovers and men with a saintly air of detachment, solid looking matrons and rosy-cheeked girls. Each of them had an exceptional look that reminded me of the rough finish and rich pigmentation that gave my earthenware dishes their beauty; but if everyone there looked original, I also felt that collectively they amounted to a matched set" (186). It is through this vision as the narrator, emotionally distanced, that Ann locates herself culturally as Other: "Fascinating as this island was to itself (and to me) it wasn't the whole world—not my world anyway" (187). Ann attends multiple masses at various churches, however, looking for a way to heal from the end of the affair, for a home, and for her identity in the Irish cultural landscape. Having attempted to establish a sense of belonging to Ireland in her journey, she has instead found herself in a state of ethnic absence. Her heritage and her community, she decides now, are religious: "I solved the dilemma by hearing Mass at a series of different churches—the Carmelite off Grafton St., the University Church on Stephen's Green . . . Attending Mass in Ireland was my own kind of certification . . . I could feel as Catholic as the rest" (186). She finally finds familiarity here among these strangers. Having discovered that traveling to Ireland was not, in fact, a homecoming, Ann returns to her Catholic traditions for identity and community, but it is an ambivalent arrival.

Indeed, Ann gains, finally, not a pleasantly bicultural perspective or enriched sense of her own ancestry from her ten months in Ireland but rather an unsettling experience that leaves her with her sense of identity as a gap. This is in contrast to Cullinan's later short story, "Commuting," whose central metaphor, Charles Fanning argues, is "beautifully appropriate" to the "doubleness of ethnic consciousness," suggestive of seeing "everything twice and more clearly—as the Irish girl from the Bronx that she was and the New Yorker that she is now" (374–75). The character announces on one train ride: "I've escaped!" (35). As Fanning writes, commuting is not a "repudiation of the ethnic world but an expression of the potential dynamic worth of interchange between two worlds" (374–75). Here we have a narrator more at ease in her world and with her identity, but it is through the act of the narrative—of the telling—that she can begin to identify and name the layers of experienced identity.

Ann's experience in church at the close of A *Change of Scene* is also painfully complicated by a disturbing memory of an earlier encounter with the priest, Father Broderick, who is saying mass this particular day. A few weeks before, Father Broderick had invited Ann to visit him and discuss literature, attempting to persuade her to read a popular writer of the day, Maurice Walsh, rather than, as Father Broderick says, "that reprobate Beckett" (174). In his room at the rectory of Sacred Heart, Ann and Father Broderick are having a conversation and drinking sherry when he comes up behind her and gropes her breasts. Ann sets down her glass, smoothes her skirt, and announces she must go. "Thank you for the sherry," she says. Father Broderick then asks, compounding the disturbing event, "Is there anything you need? Do you want confession?"

No more is made of this encounter until the last scene in church, where Ann, upon seeing Father Broderick at the altar, wonders how he feels. She hopes that the "whole business wouldn't eat away at him" (186). Ann expresses no anger or fear—she does not even suggest that she has questioned what he did—but rather responds dispassionately. Ann effaces her experience of self; the experience becomes an unexamined elision, or gap, in her experience and understanding of Ireland, one of many such elisions on Ann's part. While Cullinan finds the character's failure to reflect a flaw of the novel (personal interview), I would argue that Ann's lack of analysis and vague subjectivity as well as her approach to being Irish or Irish American as performance are important and necessary in the psychic development of the metacharacter. And, certainly, the narrative voice is aware, framing the dark irony of Father Broderick's offer to hear Ann's confession. Cullinan's representations of clerical failure and immorality are thematized in other works as well.

"Voices of the Dead," published in *Yellow Roses* (1977), recalls *House of Gold* in its presentation of another version of the Devlin family, here called the Nugents, as they gather at the matriarchal home to celebrate Easter mass. Father Clement, seen before as Father Phil, has been given permission to celebrate mass in Mary Nugent's home because she has become too ill to leave the house. Cullinan's choice of names for this priest figure suggests an ironic dimension of magnanimity to his patriarchal authority, an authority he is seen to exert with an arrogant harshness. In another story, "The Ablutions" (in *The Time of Adam*) the narrator offers a portrait of Father Fox, yet another version of the priest figure, and reveals to the reader his sense of self-importance and omniscience: in Father Fox's view, "God's will almost always coincided with his own" (101). Fathers Phil, Clement, and Fox exemplify the dangerous personality traits that can be sanctioned and supported within the context of the priesthood.

Once again, communication and interactions are controlled by the priest. In "Voices of the Dead," Father Clement displays his power in an attempt to mute his mother's demonstrative exuberance at this family gathering. She hugs Father Clement upon his arrival that morning: "He delivered himself to her embrace, which was almost violent," and, pulling away from her and smoothing his hair back into place, he says, "Now Mother . . . I think you ought to have something to quiet your nerves" (*Yellow Roses* 106). Sedated with a sleeping pill, Mother drifts off and back to her Irish childhood, mumbling, "Suffer the little tinkers," snoring softly through mass, and waking abruptly at the end to yell out, "What part are we up to?" (112). The symbology of the mass commingles with family artifacts and the sacred symbology of the matriarchal home. The church, again across the street, is Holy Family Church. Mrs. Nugent recently had taken to watching the services from her front porch, and she becomes, in her mind, coupled with the martyrs: "She was able to make out the gleaming gold vessels, to identify each passing liturgical season by glimpses of the vestments—creamy white, or violet, or emerald, or red, glowing like the blood of the martyrs, like her own bright blood" (103). The domestic scene of Easter morning becomes a garbled collision of dysfunctional communication and events. The television becomes the makeshift altar, and the photographs of dead family members are "strung like Stations of the Cross" on the walls (109). Mother, in her medication-induced fog, says loudly during mass, "It's a wonderfully happy day." Father Clement responds, "I believe in one God." Liturgical music gives way to a grandchild's spontaneous singing of "Happy Birthday." A dog under the loveseat barks and pants. Mary Nugent then begins to sing the popular song "Somewhere a voice is calling, calling for me." Leo, the son-in-law, argues "What is this anyway? Mass or a concert?" as he takes out a cigarette. Soon, however, all the family joins in with a "terribly excited" Mary Nugent to finish this song. While the final moments of the mass are portrayed comically, with the confusion of dogs, children, and a drugged Mrs. Nugent, it is clear also that Mrs. Nugent is failing at caring for the living as much as she does the dead: "The wonderful sons she had lost! And the good husband! How fresh they seemed, smiling out at her and how close—closer even than the living children there with her. Death took the bodies but left behind the images that were never disappointed or cross, tired and unlucky, sick and even the unbelievable thing she was—old" (109). Empathy for her is evoked briefly, early in the story, in the litany of children she had sacrificed: six out of nine, including three who had died young, two nuns, and a priest. "'How I miss them,' she thinks, 'the little bits of nuns in their cold cloister, the handsome boys in their cemetery gardens'" (111). Empathy quickly evaporates, however, with the unfolding revelations of Mrs. Nugent's self-sanctification and the privileging of her relationship with her deified, absent children—her offerings to God—rather than those caring for her.

Motifs of failed communication with families, the obligations of the dutiful daughter, and the unresponsiveness of the church to a family's and a child's pain are also poignantly portrayed in "The Power of Prayer." The act of prayer, in the experience of fourteen-year-old Aileen, is rendered an empty promise and a source of humiliation. Here the relationship between Aileen's mother and father is explored through the child's eyes, as she begins a school day preoccupied with her parents' marital problems and the event of her mother's birthday: "Please let him come home tonight. Please let him come home soon" (*The Time of Adam* 61). Caught up in her worries, Aileen laments not only the silence and sadness of her home these days but also fears the possibly shameful future: "If my mother gets a separation, there'll only be one signature on my report card. Mid-terms are next month. Everyone will know" (52). During the day at school, Aileen is reprimanded by her Latin teacher for passing a note, an "irreverent" one; the words she writes and utters become ominous to Aileen. Her note is shameful; her petitions come out wrong, she thinks, so she lies to Sister Alphonsus, saying her father is ill. Aileen's language, however, is oppositional in its contesting the notion of what is reverent and sanctioned. Aileen's punishment for the note is to say a rosary in the chapel after school, but she sees herself as failing even in the virtuousness of her prayers: "She never prayed as the nuns recommended, for the missionaries, or for the conversion of Russia, for the souls in Purgatory, or the poor and oppressed of the world" (6). The church offers no solace to a young girl afraid her parents will divorce; she feels "cheap and dishonorable" because of her "selfish petitions." Praying to be worthy, "'Let me be reverent,'" she tries to act accordingly but the prayer flies off as she thought it. There was only one thing she could ask, one thing to pray about. She would have to take the chance. "'Just this once,' she said, 'and I'll promise not to beg again.'" She pleads once again for her father to come home for dinner and to celebrate her mother's birthday (60).

At home, Aileen and her mother eat alone. Shutting off the hallway lights, Aileen kisses her mother and then pauses by the statue of the Infant of Prague. "Perhaps he was among them—the Father, the Son or the Holy Ghost; Jesus on the cross, Christ the king, transfigured and radiant, or the Sacred Heart, opening his chest for all to see" (62). Abruptly, Aileen's thoughts shift from paternal images to her mother: "I think you ought to take a sleeping pill," she tells her mother. Questions of faith are mixed with questions of obligation, and Aileen is unprepared to answer either set; rather than communicate her uncertainty, Aileen assumes the parental role of her absent father, who would, as do so many male characters in Cullinan's fiction, silence women. Late that evening, Aileen hears her father coming home; she fears he has been drinking, as before, but he has not. Yet her prayers have been subverted: "What a way to answer the prayer, God—to let him come early, but not early enough!" (63). The failures of the earthly father are mixed in with the failures of the spiritual Father, leaving young Aileen as an ill-equipped substitute for both—a pattern that, in Cullinan's fiction, underscores the heavy burdens of the dutiful daughter.

"Sum and Substance," from *Yellow Roses*, depicts the trauma of the family visited upon the daughter. Twenty-three-year-old Ellen MacGuire is in the hospital for exploratory surgery. The surgery turns out well, but when her parents visit after the surgery, Ellen is curt and asks them to leave. Her physical pain reflects her psychic pain, and the dutiful daughter theme re-emerges: "One night in bed, they'd created a different love, a different need—this Ellen, this she who was to make up for everything. But she had failed them too" (37). Ellen is haunted by failure—her own needs and limitations—and the surgery comes to represent the traumatizing effects of her family life on her self-development and her inability to articulate her pain: "Touching the wound . . . the body took the blows. The body had its own insights, its own learning . . . it knew what happened and what to make of it. The body might take its time, but the body understood, the body remembered" (38). While Ellen's pain can be explained in terms of her family history and psychic inheritance, the depth of trauma described here, if we read across Cullinan's fiction as a connected narrative, becomes clearer in the last story to be discussed.

A most haunting story, "Only Human," published in *Yellow Roses*, is yet another counter-narrative challenging the myth of the happy, blessed family and interrupting the destructive family code of secrecy and silence. In the portrait of an evening in the life of Marjorie Cunningham, a young woman in her twenties, she is seen attempting to reconcile with her personal history and her uncle, Father James Murray, on his deathbed. It becomes clear that Marjorie had been repeatedly sexually abused by her uncle when she was a child, and this story delineates Marjorie's ongoing pain, particularly horrific because the abuser is not only a family member but also a priest revered by her family and community.

Opening with the familial mythology, the story introduces Mrs. Cunningham, sister of Father Jim and mother of Marjorie, as she recites Father Jim's virtues to an audience of nuns at Father Jim's wake. "He was forever thinking of others, never of himself, and that was how he spent his last day on earth, thinking of others" (144). The narrator reveals, however, that Mrs. Cunningham has inadvertently reversed the culminating line of the Father Jim story and, rather, opened with what traditionally had been the conclusion; here, it is suggested that the powerful family stories are vulnerable to Mrs. Cunningham's narrative unreliability. She attempts to repair the narrative structure: "She had to stop and collect her thoughts, and the nuns took her to be overcome with feeling" (144). The family's eulogizing is rendered as performance and affirms the story's value as an ideal rather than accurate reporting. The narrative's reversal mirrors the structure of the short story as well, which begins with the wake and moves backward to Father Jim's death.

In "Only Human," Marjorie is most clearly defined as an outsider to her family, resisting the code of secrecy and preservation of the happy/holy family myth—the privileged narrative constructed to protect the family, as seen earlier in *House of Gold*, with a shield of propriety and virtue. Early on it is revealed that Mrs. Cunningham is displeased with Marjorie. Mrs. Cunningham says to the nuns, with a voice that "had an edge to it . . . 'there was no use in calling Marjorie,'" depicting Marjorie as an unreliable family member who could not be called upon for help when Father Jim became ill (146). Later, however, Mrs. Cunningham says that Marjorie was not called simply because she had no car to drive her mother to the hospital. The narrator also tells us that Marjorie was "someone who would always look the way she was supposed to look, someone who had a horror of standing out" (146), referencing the psychological consequences of abuse for this character and establishing events to come. The structuring of events and memory galvanizes the durability of trauma in Marjorie's life and identity.

Arriving at the wake, held in the administration building where Father Jim had been assistant superior and rector, Marjorie ponders a dispute that had involved herself and Father Jim: "he'd been of the old school, not quite ready for the change [in the Church] and not quite able to stand up to it or back down from it" (148). A "breath of scandal" is also invoked. The issue now preoccupying Marjorie begins to be exposed: "But now the Church had had a real dose of scandal. Defections, heresy, a generalized discontent and disorder in the ranks—all that gave Marjorie the sense of having been ahead of the times, which . . . was the last thing she wanted" (148–49). Marjorie is, by self-definition, undefined. When asked what she does, she replies, "I don't do anything. I'm divorced" (155). Here she adds a layer of transgression to her psychic absence.

Reversals, disorder, and distortion continue as the story unfolds: Marjorie "wanted to lose her way and then find it again, find it for herself, if the way was there and could be found. But while her back was turned a trick had been played on her, everything was switched around" (149). She finds herself joining her mother and the group of nuns, compelled back to family and clergy. One of the sisters engages Marjorie in a conversation about her Uncle Jim, and she silently offers a sarcastic and painful counterpoint to each of the nun's statements: "He was a terrible tease," says the nun, and Marjorie thinks, "And in ways this nice nun wouldn't have come up against." The nun continues, "But he had tremendous warmth, too," to which Marjorie silently responds, "Always taking you aside and telling you, in that beautiful, cultivated voice, some dirty joke; always when he kissed you, touching you in some place he shouldn't have touched you; always those wet kisses" (150). The reader also learns that Marjorie has, sometime in the past, revealed the secret, to her family and others, of her uncle's abuse, and we see the humiliating and isolating consequences of having done so—as well as more silencing. Marjorie is at a table, talking with the priest next to her, when her conversation is interrupted by her Uncle Joe: "Joe cut her off—in his opinion Marjorie should have been cut off altogether; he couldn't see that she was anything but a troublemaker—a proven troublemaker." When the priest asks which of the Cunningham daughters she is, she replies "the younger one." The interior monologue of shame and truth-telling continues; she thinks, "The one who caused the trouble." Aware of his reaction, she sees she is stigmatized: "Something told her he knew very well—something alert and knowing in his eyes and in his voice" (153). A narrative of shame emerges for Marjorie. Surrounded by priests who had lived with her uncle, the adored "soul of kindness" who gave of himself "unstintingly" (155), Marjorie finds herself at the center of attention, as unwanted as the incestuous abuse from her uncle. A repetition of humiliation emerges as Marjorie is demonized for having broken the silence, shamed the family, and threatened the hallowed reputation of Father Jim and the holy family. In this story destructive family relationships and the oppressiveness of the Catholic Church are seen clearly as inherited damage visited upon this Irish American Catholic girl—cultural, and perhaps even inevitable, damage. There is no resolution for Marjorie, only continuing alienation, pain, and shame.

Cullinan's characters help us map the evolving identity of a young Irish American woman and her experiencing of identity(ies) within and beyond the family. In *House of Gold* the adolescent character of Winnie evokes great sympathy in the reader for her courageous refusal to participate in the family's obsequiousness to authority and her challenge to the values, beliefs, and narratives that have created so much damage in the novel's characters. The metacharacter, as she evolves into Marjorie Cunningham, Louise Gallagher, Ann Clarke, etc., is older, but she is even less certain of self—more liminal—than the rebellious adolescent, and, at times, less able to reject or adopt new definitions of self now inclusive of and beyond family. Maureen Murphy quotes Cullinan's remarks on her Irish Catholic girlhood in New York: "You were given a context to grow up in and that was supposed to be your identity. That's what you were. You were fortunate. You didn't need anything else" (139). Yet the older version of Winnie finds herself in need of something else. She has had to revise her own claims and categories, complex within her own family, redefined by the author's personal history at the *New Yorker* and finding herself to be Irish American, and finally, her emergent desire to discover deeper understandings of identity in Ireland. In contrast to the celebratory hybridity in "Commuting," published after *A Change of Scene*, we see the still evolutionary and incomplete sense of self(ves) for an Irish American woman writer. Her ambivalence and alienation help us to chart the shape and course of the cultural legacy, artistic consciousness, and literary traditions of Irish American women writers. Elizabeth Cullinan articulates a compelling vision of the powerful relationships between culture and character for an Irish American woman in her quest for agency, identity, and voice. Brilliantly skilled at portraying the interiority of experience and the emotional complexity of her characters, she opens a wide window onto the grounds of identity creation within the Irish American, Catholic family and beyond in the latter half of the twentieth century. In revealing the trajectory and felt life of a young Irish American woman within the context of gendered, ethnic, and religious culture, Elizabeth Cullinan describes the reinvention of identity that comes with challenging the familial and cultural narratives and having the courage to authorize self in and through the retelling.

Works Cited

Brennan, Maeve. "Through a Lace Curtain, Darkly." *New Yorker* 14 Feb. 1970: 130.

Cullinan, Elizabeth. *A Change of Scene*. New York: W. W. Norton, 1982.

———. "Commuting." *Irish Literary Supplement* 2.1 (1983): 34–35.

———. *House of Gold*. New York: Random House, 1969.

———. *In the Time of Adam*. Boston: Houghton Mifflin, 1971.

———. Personal Interview. 10 April 2002.

———. *Yellow Roses*. New York: Viking, 1977.

Fanning, Charles. *The Irish Voice in America: 250 Years of Irish-American Fiction*. Lexington: University of Kentucky Press, 1990.

Howard, Maureen. Foreword. *Cabbages and Bones: An Anthology of Irish American Women's Fiction*. Ed. Caledonia Kearns. New York: Henry Holt and Company, 1997. xi–xiv.

Murphy, Maureen. "Elizabeth Cullinan: Yellow and Gold." *Irish-American Fiction: Essays in Criticism*. Ed. Daniel Casey and Robert Rhodes. New York: AMS Press, 1979. 139–52.

Oates, Joyce Carol. Review of *House of Gold*, by Elizabeth Cullinan. *New York Times Book Review* 7 Feb. 1971: 6.

CHAPTER 5

Alice McDermott's Narrators

BEATRICE JACOBSON

The novels of Alice McDermott share common themes and concerns developed with a richness of language and narrative skill located, usually, in a female persona who serves as both character and narrator. This figure, whose ironic, witty, intuitive, and ultimately wise voice guides the reader through events and reflections, is typically a woman of Irish American heritage and Catholic upbringing. Yet McDermott has distanced herself from her ethnic world—or she has been distanced from it. Thus, in the course of her storytelling, she often seeks to make sense of that world by revisiting the past and, in several books, by revisiting the Irish American culture out of which she emerged. This theme of return suggests the positioning of McDermott's narrators as women on the margin between past and present, and between home (Irish American and Catholic) and the larger world (secular and materialistic). This voice from the margin resonates both with the contexts of Irish American literature and, more generally, the circumstances of women writers.

Marked by a sense of loss, Irish American culture echoes experiences of exile and separation from home and family—from Mother Ireland—resulting in a search for connection and belonging. For the second and third generations of Irish Americans, this loss evolves to reflect other kinds of alienation—a loss of faith or the thinning of family or community ties—that are further complicated by struggles to make one's way in a culture resistant to Irish Catholics. By the middle of the twentieth century, Irish Americans were experiencing increasing acceptance, epitomized by the election of an Irish American Catholic president. Yet this progress failed to completely resolve feelings of alienation. Further, social and political movements in the 1960s and 1970s encouraged the post–World War II generations of Irish Americans to resist traditional Irish behavior patterns. As one of McDermott's narrators observes, "Even when I married Matt . . . we headed for Seattle. Lives of our own, we said. Self-sacrifice having been recognized as a delusion by then, not a virtue" (*Charming Billy* 132).

In different but equally important ways, women writers, who are located on the margins of patriarchal society, also have understood themselves as alienated. For Irish American women writers this sense of difference, coupled with ethnic identification, has posed multiple challenges as well as multiple opportunities. Maureen Howard, in her foreword to Caledonia Kearns's *Cabbage and Bones: An Anthology of Irish American Women Writers,* delineates the challenge that McDermott and others have embraced: "The duty that many of these writers take upon themselves is to discover what is wayward in their women's souls, where transgression in thought or deed may lead to a finer, at times, more generous understanding of a limiting world or to self-discovery" (xi). This challenge is made more daunting by literary scholarship, which has traditionally reflected *ad hominem* concerns, a politics described by Sandra M. Gilbert: "Not only have examinations of literary history tended to address themselves "to the man"—that is, to the identity of what was presumed to be the *man* of letters who created our culture's monuments of unaging intellect—but many aesthetic analyses and evaluations have consciously or unconsciously appealed to the "personal interests, prejudices, or emotions" of male critics and readers. (ix)

Thus, in their attempts to negotiate both the world of literature and their social contexts, Irish American women novelists have had to invent strategies that strive for community on the one hand and that affirm artistic identity on the other. In her remarkable series of novels, Alice McDermott provides ongoing lessons in such work. Her use of a variety of narrative techniques, her explorations of the meaning of story and storytelling, and her examination of the connections and the conflicts between life and art provide the grounds for a "generous understanding" of the Irish American world and its women storytellers.

McDermott's upbringing in an Irish American family in Brooklyn and her education in Catholic elementary and secondary schools account for the focus on Irish American life in several of her novels. Yet McDermott de-emphasizes the role of Irish American culture in her family: "My parents were first generations; their parents had all been born in Ireland but we didn't talk about Ireland; my parents had never been there. There was no yearning for it. We were *American*" (Roberts). Similarly, while acknowledging her grounding in Catholicism, she recalls distancing herself from the Catholic Church in young adulthood; she experienced years of "semi-indifference, occasional rejection, political objection, and unshakable associations" until she found herself "at middle age, a practicing Catholic. A reluctant, resigned, occasionally exasperated but nevertheless practicing Catholic with no thought, or hope, of ever being otherwise" ("Confessions" 13). Such ambivalence is not uncommon among second-generation Irish, though it is ironic for a writer who has focused so much attention on the materials and themes of Irish American life in New York, as well as on questions of faith, love, and, religion. Yet it is understandable: by the time Alice McDermott began her writing career, Irish immigrant traditions were vanishing or at least had been drastically modified. While the previous generations endured poverty and abuse, the contemporary generations depicted in her novels are not starving; they are not oppressed as were their parents or grandparents. As their middle-class aspirations were realized, families became less closely knit and less responsive to their identity as descendents of immigrants. For the second and third generations, memories of Ireland have become part of the mythical past; when Ireland appears in a novel, as in *Charming Billy*, it plays a sad or even perverse role, serving as the site of secret and cruel betrayal. Thus, in McDermott's novels rejecting or embracing traditions—of ethnicity, religion, or, ultimately, art—is deliberate and deliberated.

Through the voices of her women narrators, Alice McDermott responds to this transitional period of Irish American culture and the options for self-definition it offers her generation. Part of this process involves recovering the past—both personal and historical—and rendering it as story. Mary Paniccia Carden notes that in *At Weddings and Wakes* and *Charming*

Billy McDermott connects stories of romantic love with larger cultural concerns, overlayering both "with the hopefulness of immigrant dreams and the possibilities of America, a romantic love that stands as a metaphor for the historical processes that create Irish Americans" (12–13). In fashioning her narrators and protagonists for this project, McDermott distances them from their culture, paralleling the strategies of earlier Irish American women writers. In her survey of works by Irish American women, Bonnie Kime Scott identifies a strategy and an objective shared by them:

> By choosing the critical perspective of the young woman—an outsider in sex as well as ethnic group—and by insisting on daily details and commonplace crises of individual characters, they suggest other goals as well. In "figuring out people," they detect patterns of personally and socially induced frustration. They resent and implicitly question self-sacrifice, bitterness, anger, and defiance as the coping mechanisms for various forms of failure at every economic level. (101–2)

Most of McDermott's narrators—especially the unnamed narrator in *Charming Billy* or Theresa in *Child of My Heart*—position themselves at a critical distance from their social and kinship groups. "Figuring people out" from their particular vantage point aptly describes their work. Each of McDermott's narrators, however, is located differently. In *A Bigamist's Daughter* (1982), McDermott's first novel, a love affair allows an editor to reflect upon her own life and, most interestingly, the life of stories. *That Night* (1987) features a narrator who recalls the suburban neighborhood of her childhood and the upsetting events of one night in the 1950s when a young rebel and his gang arrive to claim his girlfriend. *At Wakes and Weddings* (1992) and *Charming Billy* (1998) share themes and contexts related to Irish American family life. In the former, seen largely through the eyes of three young children, the frustrations and hopes of an Irish American family in Brooklyn are explored. In *Charming Billy*, for which McDermott received the National Book Award, the story is narrated by a young relative who has joined her family for the funeral of a beloved, charismatic alcoholic whose life evoked the adoration, affection, and despair of his family. Finally, in *Child of my Heart* (2002), Theresa, a skillful and wise babysitter, comes of age during a summer marked by magic and death.

In different ways all of these novels work to maintain cultural memory, a project identified by Caledonia Kearns in *Cabbage and Bones* as common to the Irish American women writers she anthologizes: "In these stories, women are clearly defined as essential to the preservation of culture" (xix). In *At Weddings and Wakes* and *Charming Billy*, and more generally through her female narrators, McDermott embodies the role Kearns delineates—that of the woman storyteller refashioning the tales of her tribe. Yet she also explores the nature and purpose of storytelling, ultimately moving toward a study of the predicament of the woman who would be an artist.

Storytellers and Their Ways

McDermott's novels provide a workshop on narrative perspective. From one novel to another, or even within the same novel, narrative point of view shifts with a kind of restlessness, resulting at times in what Rand Richards Cooper refers to as a "stealth narrator" (12). *A Bigamist's Daughter* experiments with moving from third-person to first-person narration, affording Elizabeth Connelly the chance to tell only part of her story; the narrative is further complicated through the shifts from past to present and back again. Similarly, *That Night* uses a first-person narrator, an unnamed adult woman who revisits a neighborhood crisis she witnessed as a ten-year-old. Her voice occasionally fades to a third-person narrator in sections relating events of which she could have no knowledge. Again, the narration is not chronological. *At Weddings and Wakes* is written entirely in the third-person, although most events are related from the point of view of the three Dailey children.

    Charming Billy uses a more certain first-person perspective. Events narrated by Billy's niece are blended with those described in a third-person voice. This narrator, unnamed and almost completely silent at family gatherings and in conversations, is occasionally addressed by other characters, suggesting a "ghostly presence" (Cooper 12). One example of the sleight-of-hand at work occurs in the last section of *Charming Billy*. The section opens with third-person narration and a description of the Long Island house, in which a man (Dennis Lynch, no doubt) fixes breakfast for an unspecified woman. As far as six pages into this section, the man abruptly begins a conversation: "You'll have to give the in-laws a call while you're here." This line is followed by, "I said yes, I had already told them I'd stop by" (238), a revelation that switches the narration of the passage to the first-person voice of Dennis's daughter. Such stealth is appropriate,

Cooper suggests, since this young woman has moved beyond the community in many ways (12). When she returns to attend Billy's funeral, she is both part of and separate from the circle of kin—both a witness and a participant.

This narrator-witness succeeds specifically because of her insider/outsider status. She serves as the exemplar listener—the representative of the younger generation, the trustworthy listener who will not trivialize a story, who will, in fact, take the story and recast it for others. We see her at this task throughout the book, listening to and learning from one relative and then reassessing another as she becomes acquainted with the experiences of Billy and of those close to him. She works not only to preserve family truths but to make sense of them for herself as well as for the reader. Her affection for her father Dennis, Billy's cousin and best friend, prods her interest in Billy's life. She absorbs what she learns, however distressing, with understanding. Yet she is not uncritical; when she learns that her father will marry Maeve, Billy's widow, she ponders: "Was it penance, I'd want to ask him, was it compensation for an old and well-intentioned lie, for the life it had deprived her of? Or was it merely taking care, more taking care? A hand held out once again to whoever happened to be nearby" (242). The narrator never confronts her father, but these questions challenge all that he and his generation stood for.

In its focus on a largely adult world, *Charming Billy* differs considerably from McDermott's other novels, in which childhood is foregrounded. Questions raised in *A Bigamist's Daughter* encourage Elizabeth to recall in detail her girlhood and her parents' behavior, especially her father's frequent and curious absences. The adult narrator of *That Night* is fascinated with the neighborhood drama of her childhood; this opening up of the world of the child and the child's perceptions is improved upon in *At Weddings and Wakes*. Through much of this novel, the reader is looking over the shoulders of the three Dailey children as they accompany their mother on her twice weekly pilgrimage to her family home in Brooklyn. At points readers are on the floor with the children, looking up at the adult scene they find themselves in the midst of:

> In the chair above them their father slowly turned the pages of one of the dull magazines, smoking and lifting small pieces of tobacco from his tongue. . . . In the kitchen and the dining room cabinets slammed and pots rattled together, voices rose although they remained, especially on

that Christmas that Fred was there, encased in a hard, crusty whisper. At some point Agnes or May or Veronica or their mother would stride silently through the living room and shut a door. At some point the children would catch the breathy sound of tears. (103)

Despite the tensions and the sorrows surrounding them, the Dailey children enjoy a safe, ordered environment; thus, observing and decoding the behaviors of their elders requires only the patience and discipline to endure the long days and evenings at Momma's and the Towne women's anger and despair. More difficult for children is negotiating the adult world — bringing order and safety when grown-ups have failed to do so. Such is the lot of Theresa, narrator of *Child of My Heart*. Here McDermott changes strategy: Theresa, who is also the protagonist, narrates the entire story, and while there are some shifts in time, the sequence of events runs chronologically through the summer weeks of Daisy and Theresa's time together and, finally, into the fatal autumn and winter.

The most fully defined of McDermott's storytellers, Theresa is not at all stealthy and positions herself as the key actor in her story. Here the insider/outsider dynamic becomes more richly complicated. Theresa negotiates between her aspiring middle-class background and the world of the wealthy she serves as a nanny and pet-sitter, but she also negotiates the divide between the world of children and that of adults, a gap made perilous by the irresponsibility of parents. Further, she negotiates between the Irish Catholic culture of her extended family and the secular materialism of wealthy Long Islanders. Finally, she takes charge of her own initiation into adult sexuality. Through these tasks Theresa moves beyond the role of observer and, more than any of McDermott's narrators, acts to alter her world and that of her young charges, a project that involves storytelling and imaginative play. The narrative strength of *Child of My Heart* lies in Theresa's ability to move between worlds — from middle-class Irish Americans to upper-class WASPs, from the needs of childhood to those of adulthood, from innocence to experience. In doing so, she becomes not only a mature person but also a mature teller of tales.

Over the course of these novels McDermott's female narrators gain confidence. Unlike the more ambiguous narrative voices of several of the earlier novels, Theresa's unambiguous voice controls the text of the novel as well as her other "texts": the stories, festivities, songs, and jokes with which she humanizes the world of children who have been ignored by their parents. Along with these children—Daisy, Flora, and the Moran children—readers of *Child of My Heart* experience nurturing, affection, and responsibility together with self-determination, creativity, and loss.

Child of My Heart also delivers a more chronological narrative, and, like *A Bigamist's Daughter*, it depends on a more traditional plot. In other novels, notably *That Night*, *At Weddings and Wakes*, and *Charming Billy*, the narration is marked by frequent flashbacks, so that narrative structure depends on a circularity of form with one core event or situation serving as the narrative center. Like a stone dropped in water, that center generates a field of stories and reflections, both past and present, which ripple through the pages, complicating and deepening the impact of the central event. In *That Night* the event is Rick's raid on Sherry's home. Almost all of the book's sections deal with what this event meant for the neighborhood, what led up to it, and what followed. The focus in *At Weddings and Wakes* is not an event but a family, specifically the dysfunctional relationships between Momma and her step-daughters, a nexus identified with the family apartment in Brooklyn. In *Charming Billy* the death of the title character is the main focus: family members tied to the phenomenon of Billy's life and death have gathered for his burial.

Such shaping of a text is reflected in other structural elements. None of McDermott's novels, except for the first, have numbered chapters, a stylistic choice that emphasizes the non-linear structure of the novels. For instance, while the timeline of *That Night* generally moves forward, McDermott manipulates the sequence of events: about two-thirds of the way through the novel, a section describes Rick and his gang planning the raid that appears in the very first section of the book. In addition, the novel is divided into two parts, the first focusing more on the neighborhood and the second following Sheryl to Ohio. Yet the action reverts to the neighborhood when the narrator returns, years later, and again encounters Rick. Likewise, *At Weddings and Wakes* and *Charming Billy* allow time to shift forward or to relapse into the past. While this technique is not unique to McDermott, it serves in her work to support more largely thematic concerns regarding the impact of time on memory and the story-making that is not only memory's key function but also a hallmark of the Irish American literary tradition.

Placing core events at the center of her characters' consciousness— events returned to if only in memory—suggests a circumscription of experience, a strategy that focuses on what has happened. While reflecting on the past is not remarkable, as later experience informs memory, or as one character's understanding of an event is modified by another's, there seems to be more at work when McDermott's characters remember the past. Seeing the world as circumscribed by the past—and therefore seeing human experience as limited—is a form of realism eliminating the possibility of transcendence. Throughout much of Irish American literature, reality seems to be not an option but simply the hand dealt. Given those limits, despair is avoided either through escapism—in particular into alcoholism—through faith, or by imbuing reality, and especially the reality of the past, with imaginative richness so that phenomena originally perceived as limits or boundaries take on greater significance than merely the limitations of real life. Thus, the circularity McDermott employs in several of her novels encourages readers to look again, to re-see and to revise, along with the narrator, the sense to be made of the hand dealt the characters.

Charming Billy is the best exemplar of this technique since the revising of Billy's life takes place through the stories of the family gathered for his funeral as well as through the lens of his young relative, the narrator, who knows the secret truth that complicates all others' versions of Billy's life. More than an object of pity, more than a charming but tragic companion, Billy serves as the center of a web of family relations that results, ultimately, in the marriage of his widow to his cousin and best friend Dennis Lynch. By orchestrating the viewpoints through which readers learn of Billy and his extended family, the narrator deepens the significance of his life, making him not simply the stereotypical Irish drunk but a presence critical to the lives of those around him, both before and after his death.

The circularity of these novels also provides ample ground for the precise and luminous writing that has become McDermott's hallmark. She notes that writers use detail "to tame time, to step on life's receding tail. . . . We use precise detail in fiction not merely because it makes for better, more vivid writing; we use detail because the moment of conscious contact holds a drop of solace" (*"Bend"* 134–35). Both functions—to fix the moment and to console—operate in McDermott's writing. In *That Night*, for instance, the narrator, now an adult, recalls the summer nights of her childhood:

But I remember those nights as completely interesting, full of flux: the street itself a stage lined with doors, the play rife with arrivals and departures, offstage battles, adorable children, unexpected soliloquies delivered right to your chair by Mrs. Evers or Mrs. Rossi or whoever happened to climb our stairs. It's nostalgia that makes me say it, that most futile, most self-deluding of desires: to be a child again, but there was no boredom in those suburbs, not on those summer evenings, or at least not until this one. (11)

The sensory quality of this passage and the realistic details of the neighborhood anchor the narrator's "most futile, most self-deluding" desire to experience childhood again. Even as she expresses this wish, she undercuts it by characterizing it as "futile" and "self-deluding." And so, in contrast, her chief claim—"there was not boredom"—is credible given the theatrical analogy that structures the list of details—phenomena "stepped on" before they recede into the mists of the past. Elsewhere, phenomena assuage the pain of loss. The conclusion of *Child of My Heart* occurs in August, when Daisy has returned to her home in Queens where she will soon die and Theresa discovers three newborn rabbits, the fruits of a neighbor boy Petey's hunt for a gift. The ironies of new life in the season of Daisy's fatal illness and of Petey's frustrated desire to be loved leads Theresa to reflect on "the inevitable, insufferable loss buried like a dark jewel at the heart of every act of love" (242). The rabbits console Theresa, despite their own vulnerability and despite her understanding of them as finite "hopeless little things" (242).

Detail in McDermott's work fulfills yet another function, however, best described as sacramental, a trait that places her in the context of earlier Irish American women writers. In her study of early Irish American women writers of the nineteenth and early twentieth century, Marie Regina O'Brien distinguishes these writers from their Protestant counterparts through their emphasis on physical phenomena. Just as the Catholic tradition of the sacramental imbues objects with a religious function, so early Irish American women writers linked objects to faith, to the spiritual world. McDermott does likewise. For example, the introductory passage of *At Weddings and Wakes* narrates the journey Lucy Dailey and her three children make as they travel from their Long Island home to her family's apartment in Brooklyn, a trip made twice a week in the summer. McDermott renders this commute a pilgrimage by stressing ritualistic repetition: the children recognize the same signs, stores, noises, and smells each time the trip is made. As they leave the bus, "their first sight . . . was always the identical Chinese couple in the narrow laundry, looking up through the glass door from their eternal white and pale blue pile" (4).

It is a catholic world they see, filled with all sorts of people, languages, stores, and foods. They hear street sounds from people and machinery; handling the subway tokens, they feel "the three opened spaces in the center of the embossed coin" (7); they smell "diesel fuel and cooking grease and foreign spices, tar and asphalt and the limp, dirty, metallic smell of the train" (11).

The sensuous though secular world they travel through is transformed by their passing, as are they. Their mother becomes heroic as she confidently maneuvers through moving subway cars or protects them on the bus where "they squeezed together three to a narrow seat, their mother standing in the aisle beside them, her dress, her substantial thigh and belly underneath blue-and-white cotton, blocking them, shielding them, all unaware, from the drunks and the gamblers and the various tardy (and so clearly dissipated) business men who rode this bus" (6). Nearing her family home and the end of their journey, Lucy Dailey buys unleavened bread from a bakery and shares it with her children. As she sacerdotally breaks off pieces of the bread for the children, she tells them: "This is the kind of bread . . . that Christ ate at the Last Supper" (12). This reference to the Catholic mass begins a series of parallels between the patterns of their visits to the Towne apartment and Catholic ritual. Greeting Aunt May, an ex-nun, "The children kissed her with the same perfunctory air with which they wiped their feet at the door or genuflected in church" (14). Each evening, their mother, accompanied by Aunt May, carries a silver ice bucket into the living room, where "the lights seemed to go up by themselves" (27). What follows, the ritual of a cocktail hour, "was familiar and enchanting and would be remembered by the children for the rest of their lives with the same nostalgia and bitterness with which they recalled the Latin Mass" (27).

While some events in At Wakes and Weddings lie beyond the children's understanding, their efforts to make sense of this complicated web of family relationships stand out. Their attempts to resolve the mysteries of their family and the world they live in requires the ability to interpret objects, comments, sounds, and appearances as parts of a web of phenomena that bear significance. For example, by attending to details of behavior and demeanor during a walk with Aunt May, the children realize truths about their aunt and the love she has found late in her life:

In the street again, Aunt May let them sit on the low wall of the schoolyard that was once again deserted as they ate their pistachios and tossed the bright red shells into the street. She was, the children understood, cracking and tossing and leaning back against the fence to stay in the school's shade, the one of their mother's sisters most determined to be happy, and although she treated joy as a kind of contraband, sneaking them glasses of Coke, bags of pistachios, folded dollar bills, . . . she was for the most part successful. (21)

The children's ability to read Aunt May by assessing her actions, posture, and attitude suggest a Catholic way of perceiving the world that is echoed elsewhere in McDermott's novels. In *Child of My Heart*, for instance, Theresa massages the fated Daisy with Noxema, an action that amounts to an anointing of the sick.

This process of imbuing phenomena with religious significance is epitomized in *Charming Billy* by the linkage made between Billy's alcoholism and his religion. "He's got this faith—which is probably why he drinks," observes Dennis Lynch (35–36), who defends Billy against those who would see his alcoholism as a disease. At times compared to a priest, Billy, the tragic alcoholic, is a powerful presence in his family. For many, but especially for Billy, drink provides a perspective that "alleviates the discordance between faith and disillusionment, between the promise of love and the experience of loss" (Carden 16). Thus, he seeks out bars as avidly as he seeks out churches, yet even bars become sacred sites where he connects with his past love and with his faith. Visiting a bar, for Billy, is indeed a spiritual experience:

> Dark, sparkling, sprinkled with moments when the sound and smell and sight of the place, the taste at the back of his throat, transported him, however briefly, to a summer night long ago when he was young and life was all promise and she was there to turn to, to drink in, this was also the world where his faith met him, became actual, no longer as mere promise or possibility but as inevitable and true. . . . now the various bars he stopped into . . . reminded him that what he sought, what he longed for, was universal and constant. . . . And in each of [the bars], the force of his faith, of his Church, a force he could only glimpse briefly when sober—maybe for a second or two after Communion when he knelt and bowed his head . . . became clear and steady and as fully true as the vivid past or as the as-yet-unseen but inevitable future. (186–87)

This is one interpretation of Billy's alcoholism, yet this tendency to imbue his drinking with spirituality is checked in numerous other passages where the redemptive or heroic functions of alcohol are leveled by a steady focus on reality. The efforts of Dennis and Maeve as they carry the unconscious Billy into his home might echo the care of the dead Christ by the apostles and Mary, but the account of their physical struggles with an unresponsive body undermine any hagiographical lacings:

> She could manage his legs if Dennis could just get him under the arms. She could place herself between his knees, her elbows locked beneath his calves, her help bearing whatever weight she could not bear on her forearms and maneuver him up the stairs, the landing the trickiest part . . . She would be breathless by the time she got him to the bed, the backs of her legs black-and-blue from where his heels might have caught her, her arms weary, rubbed pink by the rough gabardine of his pant legs. . . . His body remained thin, the same long, thin legs and hairless chest, the same pale skin, chalk-white except for the raw patches of psoriasis . . . so he looked for all the world in that moment before Maeve pulled the sheet up over him like some broken martyr, a tortured and heaven-bound saint. (188–89)

Pressing reality for the "universal and constant," yet respecting the truth of phenomena, Alice McDermott invites both an affirmation of the religious significance of physical objects as well as a skepticism toward the tendency on the part of Billy's family to hallow his tragic life. In this novel as in others, McDermott's rich layering of sensory phenomena work to make sense—not sentimentality—of the worlds of her narrators, who collectively address the functions of storytelling.

The Uses of Stories

Appropriately, in McDermott's first novel, A *Bigamist's Daughter*, a young woman discovers the function of stories. A jaded editor for a vanity press, Elizabeth Connelly works in a business that treats stories as commodities. However meaningful these books may be to her authors, she has developed professional strategies that allow her to close the deal on a book, to mitigate the writer's frustration with the book's eventual marketplace failures, and even to inveigle the disappointed author to trust his or her next effort to the capable publishing hands at Vista Books. As the novel begins Elizabeth is also processing her mother's recent death, which leads to questions about her long-deceased father, whose absences seem to suggest bigamy. An affair with a new author-client whose novel is about bigamy allows Elizabeth to rethink the significance of stories—those of her writers, those told in families, and those shared by lovers. By listening to her own story of genuine love for a man she once lived with, Elizabeth concludes that her current lover "will know her worth, the way she is capable of loving. She and all the women before her. He will know what magic has touched her by the story she tells." (275). She begins to reconsider her clients, writers wanting to share their stories even if "words that mean something and change everything" may seem silly and inconsequential to others" (277). Though her own story fails to impress her lover, who trivializes her tale of first love, Elizabeth has discovered the value of stories.

That stories can manipulate is discovered by one of the Dailey daughters in *At Weddings and Wakes*. Fourth-grader Maryanne is infatuated with her teacher, Sister Miriam. To gain the nun's attention, she tells her teacher the story of her recently deceased Aunt May, who died four days after her wedding. When she feels that Sister Miriam's interest in her sad story is flagging, Maryanne adds another fact to her narrative—that May was once a nun. As she says this, she "feel[s] as grateful for the detail as if it had come to her through divine inspiration alone, as if she had, brilliantly, made it up in order to catch again and carefully secure Sister Miriam's complete attention" (60). The child likens her use of story to manipulate those around her—to gain Sister Miriam's attention—to inspiration. The magic of her story is so effective that it is "as if" she "made it up," a near collapse of reality and fiction. Even the ten-year-old is impressed by the power of storytelling.

In *Child of My Heart* stories intended simply to entertain eventually serve larger purposes. On the one hand, Theresa uses stories, jokes, and songs to entertain her charges, especially the ailing Daisy. All of these youngsters, including Theresa herself, suffer from the neglect of their parents. A chaotic family life has left the Moran children sad and angry. Little Flora's mother has abandoned her, so her father depends on hired help to care for her. Given the serious problems her charges face and her intuitively wise ways, Theresa's stories are not merely amusement or distraction. While her parents' neglect makes Theresa sympathetic to the children, her creativity allows her to provide effective care for their physical and psychological needs.

Some of Theresa's playful stories are fanciful, such as her claim that a magical lollipop tree provided candy for Daisy's siblings. Just the invention of this story leads to an insistence that it become a reality; thus, months later, Daisy, Theresa, and Flora decorate a tree with candy and celebrate the incarnation of this fiction. Some of Theresa's stories deal with death, often the death of children, and the plight of those left behind on earth, such as the story of the little girl who dies on the day of her First Communion and goes to heaven. She also tells Daisy her uncle's story of a ghost in the attic who sits with a boy on his lap (30), a tale that allows Daisy to resolve her own distance from her family. The boy's identity puzzles Daisy until she decides that he is the ghost's child, who was on a ship "that finally returns" (86), a conclusion that reverses a song both Theresa and Daisy heard throughout their childhoods from their parents: "No they ne'er returned . . . And their fate is still unlearned" (55). Theresa also invites Daisy to remember heaven before she was born and those she met there—deceased relatives or family members yet to be born. Thus, for Daisy, whose life will soon end, Theresa's stories offer reassurance.

Such examples demonstrate the richness of creative play in *Child of My Heart*, just as the layering and intertextuality of song, drama, ghost story, performance, and daydreams suggest the creative fecundity of child's play. More than preserving memories or manipulating listeners, stories here take on spiritual and artistic importance.

Yet McDermott's works are also haunted by story's absence, deception, and failure. Occasionally the story is written. In *At Weddings and Wakes* passages from the diary of Annie, who dies after the birth of her last daughter, are read by her daughter Agnes, who then buries the journal in a wall being constructed in the apartment to separate the bedroom of her father and the woman he has just married—their mother's sister—from the children. In *Charming Billy* references are made to Billy's poetry; he is seen writing brief messages to friends and family, a kind of fragmentation of his voice across the years. Yet even these texts are simply pointed to, not explored.

More often, the story is oral. *Charming Billy* continues to examine a theme raised in *A Bigamist's Daughter*—namely, the use of story for deception. The lie central to the novel's action is told years before the narrator's birth. When Billy's beloved Eva betrays him, Dennis tells him that

she died in Ireland. No one knows the truth for many years, and then, even
when Billy encounters Eva—and her secret—in Ireland, he does not correct the story. Of course, the lie Dennis tells is meant to protect Billy from
shame and disillusionment. His family, unaware of the truth, continues to
ascribe his alcoholism to his tragically broken heart; indeed, this mythology
turns Eva into a tragic icon for youth's first and most profound love. Thus
Maeve, his eventual wife, receives the family's silent sympathy, partly because of her fidelity to Billy throughout his alcoholism but also because of
her standing as Billy's second choice.

Yet larger deceptions loom. Questions of faith and salvation challenge
Billy's relatives, especially Dennis. In addition to the lie he told Billy, several other experiences have made Dennis question his world and his faith.
The difficult death of his wife Claire, whom he faithfully supported through
her cancer, challenges his sense of salvation and redemption:

> [He was] unable . . . to convince himself that the attention he had
> given her . . . the assurance that they had achieved something exclu-
> sive, something redemptive in the endurance of their love, had been
> any more than another well-intentioned deception, another construc-
> tion, as unbelievable, when you came right down to it, as the sponta-
> neity of a love song in some Broadway musical, the supposedly heartfelt
> supplication of a well-rehearsed hymn. (211)

Concluding that heaven is nothing more than "a well-intentioned deception meant to ease our own sense of foolishness, to ease pain," he could
only see death as "the void that met a used-up body, a spent mind" (211).
By the time of Billy's death, when he shares this doubt with his daughter,
he claims to have recovered the faith he had temporarily lost: "'It was only
a brief loss of faith,' he said. . . . 'I believe everything now . . . Again.'"
(212). To which his daughter-narrator adds, "Of course there was no way
of telling if he lied" (212).

So the enigma of deception persists, at times moving toward faith
while also inviting the skeptic's questions. Yet in the end, McDermott fa-
vors both story and faith, as Dennis and his daughter affirm. Even if heaven
is a myth, Dennis's daughter ultimately feels that it is valuable and even redemptive. She ends her narrative by announcing her father's marriage to
Billy's widow. She notes that the church where they wed is no longer called
St. Philomena's because of questions as to whether this saint had "actually

lived"; she comments, "As if in that wide-ranging anthology of stories that was the lives of the saints—that was, as well, my father's faith and Billy's and some part of my own—what was actual, as opposed to what was imagined, as opposed to what was believed, made, when you got right down to it, any difference at all" (242–43). The complexity of this last sentence suggests the narrator's difficulty in resolving these issues. In her text she has "gotten right down to it," re-inscribing and revising versions of Billy and those close to him, yet this death-centered novel that is also an elegy ends with a wedding. Story, at least when it is embraced by the teller and listener, is faith.

Portrait of the Narrator as a Young Nanny

The settings of McDermott's novels move from Manhattan and its neighboring boroughs to Long Island. This eastward movement culminates in *Child of My Heart,* whose narrator is situated in the Hamptons, far from the city and the urban Irish American community. Indeed, key to the thematic concerns of the novel is the decision by Theresa's middle-class parents to move to an expensive resort where their beautiful daughter might mingle with its rich residents. The challenging lives led by cousin Daisy's family—Uncle Jack works in law enforcement and relentlessly enforces laws at home as well, and Aunt Peg is stressed by the work of raising a large family in "Queens Village" (4)—are exactly the pressures Theresa's parents flee for the wealth of opportunities envisioned for their daughter in the rich world of the Hamptons. Though they seem well adjusted to their exile, a Sunday dinner with friends who also have moved to the Hamptons emphasizes the community ties that they have abandoned: "Even after twelve years of friendship, they were still discovering weekly it seemed, places where their paths had crossed or their histories had merged—a familiar candy store in Brooklyn, a friend of a friend's sister whom one of them used to date, another GI who also was on the *Queen Mary*" (144).

For Theresa, a teenager with no apparent friends and only occasional contact with her extended family, such networks seem foreign. Explaining her success with children, she notes that as a child, she "had been alone much of the time, as happens with only children of older, working parents" (15). Theresa's parents seem disturbingly remote. They commute together to their nine-to-five jobs, leaving Theresa on her own. As they return home from work, she observes that "They might have been visitors from another, darker planet" (3). Her father's greeting sounds "as if he was indeed surprised to see us" (94). Just as Theresa has been distanced from their world of Irish American ties, so her parents have become estranged from her. Further, the sense of neighborhood found in some of the other novels has been replaced by a natural setting—beautiful indeed, but curiously alien to Theresa and her parents.

More than any of McDermott's other novels, *Child of My Heart* depends on its seaside landscape and places its characters into regular contact with nature: residents walk along paths, bask in the sun, and bathe in the sea. An amazing amount of the novel takes place out of doors. For example, the yard of the modest cottage where Theresa and her parents live serves varied purposes: here Theresa breakfasts and reads; frequented by Theresa, Daisy, and the neighboring Moran kids, it becomes a kind of play room; blurring property borders and even the borders between inside and outside, Petey Moran occasionally sleeps in the yard outside Theresa's window. And it is within the yard's liminal space that Theresa enfolds the story she tells: the book begins and ends in that yard, with her finding baby rabbits—and a sort of resolution—on a day in August after Daisy has gone. Together, the various renderings of this setting fashion a world of imaginative potential.

Throughout the novel, the popular or folk materials of Theresa's child's play—ghost stories, folk songs, religious lore, and family stories, which she and the children intertextualize—are entwined with references to "high art," to Shakespeare's plays and the works of Flora's father-artist. As she studies his works, especially representations of his daughter Flora, Theresa begins to understand how the artistic mind works, how art is created, and what function it serves in the world. The artist, who has no name, represents for Theresa one model of the artist, one that demonstrates many of the stereotypes of artistic temperament: he is highly sexed, insecure, self-indulgent, and alcoholic. Advanced in age, he also becomes a type of Silenus, a demanding authority in a pastoral *locus amoenus*. If Theresa's developing sense of art is to mature, she needs access to the power he enjoys without becoming his victim, and she has seen women more experienced than she diminished by their relationship with him. Perhaps her parents' calculated use of her beauty as a means to capture wealthy Hampton hearts has made Theresa aware of her ability to manipulate. Perhaps her work as a protector of weaker beings has encouraged her very guarded approach to sex. In any event, she approaches this encounter with deliberation, not the passion typical of such trysts. Almost devoid of desire, Theresa understands the sex act as key to her survival as a person and as an artist. Sexual agency—not seduction or submission—will enable her to survive emotionally and artistically.

Rather than sweeping her away, sex with the artist makes her reconsider the daily world around her. As she takes leave of the artist after they have had sex in his studio, she says, "Back to my work" (226), a phrase that would seem to parallel her work of caring for children with his work as an artist. It is sex that links art and nurturing, both of which appear throughout much of the novel as separate spheres: the artist's work can continue in his barn studio largely because someone else is caring for Flora. McDermott goes to great lengths to challenge this division. She details Theresa's work with children, imbuing it with sensitivity and creativity. That mothering employs strategies of art is borne out in the creative and often witty exchanges among Theresa, Daisy, and Flora; further, the function of child's play in one's understanding of and response to experience is crucial to several children in the novel. Shifting to more formal considerations of art, however, is fraught with peril, especially, as Theresa demonstrates, for the woman artist. Immediately after her sexual encounter with the artist, she meditates on his sketches of his wife and daughter. She considers them commodities, records of life, biography, and, finally, as art—as novels. She concludes: "I found I preferred modern art, pictures of nothing, after all" (227). It's no wonder that, for Theresa, in this season of sexual initiation and imminent death, nonrepresentational art seems safer than biography or fiction. That artists can and do exploit those around them makes the woman artist's work all the more perilous, given her investment in social relationships and nurturing and given society's censure of women who reject those concerns.

McDermott's novels appeared at a time when Irish American women artists began to receive recognition; their artistic production was assumed, and the inquiry has shifted to assessing their achievements. *Child of My Heart* raises questions that in a sense precede McDermott's earlier novels, questions that concern not only women writers who have emerged from such a distinct and complex immigrant culture but also their readers: How does her socialization as a woman affect a woman's stories about her Irish American heritage? What role does that heritage—and especially its religious component—play in her art? What forms do duty and responsibility take in stories of the imagination? Collectively, McDermott's narrators thoughtfully explore these questions, working not simply to preserve culture but also to invent storytelling strategies that allow them to explore the interstices between life and art. Being marginalized—by culture, by gender, by generation—allows the voices in McDermott's novels to reconsider traditional understandings of life and art. More radically, marginalization encourages her narrators (and those who read them) to explore the ways that life—and women's experience—informs art.

Works Cited

Carden, Mary Paniccia. "(Anti) Romance in Alice McDermott's *At Weddings and Wakes* and *Charming Billy*." *Double Plots: Romance and History*. Ed. Susan Strehle and Mary Paniccia Carden. Jackson: University of Mississippi Press, 2003. 3–23.

Cooper, Rand Richards. "Charming Alice: A Unique Voice in American Fiction." *Commonweal* 125.6 (27 Mar 1998): 10–12.

Gilbert, Sandra M. "Ad Feminam: Women and Literature." *Claiming a Tradition: Italian American Women Writers*. By Mary Jo Bona. Carbondale: Southern Illinois University Press, 1999. ix–x.

Howard, Maureen. Foreword. *Cabbage and Bones: An Anthology of Irish American Women's Fiction*. Ed. Caledonia Kearns. New York: Henry Holt, 1997. xi–xiv.

Kearns, Caledonia, ed. *Cabbage and Bones: An Anthology of Irish American Women's Fiction*. New York: Henry Holt, 1997.

McDermott, Alice. *A Bigamist's Daughter*. New York: Random House, 1982.

———. *At Weddings and Wakes*. New York: Random House, 1992.

———. "Bend Sinister: A Handbook for Writers." *Sewanee Writers on Writing*. Ed. Wyatt Prunty. Baton Rouge: Louisiana State University Press, 2000. 125–37.

———. *Charming Billy*. New York: Random House, 1998.

———. *Child of My Heart*. New York: Farrar, Straus, and Giroux, 2002.

———. "Confessions of a Reluctant Catholic: Portrait of a Novelist." *Commonweal* 127.3 (11 Feb. 2000): 12–16.

———. *That Night*. New York: Random House, 1987.

O'Brien, Marie Regina. "Scribbling Brigids: The Search for Identity by Irish-American Women Writers, 1847–1911." Diss., University of Delaware, 2001.

Roberts, Roxanne. "The Accidental Novelist: Bethesda's Alice McDermott and Her Latest Reluctant Success." *Washington Post* 21 Apr 1992: D1.

Scott, Bonnie Kime. "Women's Perspectives in Irish-American Fiction from Betty Smith to Mary McCarthy." *Irish-American Fiction: Essays in Criticism*. Ed. Daniel J. Casey and Robert E. Rhoades. New York: AMS, 1979. 87–103.

ORAL TRADITIONS

CHAPTER 6

Tess Gallagher

A Network of Sympathies and Distant Connections

MARY ANN RYAN

Tess Gallagher's maiden name is not Gallagher—it is Bond—but her literary legacy is not and will not be founded on another marital connection, her eleven-year partnership with Raymond Carver, for her writing talent was clearly self-possessed years before she and Carver met. In addition, Gallagher's literary reputation is not founded in her fiction; rather, she is known foremost as an American poet. She is neither a New Yorker nor from the East Coast; she is from the Olympic Peninsula in the Pacific Northwest. Although she is of Irish descent (as well as other ethnicities, including Native American), Theresa Jeanette Bond was not raised Catholic, nor was she named after St. Teresa, whom she has quoted in epigraphs.

In fact, Gallagher's maiden name is quite appropriate since her work is informed pervasively by bonds—her exhumations, postulations, and venerations of human bonds, whether familial, marital, or social. It is her awareness of ancestral bonds that calls our attention to her work as representative of Irish American women's fictions, even though her life circumstances are in direct contrast to those of most of the Irish American women writers discussed in this volume. Gallagher possesses an Irish heritage on both sides of her family. Although she is at least a third-generation Irish American and has never bothered to trace her roots fully, she honors her ancestors, keeping a photograph in her kitchen of her great-great-grandfather, Timothy Halsey Quigley.

Gallagher's Irish ancestry informs her short story, "The Lover of Horses," the title story from her first collection of fiction. In this story the female narrator is unexpectedly overcome by atavistic impulses. The great-granddaughter of an Irish "horse whisperer," she realizes, "Suddenly, I felt that an unsuspected network of sympathies and distant connections had begun to reveal itself to me on my father's behalf" (8). *The Lover of Horses* begins with a tale of a daughter's acceptance of her incorrigible father and his legacy, which urges her to take risks in life. The collection ends with a story full of friction between a mother and daughter—both common subjects for Irish American women writers (Ebest). "The Lover of Horses," in particular, serves as an example of Gallagher's more dramatic tendencies. Her other stories are less lyrical, without the magic of horse whisperers, less dramatic and more quiet.

In this story and in many others from *The Lover of Horses* collection and her next, *At the Owl Woman Saloon,* Gallagher's characters are often "stolen" by things: horses, drink, a pair of glasses, guns, an abandoned child, hummingbirds, or other people's lives, whether these others are bank robbers or Avon ladies. Some characters commit their own thefts either literally—as in stealing a rival's poodle, $46,000 from a bank, a great fir "spar" (a necessary anchoring tree for loggers), a house—or figuratively, as in a native language, someone else's mother, another's place in line, or other people's hard-earned wages.

After reading Gallagher's works and interviewing her, it becomes clear that Gallagher herself was stolen by words at an early age. This connection to Irish writing's reputation for impressive linguistic formulations is a foremost aspect of her Irish heritage. Possessed by the power of language, Tess Gallagher—from the other side of the social track and across the Puget Sound from Seattle—re-imagined her potential. After a high school job at a newspaper, she realized her desire to pursue writing as a vocation. Against her father's expectations, she committed herself to a college education (McFarland 8). She moved across Puget Sound and enrolled at the University of Washington. Yet despite considerable artistic success, Gallagher has never abandoned nor denigrated her background, which continues to inform her sensibility and her writing.

Gallagher identifies herself proudly as the "daughter of loggers" and describes her parents' marriage as a "sweat-of-the-brow partnership" ("Tess Gallagher" 19). Her father, Leslie Bond, was born in an Indian dugout in New Mexico and was reared in Oklahoma. According to Gallagher, her father's family were itinerant subsistence farmers, horse-traders, and "Ridge Runners" running stills for making "moonshine" ("Re: Questions").

As Gallagher explained in a personal interview and in *A Concert of Tenses*, her father met her mother, Georgia Morris, in Missouri, where she was raised as the daughter of farmers. Like many of Ireland's immigrants, leaving his sweetheart behind in his search for work, Bond raked across America, hoboing part of the way by riding the rails. He picked cotton in Oklahoma, mined coal in Iowa, worked oil fields in Texas, and settled into work as a logger in the Olympic Peninsula woods of Washington State. After a ten-year courtship, Gallagher's father sent for her mother, who had left Missouri to work as a cook and nanny to a wealthy family in Colorado. Tess Gallagher was born in 1943, and she lives today in Port Angeles, Washington. Her father eventually left the woods to work in the docks of Port Angeles, where he became head of its local longshoreman's union and fished the Strait of Juan de Fuca.

Not unlike her father in his vocational versatility, Gallagher's writing ranges across literary genres. She is the author of eleven books, including seven collections of poetry and two collections of short stories. Her highly regarded collection of essays, *A Concert of Tenses*, explores the art and craft of writing poetry. With Raymond Carver she co-authored two one-act screenplays, including *Dostoyevsky: A Screenplay* for Capra Films in 1985. After Carver's death, Gallagher was an essential advisor to director Robert Altman on his film *Short Cuts*, which is based on nine Carver short stories. Her most recent work, *Soul Barnacles: Ten More Years with Ray* (2000), is a collection of essays, letters, interviews, book introductions, and journal entries from the ten years following Carver's death in 1988. In *The Sky Behind the Forest* (1996), Gallagher further expands her *oeuvre* in her translation of Romanian Liliana Ursu's poetry.

"The Lover of Horses" provides a paradigm for Gallagher's subjects, themes, tropes, and stylistic devices. Her subjects include traditional Irish topics: family connections, well-worn marriages, alcoholism, self-delusion, obsessions, the experience of exile, loss and death, and the potential for psychic and emotional resolution. Through her characters' interrogations of these subjects, common themes reveal Gallagher's fascination with the power of the imagination, its partnership with memory, and the truth of its fiction. Other stories involving themes common to other Irish writers (such as Brian Friel) explore the importance of place names, the loss of a language, the effects of mistranslation, the dialectical oppositions of myth versus history, the role of memory and the imagination in forming identity, and the need for faith in humanity. Perhaps the quality of her writing that is most identifiably Irish is its humor, linking her work to the comic tradition in Irish women writers so competently explored in Theresa O'Connor's collection on this topic, *The Comic Tradition in Irish Women's Writing*. Michael Gillespie's contribution to O'Connor's book marks the work of Edna O'Brien as employing "the convention of sardonic social commentary that has formed an integral part of the Irish comic tradition" (5). Gallagher, like O'Brien, continues the legacy of the "particularly Irish literary inclination to integrate comedy . . . into the most tragic of topics" (Gillespie 121). Similarly, Gallagher's fiction mirrors certain qualities of O'Brien's. According to Gillespie, "she [O'Brien] integrates rather than displaces the quotidian with the fabulous [and] . . . her anger retains a sense of proportion and asserts the value of plurality" (110). Some of Gallagher's characters possess an amused sense of irony in their narration of events; others are less introspective. Yet while their particular situations provide hilarity or absurdity, apart from the protagonist in "The Poetry Baron," her characters never deserve mockery.

Many of Gallagher's stories involve or resolve in epiphanies. A number of characters are dreamers who sense the mystery available in life and who risk rejection to embrace it. Other characters find themselves in an existential crisis, whether as the result of some traumatic life passage or of a cumulative chaos. Metaphysical truths are revealed to the characters who recognize, in varying degrees of perception, that they are experiencing a transcendent moment. These moments, or liminal states, often provide alternative philosophical positions that grant the characters either the opportunity for empowering action or for a surrender of power that grants them a saving grace.

When magic is invoked the sensational is humbled by the humorous. Nature often provides the vehicle for her characters' metaphorical metamorphoses. In many of Gallagher's stories the natural world, usually her beloved Pacific Northwest, is so intrinsic to the story it is almost a character itself, which echoes Irish American writers' passion for their land. So, too, some of Gallagher's characters identify with animals and birds—for example, horses, bears, and hummingbirds—in stories that dramatize human psychology and its relationship to basic instincts at the heart of complex patterns of behavior.

In "The Lover of Horses" the female narrator begins a tale ultimately about her father's last days of life with another tale of an earlier Irish ancestor, her maternal great-grandfather: "They say my great-grandfather was a gypsy, but the most popular explanation for his behavior was that he was a drunk. How else could the women have kept up the scourge of his memory all these years, had they not had the usual malady of our family to blame? Probably he was both, a gypsy and a drunk" (*Lover of Horses* 1). Juxtaposing the imaginative with the jaded, the opening paragraph represents a microcosm of subject and style that is classic Gallagher, where flights of fancy are grounded by a down-to-earth retort, thereby revealing the intimate, acerbic humor commonly attributed to Irish families.

After traveling to Ireland the narrator comes to believe her great-grandfather's social aberrance is a result of his heritage—he had most likely been a " 'whisperer,' a breed of men among the gypsies who were said to possess the power of talking sense into horses" (2). These gifted outsiders were able to calm and compel troubled animals with mysterious sounds only their equine listeners understood.[1]

The common knowledge handed through the narrator's female forebears about her great-grandfather, a "huge stallion" of a "horse poor" man himself, is that he was just a drunk who at age fifty-two abandoned his wife and eleven children (and his beloved twenty-nine horses) to join a circus. Mesmerized by a dappled gray stallion that could perform the Mazurka flawlessly, her great-grandfather became a dance partner to the horse. Although the women of the family deemed his actions the result of inebriation and escapism, the narrator has come to believe "the gypsy in him finally got the upper hand, and . . . that he was in all likelihood a man who had been stolen by a horse" (3). Numerous other anecdotes about her ancestor's unusual behaviors as a result of his obsessions are recounted and then countered by the women's unromanticized judgments.

The tale of the great-grandfather, the lover of horses, segues into Gallagher's intended subject—the narrator's father, his last days, and her inheritance from him. The narrator has come to understand that her great-grandfather's aberration is a family legacy, further evident in her father's compulsive card playing (and the complicit alcohol consumption it usually entails) and her own mother's original attraction to her father: "When she met him . . . she asked him what he did for a living. My father pointed to a deck of cards in his shirt pocket and said, 'I play cards'" (5). Gallagher's poker-faced humor continues to undermine a straightforward family history. In the present of the story, the narrator's mother's attraction to her father has clearly diminished.

The narrator is called home by her mother's entreaty—"Can you do something?"—when her father falls ill at seventy-three and is given only a few weeks to live. He is convinced that his illness results from a bad streak of losing at cards. His self-cure is to play cards and drink, and he has not come home in three days to eat or sleep. The narrator is chosen above other siblings to rescue him because her mother, rather a clairvoyant herself, suspects her daughter's instinctive kinship with her forebears. The narrator herself would not speak above a whisper until eleven years old. Since that time and until the story's present, the narrator has abandoned her own tendency toward aberrant behavior, embracing conventionality as the smoother path in life.

The rest of the story narrates her father's various superstitious attempts to keep death at bay, attempts that are kept in check by her mother's wry, yet intuitive, theories as to his motivations. Their marital banter proves to be typical Irish humor in which disparagement belies tenderness. Writing about her own parentage in A Concert of Tenses, Gallagher says of her father, also a card player and drinker: "He told stories, was witty, liked to laugh. But in those early days, . . . I was often afraid of him, of the violence in him, though, like the rain, tenderness was there, unspoken and with a fiber that strangely informed even the unreasonable" (11).

When the narrator arrives home to help bring her father out of the back room of the tavern (another reportedly common rite of passage for an Irish offspring), where he has been on a three-day winning streak, she makes a broth to bring to him at the bar. While pouring the broth into a thermos, she hears herself "utter syllables and other vestiges of language which I could not reproduce if I wanted to" (8); this is the first time her possibly gypsy blood makes itself known. Realizing why she has come, her father, his eyes fixed on his cards, tells her "I'm having a hell of a good time. The time of my life. . . . Tell the old kettle she's got to put up with me for a few more years" (9), and lights a fresh cigarette. After two more nights and days, he returns home, triumphant, completely soused, and in a state of total exhaustion.

It becomes clear that his time left is much shorter than weeks. Eventually, when his death is imminent, the narrator spends the day outdoors revisiting her father's favorite haunts. She passes the day "in a trance of silences," appreciative of what silence means "for a word-bound creature such as I was," as she waits "to know what to do for him" (13). Eventually she is propelled into an inexplicable ritual: "That night when I walked from the house I was full of purpose. I headed toward the little cedar tree. Without stopping to question the necessity of what I was doing, I began to break off the boughs I could reach and to pile them on the ground" (14). She makes her bed for the night under the "maimed" cedar tree, "under the stars, with the hiss of the ocean" in her ears, listening to the nighttime games of the grandchildren outdoors, allowed to play unusually late while the rest of the family hover around her father's bed. The narrator's making a bed of the ground suggests a sympathetic gesture toward preparing a grave.

Gallagher's talent in conjuring a portentous moment through sensuous description is apparent in this scene in its emotional prelude to an epiphany. The narrator listens as the wind whips up on the water and as the children whirl in spinning games, round and round, with their excitement reaching a crescendo, until they scatter, flinging "one another by the arms or chas[ing] each other toward the house as if their lives depended on it" (15). This symbolic scene provides a physical representation of the psychic vortex in which the narrator spins, a partner to her father in his dance with death, as her great-grandfather had been to the stallion. The story and her father's life conclude with an aesthetic arrangement that deconstructs words from their shared significations and returns to their basis in primal expressions of the anguish and joy of human bonds.

As she listens to the wind still echoing with the children's voices, the narrator realizes, "There was a soft crooning of syllables that was satisfying to my ears, but ultimately useless and absurd" (16). Pulled still by the pragmatic, but unwittingly vulnerable to the mystical, she at first reflects on the scene as dramatic yet irrelevant. She hears the diminishing sounds as a kind of keening, a false panacea that may assuage the pain of the living but fails to affect the dying. Then, the narrator's consciousness is opened to another possibility when she realizes the "unwieldy" sounds she hears are coming from her own lips:

In a raw pulsing of language I could not account for, I lay awake through the long night and spoke to my father as one might speak to an ocean or the wind, letting him know by that threadbare accompaniment that the vastness he was about to enter had its rhythms in me also. And that he was not forsaken. And that I was letting him go. That so far I had denied the disreputable world of dancers and drunkards, gamblers and lovers of horses to which I most surely belonged. But from that night forward I vowed to be filled with the first unsavory desire that would have me. To plunge myself into the heart of my life and be ruthlessly lost forever. (16)

The narrator, hearing voices that speak through nature, has opened herself to alternative potentialities, whether of her own invention or in a furtherance of an ancestral aesthetic. Gallagher's evocations of the magic or mystery available in the mundane are not simply clever contrivances designed mainly to impress with the well-wrought image—they are intrinsic to her artistic vision.

Ireland has been an influence on Gallagher since the beginning of her literary career. Her early literary mentor and teacher, Theodore Roethke, imbued her with an admiration for the work of W. B. Yeats. She first traveled to Ireland in 1968, at twenty-five years of age, to attend the Yeats Summer School and to sort out the conflicts in her marriage to Lawrence Gallagher, a pilot in the Vietnam War. The war itself troubled her greatly and strained their marriage. She has returned to Ireland every two years or so and lived for a time in both Belfast and Dublin. Her current partner and collaborator is Sligoman Josie Gray, a visual artist and storyteller.

In Ireland Gallagher formed close associations with Northern Irish writers Ciaran Carson, Mebdh McGuckian, Michael and Edna Longley, Frank Ormsby, and Robert Johnson, as well as with many traditional Irish singers and musicians: "Sean O'Faolain became a close friend of mine during these early years visiting Ireland and when I lived briefly in Dublin. He even wrote a short story based on one of my poems, 'Woman Enough,' in which I tell about climbing down into a grave being dug outside my caravan where I wrote that poem and others for [her second book of poetry] *Under Stars*" ("Re: Questions"). Composed in Ireland, *Under Stars* includes her poem "The Ballad of Ballymote," which contains the refrain "Cabbage and Bones," subsequently chosen as the title for the first published collection of Irish American women's writing edited by Caledonia Kearns in 1997. At a reading Gallagher gave in Dublin, she discovered one of its leading bookstores had placed her books in the Irish section, which she considered "one of the greatest honors I could ever get! To be in the company with Irish writers I so admire" ("Re: Questions").

When I asked Gallagher in our interview whether she considers her own writing to reflect any recognizable Irishness, in a response echoing William Kennedy's refrain "these traits, endure," she said: "I haven't pursued it as an obvious element. It has just been there like my heartbeat, shall we say? I can't separate it off from myself" (personal interview). Gallagher broaches this quest for authentication of one's heritage in her story "Venison Pie: From the Journal of a Contemporary Hybrid" in *At the Owl Woman Saloon*; it is a rather mythic story about a mixed-blood Native American woman who shape shifts into a hummingbird and in which past and present stray from a static linearity: "My bloodline can and must be thrown into question . . . because this questioning, this veering of others toward and away is also a kind of aggressive but necessary courtship. . . . One must have patience with obscured origins" (41–42).

Of course, hybridity is a classic postcolonial subject, as are the themes of exile and loss, both of which Gallagher addresses in her writing. Theresa O'Connor finds in Irish women writers commonalities that include "a hybridizing vision that engages in witty negation with established patriarchal, colonial, and nationalist orthodoxies" (4). In Gallagher's work many of her characters engage in a search for a balance of contradictory tensions. She states that those moments where "a rightness or at least [an] intrigue with the way the opposites balance each other into stasis, are fertile moments . . . A secret lives there. . . . the opposites do truthfully include the possibility of a joint perspective" (*A Concert of Tenses* 30). Gallagher has drawn connections among her experiences in Ireland, a focus evident in her writing: "Ireland, especially the North, was full of such contradictory elements that it probably did draw forth more of this kind of motion from me. With the violence in the North there is a closeness among one's immediate friends that I found very paradoxical. There are small pockets of inclusiveness and protectiveness, then enormous disparities outside those" (30). Although Gallagher's writing is not concerned with Irish nationalist issues, "Venison Pie" treats colonialism and its effects on language and perception as implicit in her hybrid female narrator's subjectivity.

Concerning the themes of exile and loss, Gallagher is expressing the experience of personal, rather than political, exile. She explains her sensibility as potentially a result of her home life.

As the oldest child, I seemed to serve my parents' lives in an ambassadorial capacity. But I was an ambassador without a country, for the household was perpetually on the verge of dissolving. . . .

Maybe this was the making of my refugee mentality. And perhaps when you are an emotional refugee you learn to be industrious toward the prospect of love and shelter. . . . You make a home of yourself. Words for me and later poems were the tools of that home-making. (A *Concert of Tenses* 10)

In her fiction Gallagher's exile is not necessarily literal but figurative, as in the familial exile she experienced, or the marital exile from the loss of a spouse, or the generational exile exhibited in her compelling story "Girls," which ends *The Lover of Horses*.

The above quote from "Venison Pie" also introduces Gallagher's theory about storytelling and the Irish style of it. For Gallagher storytelling involves "a courtship of the reader, of the readers' attention and affections and of their life," (personal interview) with an inevitable veering off from the story itself to tantalize the listener.

Gallagher's own fiction similarly courts her readers, veering off to one story while hooking them into her actual, intended one, each tale offering resonance to its companion. This style of storytelling is evident in "The Lover of Horses," in which the narrator's great-grandfather's story is imbricated in her father's story. Furthermore, the twelve stories in the collection resonate among themselves. Of the twelve, ten are told from a first-person perspective and nine have a female narrator. Three narrators are widowed in this collection, and five in her next, At the Owl Woman Saloon.[2] In her examination of widowhood, Gallagher echoes Mary Lavin, but it is not the characters' similarities of marital circumstance that create the resonances here. Narrative events are mirrored from one story to another.

In "Bad Company," for example, the narrator who lies on the ground in a sympathetic grave in "The Lover of Horses" is mirrored first by a young woman—another Native American mixed-blood character—who lies on her father's grave while seeking his guidance. But this character's actions are only a vehicle for the protagonist, Mrs. Herbert's, dilemma. They meet at the graveyard where Mrs. Herbert's husband lies buried. Though the Herberts remained together until his death, their relationship had been estranged for many years. She now tends his grave perfunctorily; however, moved by the girl's actions, Mrs. Herbert eventually attempts to reclaim a connection to her dead husband. She realizes she had shut him out of her heart as punishment for his drinking and its attendant dramas many years before. In imitation of the girl's gesture toward communion with her father, Mrs. Herbert also lies down on her husband's grave. But unlike the narrator in "The Lover of Horses," she finds no resolution, her regret is not salved, and she foresees a lonely future because she missed her moment of absolution with her husband.

Harbingers of death that affect the living, such as writing a will, provide a narrative focus in stories such as "Beneficiaries," in which the legacy of a first marriage and divorce infects a second one. Graves and graveyards reappear in other stories such as "Coming and Going" in Gallagher's first collection and "The Red Ensign" in her second. The notion of being "stretched on your grave" has further resonances in Irish culture. Sinead O'Connor's eponymous ballad comes from a traditional Irish lament, and, once again, Mary Lavin's stories are called to mind, where graveyards figure frequently.

Perhaps one of Gallagher's most Irish American characteristics is her fixation with doubles and doubling: she deems them "Those shadows of ourselves whom we need to embrace" (A Concert of Tenses 30). As Charles Fanning notes, this ethnic doubleness provides an artist "with images, history, language, manners, myths, ways of perceiving, and ways of communicating"—regardless of residence (358). This fascination is obvious in Gallagher's poetry—indeed, her first published collection of poetry is entitled Instructions to the Double (1976)—but she explores this motif in her fiction as well.

One of Gallagher's most striking stories in The Lover of Horses is "Turpentine." This quiet story about a childless couple is told from the first-person perspective of the wife, Ginny Skoyles. A self-described handy-woman who can fix and maintain a house, Ginny occupies her time keeping her home and marriage in working order, while her somewhat self-absorbed husband, Tom, makes work his priority. Ginny admits she becomes so involved with the stories others tell her about their lives that she sometimes repeats them, claiming them as her own. This provides the crux of the narrative about to unfold. This narrative "borrowing" is an Irish conceit employed by Irish storytellers, as Mary Doyle Curran writes in her nonfiction excerpt from The Parish and the Hill: "Whenever an Irishman told a story, it became his own" (qtd. in Kearns 24).

The story focuses on the visit of a young woman, Mary Leinhart, selling Avon products, who interrupts Ginny's work of painting the back stairs. Clearly the opposite in physical appearance, style, and sensibility, the young woman nonetheless becomes the narrator's double. Mary "had large dark eyes and her skin was so white it was almost translucent. I thought of the word "'alabaster'" (56). Mary offers Ginny a face cream, telling her how she had once damaged her own skin trying to cure high school acne: "I bought this lotion they were advertising. I'd try anything in those days. I rubbed it on and left it, like the directions said. When I washed it off, my skin was raw. Something in the formula had penetrated several layers of skin and scorched me" (59). This anecdote captures Ginny's imagination, so she purchases products in order to support the woman and interact with her again.

When Mary returns with Ginny's order, another conversation reveals that Mary has been to a psychic who has predicted she will have a baby, even though she is single. She admits this is something she both does and does not want, wishes for and fears; Ginny understands this ambivalence. They discuss their relative experiences with psychics and psychic powers. Mary leaves Ginny with the psychic's card and Ginny returns to painting the back steps. With her paintbrush dripping from too much turpentine, Ginny finds she has missed the undersides of the steps and crawls under them, where the paint drips onto her face and clothes. There she is reminded of her childhood activity of always "crawling under things to see what was there. Crawling to see what it felt like to be lost, to have lost yourself from everyone" (70). When her husband arrives home and calls for her, she remains silent, liking the "smell of dirt and darkness" as she watches him walk down the just-painted stairs (70). Eventually she emerges, paint-covered and repugnant to him: "I could feel his hating how I looked" (70).

Remaining outside, Ginny wipes her face and arms with turpentine: "It scalded a moment as if I'd been slapped" (71). When she enters the house her husband asks her about the psychic's card he found on the table. In the bathroom, as she cleans up, she sees "My face in the mirror was smeared with a residue of white paint. I looked pale and calm" (72). While Tom waits to hear her explanation about the psychic's card, Ginny leads him to believe she has seen the psychic and has had predictions made, thereby stealing Mary's tale, as Tom keeps watching her clean herself. The story ends here, with Ginny concluding, "He wanted to question me, to find out the things that might be about to happen" (72).

Ginny has inadvertently inserted herself into Mary's history and identity with the scalding turpentine and its skin-whitening effect. Scorched and pale, the turpentine's effects function as a mask for Ginny to disguise herself from her husband's expectations. Whether in rebelling against her husband's disgusted reaction to her appearance, or in continuing the reverie under the stairs, Ginny has crawled under another person's skin for a moment "to see what was there," to be lost from everyone, to have lost herself from everyone, particularly Tom, her all-too-eager mirror for self-deprecation. Since makeup covers as well as alters physical identity, so, too, Ginny's turpentine mask becomes a means for taking on another's identity as well as a metaphor for the act of reading itself. (Yeats's concept of "the Mask" has resonance here.)

Finally, Ginny's welcoming of Mary Leinhart into her home and her identification with her life dramatize yet another facet of Gallagher's Irish influences—their hospitality to strangers and their ability to empathize (Gallagher, personal interview). Gallagher's reflections on her experience with the Irish include an appreciation for their wit, their sense of drama, and their attraction to "chancing" or "pushing elements past usual boundaries" (personal interview). Gallagher's characters are often "chancers," as her female narrator in "The Lover of Horses" vows to become.

Many of Gallagher's descriptions of an Irish sensibility are directly evident in her final story in The Lover of Horses, "Girls." This strong piece juxtaposes a familiar Irish American theme—the chasms of misunderstanding between a mother, Ada, and her daughter, Billie—with the existential exile of Ada from her own identity when she is reunited with a long lost friend, Esther. Ada locates Esther after many years and gets a ride with the self-absorbed Billie to visit her. When they reach Esther's town and phone her, Esther does not remember Ada but invites her to visit her home anyway.

Ada is initially crushed by Esther's bluntness in declaring her lack of recognition: "'Kid, I wished I did, but I just don't remember you,' Esther said. 'I don't have a glimmer'" (171). Ada is angry and hurt, wondering "how she could have been so insignificant as to have been forgotten" (171), until Esther explains that she has had a stroke. Ada's frustration reveals a somewhat obsessed self-interest in the light of Esther's innocent forgetting. And Esther's guileless responses undermine Ada's serious endeavor in a minor comedy of errors.

Ada is becoming quite unsettled by Esther's lack of recognition when suddenly Esther says, "I don't know who you are but I like you. Why don't you stay the night?" (174). Although a rather hilarious offer in its innocent disregard for propriety and boundaries, especially unexpected in an elderly woman, this endearing gesture clearly moves Ada. Her daughter Billie jumps at the offer for her mother and departs for her motel. Ada continues to search for herself in Esther's mind, but the task becomes fruitless. Her identity is clearly tied to her need for recognition in these late years of her life, a need to claim an impact on someone for self-validation. Esther's acceptance of her own memory loss further exacerbates Ada's dilemma.

Ada comes to see that Esther's circumstances are pitiable, both physically and materially; indeed, her only assistance comes from her disabled, alcoholic son. Ada offers to massage Esther's swollen feet in a gesture of compassion, yet it is the weakened Esther who provides Ada with a more all-encompassing comfort. Needing to lie down for an afternoon rest, Esther asks Ada, "Honey, why don't you lie down with me on the bed. That way we can really talk" (177). Balking at first, Ada eventually lies down, still hoping to find herself in Esther's memory. When Esther reckons that if they had been such good friends, she must have told Ada all her secrets, Ada excitedly affirms that they had told each other everything. "'Everything,' Esther said, as if she were sinking into a place of agreement where remembering and forgetting didn't matter'" (178). The two elderly widows leave the past alone and confide in each other their worries and hardships.

Later, sleeping in the spare room for the night, Ada is wakened by the sound of Esther's drunken son, Jason, returning home. Frightened, she calls out for Esther. When Esther comes to her, Ada "put out her hand and took hold of Esther's sleeve. 'Don't leave,' she said. Esther waited a minute. Then she turned off the light and got into bed beside Ada. Ada turned on her side, facing the wall, and Esther's arm went around her shoulder" (181). Their connection now proves to be beyond specific memories and founded rather in their essential natures; their mutual need to give and receive comfort creates an unforgettable moment for Ada.

As she returns home with Billie, Ada is not ready to explain her evening with Esther, nor her failure to be recognized. "But the important things—the way Esther had come to her when she'd called out, and how, earlier, they'd lain side by side—this would be hers" (183). Ada doubts she could ever explain this to Billie and knows that she will not even try. As they travel northward toward Washington from Oregon, Ada gazes at the "wall of forest that crowded the edge of the highway"(184). Suddenly, the landscape changes to the empty swath of a clear cut, where downed trees and stumps are the only evidence of a previously dense wood. "Her hand went to her face as if she had been slapped. But then she saw it was green again, and she let her hand drop to her lap" (184). Gallagher ends the story with an appropriate visual metaphor for the nature of memory, its vulnerability, and its capacity for regeneration.

Gallagher's characters often risk their self-image in their attempts to break through barriers of oppressive propriety toward connections with others. Frank O'Connor speaks to this when he identifies as most characteristic of short stories "an intense awareness of human loneliness" (xiii). In these examples of Gallagher's narrative device of "chancing," she conjures events for her characters involving the risk of undertaking behaviors normally seen as strange or unusual, like making a bed on the ground or on a grave, or women lying in bed next to each other—behaviors that involve a threat to one's intact subjectivity and/or reputation. Yet through her subtle artistry, these actions seem not only natural but necessary and essential to the human need for communion. In this sense, Gallagher succeeds in subverting social norms and propriety, exposing their repressive, often toxic, effects.

Barriers, cultural or personal, become investigated and problematized further in the *At the Owl Woman Saloon*. In this group of sixteen stories, community is given more of an integral role, as is the setting of the Pacific Northwest. Five of the stories feature a male narrator. In "I Got a Guy Once," Gallagher's male narrator captures the hand-to-mouth existence of the out-of-work loggers of the Pacific Northwest, which is Gallagher's heritage. Lives of this sort populate Gallagher's narratives, clearly a source of both the scars and the strength that inhere in her identity.

Frank O'Connor, in *The Lonely Voice*, says of the short story that its emergence in different countries can be traced to "a difference in the national attitude toward society." He asserts: "We can see in it an attitude of mind that is attracted by submerged population groups, whatever these may be at any given time—tramps, artists, lonely idealists, dreamers, and spoiled priests. The novel can still adhere to the classical concept of civilized society, of man as an animal who lives in a community . . . but the short story remains by its very nature remote from the community—romantic, individualist, and intransigent" (xiv). America's attraction to the short story by its writers and readers attests to the logic of O'Connor's theory. Short story collections often connect these lonely voices into a community of their own, bound within its own bindings, like disparate patrons commingling in a saloon.

In Kerby Miller's essay on Irish immigration, "Class, Culture, and Immigrant Group Identity in the United States: The Case of Irish-American Ethnicity," he describes the variant experiences of the Irish in America.

For those who arrived and settled on the East Coast, large groups of Irish found identity, protection, and eventual empowerment in their commitment to the Catholic faith and in furthering its institutions. Many of these Irish had little formal commitment to the faith upon arrival but rather "found their religion" as a result of economic imperatives that favored unity in numbers in a defense against discrimination. For those who went West, often no such strong institutions existed. Dispersed among many immigrant groups, resistance to unfair labor practices served as a unifying force. For both groups, saloons were the public spaces where political power was created and concentrated and from whence decisions for activism were decreed (at least for men).

Gallagher's *At the Owl Woman Saloon* foregrounds this exclusion and then mollifies its effects. All sixteen stories begin with an epigraph. The first intimates the overall thematic framing of the collection: it is Webster's definitions of "salon" and "saloon," which show that "saloon" is an "Americanism" and a misspelling of "salon." Yet in only one story is there a scene set in a bar, while two stories are set in beauty salons. Gallagher's elision of salon and saloon, while noting their reputations for gendered exclusivity, is directly addressed in the first story. "The Red Ensign" is set in the Owl Woman Salon, named by the owner-beautician after the great Papago healer. The female narrator is a client who is initially upset by the presence of two men in her safe-haven but who resignedly comes to recognize and allow the need for renewal and communion that these spaces provide: "*Two men* in the Owl Woman Salon! . . . Are these guys illiterate or what? 'Owl Woman Salon,' the sign says. Did they think it said Owl Woman SALOON? I am thinking: saloon or salon—you walk in one way and come out another" (20–21)

Like "The Lover of Horses" does for that collection, "The Red Ensign" provides a thematic framework for many of the stories in *At the Owl Woman Saloon*. The narrators in this collection undergo small epiphanies, and their hearts, like the Owl Woman's, "will go out" toward others. Gallagher's characters cross self-imposed barriers to understanding themselves or others, swinging open the saloon/salon doors to enter into community or communion. In effect, they "go in one way and out another."

In "Creatures," the second story set in a salon, the justifiable rage that sleeps beneath the helplessness of a woman too caring to impose boundaries on others erupts. Those women who witness it respond in an unspoken pact to lean into the storm with her and for her, knowing it is somehow also for themselves. As in A *Lover of Horses*, Gallagher's narratives in her second collection address the beleaguered positions of many seemingly unremarkable people in America today.

Unlike many of the women discussed in this volume, Gallagher was not reared in a particularly church-going household, yet her work clearly has a spiritual dimension. It is full of moments of transformation, where her characters renew their faith in humanity and sense a connection to an otherness. When asked about her experiences with Catholicism, its ritual and mystery, she responded: "I do find myself very attached to the sense that ritual does make a form for feelings we might not express in any other way. . . . But because the Catholic religion, as it comes to us through Frank O'Connor ("My First Confession") and other Catholic writers, tends to be a kind of foil to expose/amplify human behavior, I think it is a wonderful character in Irish fiction, both in Ireland and America" ("Re: Questions").

Above all, Gallagher's stories are "human-spirit centered" testaments to the power of love. She has often quoted St. Teresa's philosophy that "Words lead to deeds. They prepare the soul, make it ready, and move it to tenderness." Robert Altman slyly inserts this quote into his film *Short Cuts* in what can be seen as an homage to Gallagher's aesthetic manifesto.

Taking St. Teresa's maxim as her central tenet, and adhering to a politico-spiritual approach to life, Tess Gallagher skillfully conjures an objective correlative for the transcendent moments available for those open to an awareness of alternate realities. Her stories challenge middle-class provincialism, construct compelling tableaus, and interweave unique images that transfix a reader's psychic memory and continue to reverberate long after a story is finished. Like a Celtic knot, Gallagher's writing is fascinating in its lively loops and strange shapes and mysterious in its resistance to a single identifiable source for its illuminations.

Notes

1. Gallagher's story about a "horse whisperer" preceded the book and movie by the same name. Her story was published in 1982; Nicholas Evan's novel was published in 1995.

2. Gallagher was not made a widow until Raymond Carver's death in 1988, well after *The Lover of Horses* collection was published as a whole in 1982. *At the Owl Woman Saloon* was published in 1997.

Works Cited

Ebest, Sally. "These Traits Also Endure: Contemporary Irish and Irish American Women Writers." *New Hibernia Review* 7.2 (2003): 55–72.

Fanning, Charles. *The Irish Voice in America: 250 Years of Irish-American Fiction.* Lexington: University of Kentucky Press, 1990.

Gallagher, Tess. *A Concert of Tenses.* Ann Arbor: University of Michigan Press, 1986.

———. *The Lover of Horses and Other Stories.* New York: Harper, 1986.

———. *At the Owl Woman Saloon.* New York: Scribner, 1997.

———. Personal interview. With M. A. Ryan and D. Cole. 10 July 2003.

———. "Re: Questions." Email to M. A. Ryan. 31 Oct. 2003.

———. *Under Stars.* St. Paul: Graywolf Press, 1978.

Gillespie, Michael Patrick. "(S)he Was Too Scrupulous Always: Edna O'Brien and the Comic Tradition." *The Comic Tradition in Irish Women Writers.* Ed. Theresa O'Connor. Gainesville: University Press of Florida, 1995. 108–23.

Kearns, Caledonia, ed. *Cabbage and Bones: An Anthology of Irish American Women's Fiction.* New York: Henry Holt, 1997.

Miller, Kerby. "Class, Culture, and Immigrant Group Identity in the United States: The Case of Irish-American Ethnicity." *Immigration Reconsidered.* Ed. Virginia Yans-McLaughlin. New York: Oxford University Press, 1990. 96–129.

O'Connor, Frank. *The Lonely Voice.* 1963. New York: Bantam Classic, 1968.

O'Connor, Theresa, ed. *The Comic Tradition in Irish Women Writers.* Gainesville: University Press of Florida, 1995.

McFarland, Ron. *Tess Gallagher.* Boise State University Western Writers Series No. 120. Boise: University of Idaho Press, 1995.

"Tess Gallagher." *New Statesman and Society* 15 Mar 1996: 1.

CHAPTER 7

"I'm Your Man"

Irish American Masculinity in the Fiction
of Joyce Carol Oates

SUSANA ARAÚJO

Joyce Carol Oates was born in Lockport, in upstate New York, but her family's background epitomizes the ethnic diversity of America's immigrant history. Oates's maternal grandparents, Stephen and Elizabeth Bush, were born in Hungary and arrived in America in 1902, settling in Buffalo, New York. Her paternal great-great-grandparents, the Oateses, were Irish who arrived in America in the late nineteenth century. Her father's great-grandmother (whose maiden surname, Mullaney, resonates with the title of her popular novel *We Were the Mulvaneys*) emigrated from Ireland to America with her six children after the death of her husband, Dominic Oates (Oates, letter to the author).

This genealogy helped fuel Oates's sociohistorical inquisitiveness, informing the rigorous depiction of the immigrant working classes that marks so many of her works. The representation of Irish experience in Oates's work is more obviously conveyed in her portrayals of second- or third-generation

157

Irish male characters. Oates's depiction of Irish American masculinity can be seen, for instance, in the figure of Michael Senior[1] in *We Were the Mulvaneys* (1996). Michael is a second-generation Irish emigrant who, faced with the rape of his daughter, sinks gradually into alcoholism, contributing ultimately to the exclusion of his daughter from the family. However, it is in an earlier novel, *What I Lived For* (1994), that Oates's portrayal of the Irish American experience is more thoroughly conveyed. *What I Lived For* has, in fact, been described by Oates as the "most Irish of [her] novels" (personal interview)—a claim that begs for our critical attention. In this chapter, therefore, I will examine how Irish history and experience are depicted in this novel and will analyze, in particular, the ways in which the narrative allows for interrogation of a specific type of masculinity.

What I Lived For describes the life and times of Jerome Corcoran, a successful real estate developer and broker of Irish descent. Brought up in Irish Hill, Union City, Jerome gradually moves up the social ladder, leaving his working-class neighborhood behind to break into wealthier and more influential social circles. In his forties, Jerome Corcoran, also known as "Corky," is already seen by friends and commercial partners as a successful businessman with a promising future in local politics. Corky is also a ladies' man with striking misogynistic tendencies. By accumulating property and women he attempts to achieve a sense of power and control that had been lacking in his childhood and tries to make up for the sense of social displacement that he associates with his family history. The novel opens when Corky is seven years old, with a depiction of the tragic murder of his father, Timothy Corcoran. Timothy had angered his trade union leader by hiring black workers for his construction site. He was later found dead in front of his house on Christmas Eve, 1954. Jerome's mother is hospitalized for depression and never fully recovers her mental capacities, dying later in the hospital. Corky is brought up by his uncle, Sean Corcoran, but the memory of his parents—particularly that of his father—continues to haunt Corky throughout his life, even after he leaves Irish Hill.

The narrative moves forward to 1992 to give a detailed picture of three days in the life of the forty-four-year-old Jerome. Corky manages to fulfil his father's desire to escape Irish Hill, but this separation only serves to widen the gulf between his "integrated" self-made-man persona and the social eccentricity that he associates with his family roots. Oates satirizes the clichés of Irishness interiorized by Corky—the drinking, blarney, and fighting—as much as she derides the image of America as a buoyant land of opportunity, a myth that Corky recognizes as fictitious but that he is unable to let go. The history of Corky's family is set alongside America's own as a powerful if contradictory influence on the definition of his identity and social position.

Union City, the fictional town where Corky grew up, is mapped out in rigorous topographical detail. Oates describes the different neighborhoods populated by black, Irish, Hispanic, and "white trash" working-class communities, as well as the tensions inherent to the occasional coexistence of these diverse ethnic groups. We witness how Irish Hill, originally an Irish community, gradually is populated by African Americans, which is very much resented by its former inhabitants. Corky's real estate expertise informs the narrative with facts about the migratory housing patterns affecting Union City. As he drives around the city, he muses about the changes in those "solidly Catholic areas," such as Washington Park, which was once locally renowned "for its citizenry's unflagging resistance to the post-ward phenomenon of 'integration'" (*What I Lived For* 386). These Italian and Polish areas, as Corky explains, were now emptied of their white working-class population: "the riots of 1967 and the eruption of inner-city vandalism, looting and fires of the following year in those days after the assassination of Martin Luther King threw the community into a panic, and Washington Park lost its white population to the suburbs" (386).

Joyce Carol Oates has described *What I Lived For* as "a novel that celebrates its landscape and its historic moment," and she has pointed out that "Corky's fascination . . . with the physical world, the world of his boyhood, in a neighborhood intersected by the Erie Barge Canal, is modelled in certain of its graphic details upon [her] own memories of growing up near Lockport, New York, where [her] grandmother lived, and where Oates attended junior high school" (Johnson). There is, indeed, in this novel a melancholic revisiting of the past that evokes the tone of Oates's early story collections, such as *By the North Gate* (1963) and *Upon the Sweeping Flood* (1966), works that are firmly grounded in the idea of home. As an adult Corky always feels socially estranged from his original background and makes persistent—if unsuccessful—attempts to bridge the gulf between the world of his childhood and that of his mature self. Despite the satirical nuances of the novel, there are also quasi-philosophical and plainly autobiographical references to the inevitably of change: "what *is* passing so swiftly so irrevocably into what *was*" (604). If Oates's early stories reveal an intense fascination with an original and primal space, in *What I Lived For* this is experienced from a more tangible perspective because Corky's sense of exile is that of the *immigrant*, who knows home to be another country not only psychologically but also geographically.

The narrative, vocalized in the third person, often adopts Corky's own language and point of view and shifts through the four main themes that Charles Fanning considers typical of the Irish American novel. In his seminal study, *The Irish Voice in America*, Fanning identifies four narratives in the Irish American novel, the basic patterns of which help to identify the genre: accounts of past lives, public lives, private lives, and stylized lives. It is difficult to place *What I Lived For* in only one of these categories, as all four of these thematic areas are simultaneously covered by Oates's novel. It is under the "public life" heading, however, that the novel is most comfortably located. *What I Lived For* corresponds fittingly to Fanning's definition of the public novel, a genre chiefly concerned with Irish American experience outside the home and one that has dominated the Irish American male canon since the nineteenth century. But *What I Lived For* is also a feminist revision of the public novel. As such, the novel shows how *public* constructions are only very superficially separated from private experience. Indeed, even though *What I Lived For* reveals a strong emphasis on the protagonist's professional achievements and political ambitions, it is precisely Corky's attempt to undermine and subordinate his personal origins and his family history to the construction of his public image that weaves the tragicomic axes of the novel.

In this sense the portrayal of three days in Corky's life is inescapably also a narrative of private, past, and stylized lives. References to private lives emerge in the story of his parents and relatives, in the reminiscences of his marriage, and in the descriptions of his recent flirtations and love affairs. The narrative of *What I Lived For* is also intersected by accounts of past lives, in particular the arrival of the first Corcorans in America in the nineteenth century. These meticulously informed and highly humorous stories contribute to the narrative a wider historical background of the Irish American immigrant experience. Finally, the novel is also shaped by metafictional allusions to the modernist tradition, which, according to Fanning, mark the beginning of the Irish American tradition of stylized narratives. A quote from James Joyce's *Ulysses*—"He rests. He has travelled"—is used as an epigraph to Oates's novel, revealing her parodic use of the modernist-epic tradition. A different kind of literary allusion, which also conveys a stylized use of parody, can be found in the very title of the novel, *What I*

Lived For. This phrase was taken from a chapter of Henry David Thoreau's *Walden*, fully entitled "Where I Lived and What I Lived For." Thoreau's reaction against materialism and social exploitation contrasts sharply with Corky's lifestyle, yet they both follow, rather paradoxically, a similarly strict code of ethics. By inviting these different narrative layers and this interchange of perspectives, Oates allows Corky's characterization to develop from a supposedly formulaic emblem of Irish masculinity into a more multifaceted portrayal of Irish American experience in the early 1990s.

Corky's feelings toward his roots are deeply ambiguous. He is fascinated by the history of his family but is deeply ambivalent about his working-class background. He is constantly promising to visit his uncle, Sean Corcoran, and his aunt, Mary Megan, in Irish Hill, yet these promises are recurrently broken. His paralyzing anxiety about meeting his relatives is emblematized by the plant he buys to give Aunt Megan, which remains neglected in Corky's car for weeks because he is psychologically unable to visit the old lady at the hospital. Corky is all too aware of his private angst: "It makes him almost panicked to think of it: driving to Irish Hill, the old streets, passing Borrow street, that house, the only house of his dreams, then to Roosevelt, and *that* house, the house following his father's death. Maybe he dreams of *that* house too, but he doesn't want to remember" (254).

By repeatedly postponing his visits to Uncle Sean, Corky knows he will disappoint the old man, but he believes that his own behavior has been determined by his Irish traits: "The Irish break your heart, break one another's hearts. It's in the blood. Can't be helped" (245). Corky's personal philosophy is an amalgam of contradictory messages, best illustrated by the clash between New World psychology and the belief in an Irish fate. While Corky holds on to the old American truism "you're an American, you're an optimist" (188), he cannot avoid seeing himself as an inheritor of "the secret of the Irish: bad luck" (76). The shadow of his father's death hangs over him, as Corky is insistently, if comically, followed by a man called Maynard Teague who wants to make a deal with Corky in order to build the disturbing "Union City Mausoleum of the Dead." In his rehearsed self-confidence, drinking, and "personal style" grandeur, Corky follows dangerously in his father's footsteps.

However, Corky's father, Timothy Corcoran, is far from being the only ill-fated Corcoran in the family's history. One of the most entertaining digressions from the main plot is provided by Uncle Sean's chronicles about the lives of the Corcorans. The hyperbolic tone of these antiheroic fables, narrated against the background of Memorial Day celebrations, adds a spark of humor to the ceremonious atmosphere of the festivities. Sean recounts in detail the odd and tragic tale of one of their first relatives in America, Dermot Corcoran, who had immigrated to Union City, New York, from County Kerry, Ireland, in the 1880s. Also known in the boxing ring as the "Irish Charger," Dermot is forced to fight a heavyweight title holder, and after an inauspicious match he begins to lose most of his fights. His increasingly damaged reputation as a fighter becomes a strain on the family's pride. One day his brother Joseph, harassed by his co-workers, tries to defend his brother's honor and involves himself in a fight, in which he dies. When Dermot finds out about his brother's bereavement, he tracks down Joseph's killer and takes his life in revenge. Dermot is then judged and sentenced to death by hanging.

At this point the story becomes increasingly implausible and ambiguous; however, its extraordinary developments are worth describing here in closer detail. The first and more flattering version of the story describes how, after the hanging, "Dermot's muscular young body was so heavy that his head was torn from his body—there was a geyser-like torrent of blood from the neck as the body fell to the ground, followed by the head which bounced, and rolled, its eyes starkly open and, according to some onlookers *seeing*" (549). The second version is less complimentary but no less bloody. According to this account, at the time of the hanging Dermot's body was so thin that they had to pull his legs down to stop his slow strangling; but they pulled "so hard, putting so much weight into it, that Dermott's body was torn away from his head—there was a geyser-like torrent of blood from the neck as the body fell to the ground, followed by the head which bounced, and rolled, eyes starkly open and sightless" (550).

In this chapter, entitled "In Memoriam," Oates recovers the cadence of the overplotted tragicomic stories of Irish antiheroes disclosing, through the words of Sean Corcoran, their implicit wisdom: "telling a story, you're in charge. Telling a story, you're listened to" (551). The narrative gains a quasi-mythic and musical quality, contrasting significantly with the broken and nerve-racking narrative discourse that had throughout the previous chapters translated Corky's inner rhythm as he drove around Union City ticking off his daily tasks. Thus, the Corcorans' stories cut through the core rhythm of the novel, evoking momentarily a sense of personal transcendence; images of national fate are projected in repetitive and continual sequences, resembling the recurring imagery of religious prayer:

Every Irish family knows these griefs, like a secret rosary. Every Irish family has said this rosary. The saintly who die young, the drinkers and shouters and abusers who live into old age. The hardworking silent ones who die of heart attacks where they stand, uncomplaining. The good girls who run off and return home pregnant and humiliated and their young lives ruined forever. The seminary student, passionate for God, who inflames the lust of one of his superiors and ends trying to commit suicide. The nun, safe in the convent, who goes laughing-mad and is sent back home again. The mother of six, or nine or eleven children who dies of the last-born, mother and infant burning up together in fever, given the sacrament of extreme unction by the parish priest, and buried together. Forever and ever, amen. (547)

Corky's misogynistic gestures and concealed racism are disturbing traits in his otherwise sociable and generous personality. As a child Corky had revealed a notable integrity: after the death of his father, in an episode that he recalls incessantly throughout his life, Corky had been interrogated by the police to identify his father's murderers. Corky is pressured by his family to identify his father's killers. The anonymous phrase, "Son, you're our only witness," is a memory that will continue to haunt Corky throughout his life (26). Corky remains, nevertheless, daringly faithful to his original words and refuses to identify faces that he had not really seen. This sense of integrity proves, however, to be both quixotic and futile in the tough social world that Corky inhabits, contributing ultimately to the deterioration of his already damaged sense of belonging.

From his adolescence onwards Corky tries to "repair" this fault by becoming the "nicest guy in Union City, New York" (53) and by presenting himself with that current all-American cliché of belonging, the phrase that becomes his personal staple: "I'm your man." (451). Sexist and racist gestures also become part of a covert reinforcement of his own identity, a ticket for white male membership, and a way of blending himself with his "superior" lot by "othering" those actually not so different from himself. These tendencies are visibly at odds with his supposedly liberal politics. He shows a condescending dislike for the racist comments of his relatives in Irish Hill, but he is dominated by racist impulses as well when he feels that his own individual interests are being threatened. Despite presenting himself as a Democrat who openly advocates civil rights, Corky is fast and firm in reproaching and wrongly condemning Marcus Steadman (a local black activist and a political opponent of Corky's friends) for crimes he did not commit. This hypocritical behavior discloses again Corky's hidden inferiority complex. One instance of his ingrained sense of social inferiority is conveyed in Corky's relationship with his current lover, a married woman named Christina Kavanaugh. Corky compares himself with Christina's husband, Judge Harry Kavanaugh, by acknowledging his own lower status: "I'm shit on his shoes . . . You think I don't know how you feel about me?—about guys like me?—from Irish Hill?" (89). Oates's study of "white" middle-class masculinity is more than a parodic portrait of the self-made macho male of the 1990s. It conveys in depth the social and private backgrounds that define Corky's self-image.

Initially Corky is only threatened by the spectre of other male figures. For Corky, women are at the bottom of the social ladder, deserving their own scatological label: while the Irish are "niggers of Union City, shit on the WASP shoes" (370), women are interestingly depicted as "Kleenex, toilet paper, you use it and as soon as you're done you're done" (96). His mother's madness and her consequent absence from Corky's life has striking effects in terms of his psychological structure, leaving him with highly contradictory feelings toward women. As a child Corky secretly desires that "he wouldn't have to take care of or see his crazy mother, shifting back and forth between her wearying kin the Corcorans and the McClures, and St Raphael's hospital" (386–87). This image has two conflicting projections in his adult self: an anomalous sexual/maternal dependency and a deep-rooted disdain of all women. Oates highlights the comic depth of Corky's love affairs by showing how, despite thinking he is in control, he is ultimately always controlled, if not exploited, by "his" women. Corky also finds out that, in the influential social circles he so much aspires to, sexual and political games are intricately connected. He acknowledges the value of women as a form of homosocial exchange but recognizes that he too is susceptible to being manipulated by the powerful men he emulates. His marriage to Charlotte Drummond is blatantly arranged by the young woman's father, Ross Drummond, Corky's boss and a wealthy businessman, for whom Corky is a new investment. Drummond's use of possessive adjectives does not leave doubts about his sense of ownership: "'my daughter's fiancé'—'My daughter's husband'—sometimes 'my son-in-law.' My, mine" (418). Cunningly, Ross Drummond has other uses for his son-in-law: he is to be employed as a middle-man in possible deals with the "Irish Mafia" (421).

Despite his inflated masculinity, Corky perceptively acknowledges the more ambiguous contours of homosociality.[2] Corky refers to his relation to

Vic Slattery, a friend and influential politician, as a marriage: "friendships are like love affairs, marriage itself. Always one part is deeper more dependent upon the other. More jealous . . . An imbalance of love means an imbalance of power" (276). He is also well aware of his homosocial needs and tendencies. When watching the Memorial Day parade and thinking about his father fighting in Korea (while he himself had not gone to Vietnam), he curiously relates his own womanizing predisposition with his feared lack of manhood: "His dad would have been ashamed of him doing everything he could to stay out [of Vietnam]. *A man among men:* he'd missed it forever. Why Corky runs off at the mouth so much, maybe. Chasing pussy like he's desperate to prove something. That's it?" (557). It is his stepdaughter Thalia, however, who more aptly denounces Corky's homosocial strategies when she accuses him of being "the kind of man who has to prove he's a man by way of women" (295). Yet she aptly explains to him "it's other men you're proving to, like they're proving they're men to you" (295).

It is significant that a woman—his stepdaughter Thalia—is the only character in the novel able to challenge Corky's misogynistic and racist tendencies. Thalia, the daughter of his ex-wife Charlotte Drummont, is a rebellious and idealistic young woman; she graduated from Cornell and is now engaged in social work. Thalia becomes obsessed with the death of her friend, Marilee Plummer, a mixed-race girl who—as we later find out—had been bribed and used as bait in a case of political manipulation. Plummer's death is presented to the public as a suspected suicide, but Thalia believes her friend's death has to do with premeditated murderer.

With the figure of Thalia leading the second part of the novel, the three-day portrait narrative of Corky shifts into the crime-mystery genre, releasing an unexpectedly intricate plot. The secrets unveiled by Thalia disclose a drama of corruption and blackmail involving many of Corky's friends, who are political leaders of Union City. Fearing being pursued by those involved with Plummer's murder, Thalia flees from home but keeps leaving crucial hints about the case on Corky's answering machine. From this point onward, the narrative assumes the pattern of a race against the clock, whereby Corky apparently assumes the heroic role of finding and rescuing his innocent but inquisitive stepdaughter. Corky finds photos in Thalia's house that incriminate his old friend and politician in the death of Marilee Plummer. Plummer had publicly accused Marcus Steadman (the African American councilman referred to above) of charges of rape. Since Steadman was an old political enemy of Oscar Slattery (Vic Slattery's father) Corky had been, at first, secretly delighted in condemning Steadman for the supposed crime. In his search for Thalia, however, Corky realizes his conjectures were hasty: Steadman was innocent, having been falsely incriminated in a blackmail scheme organized by the Slatterys. It was not Plummer's involvement with Steadman but her connection to Vic Slattery that had led to her death. This acknowledgement marks the beginning of Corky's second loss of innocence, as an initial scratch is made to the image of the second paternal figure with which Corky had established a crucial homosocial bound.

Thalia is far from being the over-sexualized female type Corky would typically choose as a lover, but he is nevertheless strangely attracted to his stepdaughter. Thalia rejects not only her family's upper-class lifestyle but also the conspicuous investment in sex appeal exhibited by women such as her mother. Instead, and not unlike many of Oates's female characters, Thalia shows signs of anorexia while exposing an uncompromising and determined personality. Physically, Thalia resembles another figure of Irish descent in Oates's canon—Marianne in We Were the Mulvaneys, who having been raped by her prom date and ostracized by her family, similarly becomes increasingly thin and cuts her hair short in a bold but unfeminine way. Unlike Marianne, however, who decides to forgive and forget, Thalia does neither. Rejecting the role of female martyr, Thalia becomes a prominent character in the last part of the novel, and it is significantly she who determines its conclusion.

The apparent rescue pursuit is inverted when Thalia, in the last chapter, appears unexpectedly at Vic Slattery's cocktail reception. In a bewildering scene, described in slow motion, Corky finally finds Thalia in the middle of a private party honoring Slattery at the exclusive Chateuguay Country Club. The scene is described as a series of flashes that Corky's vision cannot fully register: "Thalia moves in a straight unerring line toward Vic Slattery removing from her bag the Luger she had stolen from Corky's bedside table, lifting the long-barreled heavy weapon with her right hand and steadying it with her left in a pose, a gesture practiced to grim perfection. . . . And in this same instant calling out 'Vic Slattery! Murderer!' in a voice high, soprano-clear, unwavering as if much practised too" (594–95).

Instinctively, Corky shields Slattery's body, so it is Corky who is shot in the heart. The epilogue is, not unlike the typical ending of the classic Irish American novel, a deathbed episode.[3] The novel concludes with a final paradox. On the one hand, the ending confirms Corky's prediction that death was imminent, reinforcing the fate motif that runs through the narrative: "the secret of the Irish: bad luck," or "the craziness of Fate, what's called Fate" (76). On the other hand, it contradicts that fate by recovering and elaborating the notions of American optimism and capitalist ideology. In the hospital, feeling that "he can bring his life back under control again" (607), Corky thanks the doctors and nurses, thinking disingenuously both about his political image and about his insurance: "not just that these people are voters but they've done a good job . . . this fancy medical technology—it costs you, but it's worth it" (607). Despite his hospitalization, Corky is still an aspiring politician for whom it is vital to seize every opportunity, particularly now that Oscar Slattery will be resigning. As luck would have it, his political aspirations seem to have finally materialized, and Corky's accidental heroism has paid off: "they're talking of Jerome A Corcoran for Mayor of Union City" (603).

The final images of the novel are as much transcendental as surreal, parodying the precarious balance between the two opposing systems of belief on which Corky had tried to frame his identity: Irish fatalism and American optimism. The anonymous man—described by Corky as "that little prick Teague or Tyde" (607)—who had been pursuing Corky for three weeks in order to sell him his project, the Union City Mausoleum of the Dead, is waiting for him in the hospital's corridor. Having tried to avoid him for months, Corky finally welcomes Teague with his own favorite expression: "Hell come on in, I'm Corky Corcoran, I'm your man" (608). Is Corky promoting his political image in this final gesture of inclusion? Or is he coming to terms with the ideas of death and Irish fate? This remains unresolved, giving an ironic twist to the idea of "ethnicity as a liberating doubleness" (Fanning 371). It is this, along other uncomfortable ambiguities, that make Corky such a remarkably complex character and *What I Lived For* such a complex novel.

What I Lived For does more than satirize clichés of Irishness or mock stereotypes of the American way of life; it explores the complex realities running through these national labels, creating a self-reflexive Irish American tragicomedy. The narrative offers several traits of the Irish emigrant experience (references to past lives ruined by violence and alcoholism, the influence of the Catholic Church, the impact of family ties, the belief in an Irish fate, etc.) but it is, primarily, the influence of these various traits on the construction of Corky's masculinity that is more carefully explored in the novel. Through the figure of Corky Corcoran, Oates interrogates the personal and public histories that sustain the macho façade of Irish masculinity. The crucial incongruities of Corky's character disclose intricate links between power and gender, between sexism and homosociality, between masculinity and status, between racism and ethnical anxiety. *What I Lived For* provides a defiant and inquisitive portrayal of Irish American masculinity in the closing decade of the twentieth century.

Notes

1. Irish male characters in Oates's work tend to be fatherless. If Corky's father is killed during his childhood, Michael Senior is, similarly, a disowned son of an Irish steelworker from Pittsburgh. This absent father corresponds, autobiographically, to the image of Oates's own absent great-great-grandfather, Frederick Oates, Senior. Oates points out that her "prime motivation when writing about the Irish has to do with the mysterious absent handsome Irish father and grandfather who is out of the orbit of the family and what's left behind are the women who remember him and his children" (personal interview).

2. The terms *homosocial* and *homosociality* are used here to indicate the use of women as a form of male exchange as described by Eve Kosofsky Sedgwick. For Sedgwick homosociality represents the means of establishing the power in society in a patriarchal sense. It determines the assignment of gender roles, where women become property with the purpose of balancing society and filling the sexual role.

3. Charles Fanning points out that "dozens of nineteenth-century Irish-American novels follow the convention of the climatic happy death, which heralds the beginning of eternal life for the dying soul and a rejuvenated moral life for those left behind" (275–76). This motif is reverted, however, in later novels such as James T. Farrell's *Judgement Day* (1935) which describes Studs's delirium as a moment of suffering and void, in a subversion of the Christian deathbed convention. This subversion is taken one step further in the paradoxical conclusion of *What I Lived For*.

Works Cited

Fanning, Charles. *The Irish Voice in America: Irish American Fiction from the 1760s to the 1980s*. Lexington: University Press of Kentucky, 1990.
Johnson, Greg. "A Brief Biography." *Celestial Timepiece: A Joyce Carol Oates Home Page*. 12 Sept. 2006 <http://www.usfca.edu/fac-staff/southerr/what.html>.
Oates, Joyce Carol. Letter to the author. 29 July 2003.
———. Personal Interview. 25 May 2005.
———. *We Were the Mulvaneys*. New York: Dutton, 1996.
———. *What I Lived For*. 2nd ed. New York: Signet, 1995.
Sedgwick, Eve Kosofsky. *Between Men*. New York: Columbia University Press, 1985.

SEXUALITY

CHAPTER 8

Hardly Sentimental

The "Bad Girls" and Lonely Men of Mary McGarry Morris's Fiction

PATRICIA GOTT

"In this life we're all poor bastards"
—*A Dangerous Woman*

Sometimes compared to William Faulkner and Charles Dickens (Gilbert) and echoing the regionalism of Flannery O'Connor and Carson McCullers, Irish American novelist Mary McGarry Morris provides readers with a wide array of variations on quintessential Irish and Irish American traits and themes. One such theme is the underdog-cum-survivor motif. Essentially, this motif consists of an antihero, a figure inhabiting the margins of her community who emerges as a survivor of narrow cultural perceptions of gender- or class-linked behavior. The word "behavior" is significant in this context because Morris's women and men do not always behave themselves, at least according to societally determined norms. Indeed, her antiheroes can be seen as transgressive but essentially redemptive. As

Maureen Howard notes, "The duty that many of these [Irish American women] writers take upon themselves is to discover what is wayward in their women's soul, where *transgression* in thought or deed may lead to a finer, at times more generous, understanding of a limiting world or to self-discovery" (Howard xi; emphasis mine). With a hybrid voice emanating from both her Irish American and New England roots, Morris fulfills this goal and more.

To what degree do Morris's works resonate as recognizably Irish American? While her characters (like Morris herself) rarely allude to their Irish voice and ancestry, the undercurrent of this ancestry is always evident. Morris's novels break free from the forms of the conventional bestseller genre while providing elaborate variations on themes set forth by other Irish American women novelists writing today. Determining the degree to which the traits and behaviors manifested by various characters can be regarded as particularly Irish or Irish American provides a lens through which we can better understand recurrent themes in Morris's works. Of these traits, I will focus in particular on the valorization of the underdog or the social misfit, the tendency in Irish American culture to produce strong women, the depiction of Irish Catholicism, the primacy of the family in Irish culture, and the deep-seated desire for characters to create a better life for themselves in the face of overwhelming odds.

In her forward to *Cabbage and Bones*, novelist Maureen Howard foregrounds the notion of transcendence in her telling observation that Irish American authors "yearn to cross boundaries that will protect them beyond the prescription of dailiness" (xii). Indeed, Morris's characters could hardly be described as exemplifying "dailiness" or normalcy. Howard also points to the storytelling gifts that have been (sometimes stereotypically) ascribed to the Irish, noting, "The Irish had the advantage of language when [they] came to America" (xii). Morris's Irish roots are evident in the efficacy and ease of her natural-sounding dialogue, which contributes to the realistic tenor of her novels. Howard further observes that "[t]hroughout Irish American authors, there is a strong vein of the confessional" and "church-ridden women" (xiii). Although these traits are not explicitly mentioned, latent Catholicism and Irish ancestry are implicit among Morris's characters as they profess both pleasure and pain.[1]

Until fairly recently there has been a paucity of scholarly criticism about Morris, but in the existing critiques of her *oeuvre* several reviewers have commented on her deftly plotted character studies and her cogent ability to fathom the depths of characters who are castoffs and misfits. As

Susan Lynn Harkins puts it, "Morris establish[es] herself as a master in portraying the hapless victimization of the intellectually limited and emotionally disabled, people whom society would like to push conveniently through
the cracks, but who stubbornly insist on straddling them instead." One of
Morris's myriad strengths is her ability to bridge the gap between popular
fiction and fiction amenable to scholarly inquiry. Traces of potboilers like
Grace Metallious's *Peyton Place* are apparent in places, especially in the
extreme behavior, multiple betrayals, emotional complications, and lurid
scandals of Morris's plots and characters. Such vivid characterizations make
Morris's characters among the most memorable conjured up by novelists
writing today. But Morris sees them as normal. In an interview concerning
Songs in Ordinary Time, she notes that one of her key goals was "to try to
portray the humanity in each character. There are very few people in this
universe who are all bad or all good. We're just a mix" (Edwardsen).

In a 2003 interview Morris mentions her background as a native New
Englander, indicating that her regional ties may influence her choice of settings and characterizations (Penguin, Reading Guide for *Fiona Range*),
for the majority of her works take place in rural Vermont settings (two in
the mythical town of Atkinson, Vermont).[2] Born in Meriden, Connecticut,
Morris grew up in Rutland, Vermont. After her parents separated, Morris's
mother worked as a supermarket cashier during the day shift and a waitress
at night. Later, Morris attended the University of Vermont and the University of Massachusetts, where she studied creative writing in the early 1960s.
After meeting her future husband Michael on a blind date, the two married
and settled in Andover, Massachusetts, where Morris still lives today. Morris honed her writing craft while raising five children and working full-time
for the Massachusetts Department of Welfare as a financial assistance social
worker (Edwardsen). During this time period she felt some hesitancy about
identifying herself as a writer. Yet in a 1991 interview charting her writing
trajectory, Morris indicates that she could barely recall a time when she was
not a writer. Paradoxically, locating her identity as a writer produced "a
terrible confusion. . . . I knew that these feelings I felt must be what writers
felt. But I hesitated to call myself a writer when I had nothing published"
(Mehren). Perhaps not surprisingly, no one save her family knew she was
writing her first novel: "I think people just felt I was very, very busy with a
good-sized family and just a quiet person" (Edwardsen).

Despite being thought of as "a quiet person," Morris has achieved a
healthy level of popular accolades and enjoyed a certain level of celebrity
early in her career. The recipient of various literary awards, her first novel,

Vanished, received a National Book Award nomination (1988) and a PEN/
Faulkner Award nomination (1989). She made her imprint on popular
culture when her third novel, *Songs in Ordinary Time*, had the distinction
of being chosen as an Oprah Book Club selection ("Mary McGarry Morris"). The film adaptation of her second novel, *A Dangerous Woman*, was
released in 1993. In 2004 she released *A Hole in the Universe* and 2005
ushered in *The Lost Mother*, both of which have been met with extremely
positive reviews and scholarly acclaim. Evidently, Morris is more than just
a "flash-in-the-pan"; her bestsellers appear to possess true staying power.

In Morris's early novels—*Vanished, Songs in Ordinary Time, A Dangerous Woman*, and *Fiona Range*—her most memorable characters emerge as
distinct individuals but are facets of the same archetype: the "bad girl"
(and occasionally the "bad boy") who must redeem herself in order to find
transcendence. The dual specters of hypocrisy and secrecy surface repeatedly in Morris's novels, most prominently in *Fiona Range* and *A Dangerous Woman*. Additionally, all four novels center around the theme of betrayal (men betraying women and vice versa, as well as women betraying
other women, but, most importantly, women betraying themselves). Although Morris's early works are occasionally weakened by contrived plot
twists, the driving momentum and rising intensity that characterize her
work keep the reader furiously turning pages. In my view, Morris's most
singular achievement is her talent at chronicling in poignant detail the
struggles faced by her protagonists, most of whom who have been cast off
and discarded from mainstream society. Morris herself notes that she is fascinated with people who follow their own drummer: "There's something in
me that reacts quickly to other people's discomfort or pain. . . . And not
just dysfunctional people" (Weinraub). While nearly all of Morris's main
characters are violated and violate others, most remain resolute in their
quest for redemption, a common trait among the work of Irish American
women writers.

In addition to starkly depicting characters who somehow manage to
achieve a greater level of self-understanding despite the odds against them,
Morris excels in placing her characters *in media res*, as if they were a part
of a longer cycle. This technique allows the works to reflect back on themselves, mirroring their own reality. The novels' endings function much the
same way, lacking a sense of closure, much like life itself. By leaving readers wondering how these very flawed human beings will comport themselves in the future, Morris has achieved a goal many writers crave: making her characters live in the reader's mind long after the book is laid aside.

One of the most perceptive critiques of Morris's work comes from writer Alice McDermott, who notes: "Morris does not devise plots, but traps: steel-toothed, inescapable traps of circumstances and personality against which her characters struggle . . . and fail" ("Mary McGarry Morris"). Morris's ability to render a particular time and place so vividly that it functions as a sort of supporting character contributes to the staying power of her works. The settings of *Vanished* and *Songs in Ordinary Time* evoke a 1950s atmosphere; Morris depicts small towns that do not seem to exist anymore in the manic and *uber*-mechanized twenty-first century. Her works provide readers with vignettes of lunch counters festooned with short orders, dilapidated cabins rented by the week, and towns populated by nosy residents who keep their eyes trained on their neighbors. *Vanished*, in particular, suggests the allure of a distant past. The few clues indicating a more contemporary setting come in the way of cultural references, such as descriptions of apparel, or a reference to a child watching an episode of the television show *Love Boat*. In a *New York Times* review of *Fiona Range*, Maggie Paley notes that "Morris is a deliberately old-fashioned novelist. She's not interested in contemporary culture, and her characters don't make ironic references to it; instead they talk about what matters most to them—family, their own and one another's. Morris regards their emotional distress and moral failings with sincerity and compassion."

In *Vanished* (1988), arguably her most poignant work until *The Lost Mother* (2005), Morris provides the reader with a tale of wistful yearning for innocence in a world that will not exist again. The situations in which she places the characters in *Vanished* are at times so extreme as to be improbable, and the predicaments the characters enmesh themselves in occasionally reach melodramatic proportions. As a first novel, *Vanished* does not fit the mold of the rest of Morris's work, yet her characters possess the Irish American characteristic of emotional extremes simultaneously expressed and repressed (Dezell).[3] Other staples of Irish American women writers—Morris's emerging strengths as a stylist and her recurrent use of dispossessed individuals who clearly do not fit into the larger society— also make their first appearance in *Vanished*. In this novel events coalesce around a central female figure, the disturbed and provocative Dotty, although the protagonist, Aubrey Wallace, is male. He functions as Morris's most pathetic character even as he manages to retain some modicum of dignity. As Aubrey struggles in vain to protect Canny from predation, Morris juxtaposes his outer quietude and passivity with an internal state that is almost "choking with feeling" (Posesorski). Morris's works provide us with a "spontaneous overflow of powerful emotions"; however, unlike those of Wordsworth's humble rustics, these emotions are *not* "recollected in tranquility."

From the beginning of the charade that is the novel's focus, an illusion must be maintained, yet it eventually implodes from the sheer weight of implausibility. Perhaps to counteract charges that the forthcoming events are too outlandish, *Vanished* begins by stating "This is the true story" (1). The novel opens with Dotty abducting Aubrey from his wife and Canny from her family, suggesting that Aubrey and Canny are doubles of a sort, for both are innocents. Aubrey behaves as if he is mildly mentally impaired (much like Martha Horgan in *A Dangerous Woman*); in contrast, Canny, a toddler, demonstrates infinitely more common sense than the man she calls "Poppa." Dotty and Aubrey travel from town to town, scraping out a meager living selling stolen goods at flea markets. While squatting on his property, Dotty becomes involved with Jig Huller, an ex-con who has his eye on Canny. In Huller, Morris provides us with the template of the sadistic abuser she returns to with Getso, the catalyst for Martha's anger in *A Dangerous Woman*, and Omar Duvall, the con man with a hazy past in *Songs in Ordinary Time*. Intuiting that they are hiding a secret he can exploit, Huller quickly wins over Dotty's confidence by plying her with liquor, drugs, and sex, then proceeds to destroy any trace of her maternal feelings for Canny. While the characters become increasingly alienated from one another, Aubrey's attachment to Dotty remains intact. Even after he belatedly realizes that Dotty has betrayed him and Canny in a vicious attempt to garner the reward for returning Canny to her birth family, Aubrey reflects on his love for Dotty: "[She] was all he had known of mystery and dreams and wildness and chance" (209).

From the onset of her writing career, Morris has explored the theme of the divided self (what Jung might call "the shadow") (Stevens 47). Often this divided behavior is exhibited by characters who act or appear visibly different than those around them. In *Vanished* Aubrey notes that Dotty possesses a side that desires to do good for others, but her halting attempts at kindness toward him and Canny are all too often overwhelmed by a grasping, impulsive side. Dotty provides one version of the mentally unstable character so prominently featured in Morris's works. Dotty (like Martha Horgan) may well be mentally ill—or she may not. In any case, she metamorphoses into the most unstable character in Morris's canon: "The crazier life got, the better Dotty liked it. She thrived on turmoil and confusion" (97). Aubrey is similarly a divided individual. He observes that "parts of him were breaking off, falling away and missing. He was conscious of his thousands of different pieces. His brain had grown staticky and sore with the effort of having to keep track of all his parts. The sense of loss he felt was both strange and frightening" (130). Later, he reflects on his childhood drawings and those he had drawn for his boys and Canny: "his pictures always showed a man without an arm or a face without a nose or a dog without a tail" (189). Much like his drawings, Aubrey falls prey to Dotty's betrayal, losing his life in the end as a sacrificial victim of her insatiable hunger for fame.

In *A Dangerous Woman* (1991) Morris creates her most original character with the odd and memorable Martha Horgan. One reviewer calls Martha "at once the most irritating and engaging character to inhabit a novel in a long time" (Carlson 89). Even as an adolescent, Martha cannot help but realize she is not like her peers. In a rush of emotion, she reflects:

> She had never been all right. Never. No—always the butt of everyone's jokes perfect strangers children were the worst nipping at her heels like savage dogs all the way along the streets calling her name so that it had become a NAME, a bad word, MARTHORGAN a taunt synonymous with bogeymen and bums and crazed old women in unpainted, crooked old houses." (37)

Even as a child, Martha's classmates felt uneasy sitting by her in the classroom, as if she were constantly staring at them (197). Later, in high school, Martha endures lasting scars when a gang of teenage boys assaults her in the woods; they throw beer cans at her naked chest, only to later claim that she spurred them on.[4] Sadly, at age thirty-two Martha is still learning to negotiate her way in a world that at its worst expresses little more than outright viciousness toward her, and at its best indifferent contempt.

As is the case with many of Morris's other characters, Martha reads some people accurately, but not everyone. While she is capable of seeing into the heart of hypocrisy, she cannot always protect herself against the ridicule and cruelty of others. One scene that both advances Martha's desperate need to fit in and provides a pointed critique of domesticity involves her attempt to obtain status via her transparent grab for PlastiqueWare, a faux Tupperware product line marketed as high-end kitchenware that is little more than overpriced junk. Martha's emotions come to a head when another woman grabs the forty-five piece set, upsetting Martha so deeply she flees the plastic party.

Many other scenes help explain why Martha is considered "dangerous" in the eyes of others. Perhaps her most defining feature is that she (even more so than Fiona) never lies. One example of this occurs when she insists on informing a customer that his garments were not properly dry cleaned, despite her boss's protestations to the contrary. Meanwhile, Martha's stunned coworkers lower their eyes and dismiss her derisively. Not surprisingly, her behavior results in her banishment from the dry cleaners. As Harkins notes, "In addition to her explosive, unpredictable temper, Martha's basic and unwavering sense of honesty make her a very dangerous woman indeed." To their credit, neither Martha (nor Fiona) brook any patience with poseurs, and both actively attempt to deflate the arrogance they see around them.

Other characters in the novel are also irritating and quite flawed but starkly rendered. After Martha's father dies, her Aunt Frances is obligated to take her in, even though Frances clearly resents Martha's encroachment on her time and personal space. Frances also comes off as strident and overtly status-conscious in her battles to control Martha's unbridled sexuality while feebly trying to gain a small measure of acceptance from the other socialites in her narrow community. But it is Frances's quest to win over Colin Mackey, or Mack (played by the Irish actor Gabriel Byrne in the film version), the handyman-cum-writer, that leads to the two women's conflict. With Mack, Morris provides the catalyst by which Martha is transformed from a very troubled and yet invisible misfit to a woman who finally forces others to acknowledge her humanity. After watching Martha serve as the butt of repeated jokes, Mack takes Martha's side, primarily to put Frances in her place (193). Although he is alcoholic, manipulative, and self-aggrandizing at times, Mack tells Martha she should not be ashamed of being different.

However, Mack is neither Superman nor a white knight; he cannot rescue Martha from herself. When Martha tells Mack that she "aches for him," he shrugs her off and says he is only interested in friendship; he is more fascinated by his writing (243). In a rare moment of self-disclosure, the alcoholic Mack reveals the extent to which he is willing to use others. About sleeping with Frances, Mack observes, "It's a fuck. I fucked her like I fucked you. . . . And the only time I love is when I fuck myself" (250). Martha's inability to understand that a night of carnal sex does not automatically translate into a relationship contributes to Mack's unease; her interpretation of dancing as a substitute for sex similarly disturbs him (200–201). Nevertheless, while both Frances and Mack are troubled individuals (the two become lovers in the wake of Martha's tumultuousness), the pair display some positive attributes in their relationship to Martha. Both characters support Martha as she prepares to stand trial for killing Getso, another coworker in a long line of individuals who have betrayed her, and they do not waver when Martha is pressed to decide whether she will keep her and Mack's baby or give it up for adoption. These two scenes in particular demonstrate Morris's talent for showing that weakness in flawed individuals may sometimes paradoxically become a sort of strength.

At a voluminous 740 pages, *Songs in Ordinary Time* (1995) is Morris's most prodigious novel and perhaps her most overtly Irish. On the surface it involves the turmoil of some fifty characters cast against the backdrop of scandal unfolding in a small Vermont town; at its center the novel chronicles one family's struggle to keep itself together against relentless external forces and ruthless individuals threatening to split it apart.

The events take place during the early 1960s, well before the ensuing turmoil of the Kennedy assassinations or the burgeoning civil rights movement. The significance of the title is brought out in a short exchange between Howard Mencak and a clerk in the Holy Articles Shoppe: "This summer, it's ordinary time. There aren't any special feasts then." Of this period, Howard thinks: "It was ordinary time, and there was nothing to look forward to and no one to love" (299). Morris notes that the title functions on several levels: "The Songs are various stories of ordinary people in Atkinson: I wanted them to have a lyrical feeling so that each character's voice could tell their story, and as the various segments of these stories ended there would be this subtle ebb, and then another character's tale could take up the melody, and I envisioned the effect of this being a kind of chorusing, a consonance of pain and joy" (Putnam Penguin Reading Guide for *Songs in Ordinary Time*).

Like all of Morris's characters, the members of the Irish Catholic Fermoyle family are enmeshed in a battle for self-worth and financial stability. In many respects the novel is a testimony to Marie's ability to keep her family intact while various external and internal forces threaten to break it into bits. (This emphasis on the family is echoed by the plight of the Talcott family in Morris's most recent novel, *The Lost Mother*.) The three Fermoyle children and their mother face both physical and emotional impoverishment arising from the desertion of their alcoholic father and husband Sam Fermoyle. Regarding familial struggles—a common Irish American theme—Charles Fanning notes that the depiction of family life in the Irish American novel "can be constricting as well as supportive" (340), a claim that can be substantiated in each of Morris's works.

Another motif that Morris repeatedly returns to her in her works is the pattern of manipulation faced by female characters—a feminist theme typical of Irish American women writers. In *Songs in Ordinary Time* this is most relevant to Alice and her mother Marie. When Alice has sex for the first time, her boyfriend Lester waits until after the encounter to inform her that girls like her are "confused . . . kind of mixed up, not just emotionally, but you know—morally. . . . They're . . . always trying to find love" (90). Despite this insight, unwilling or unable to realize the ramifications of his behavior, he repeatedly seeks out Alice for sex. Worse, Father Gannon considers it his prerogative to take advantage of his position, finding in Alice both a confidante and a prospective lover (157).

Alice also becomes the target of her mother's wrath. Marie's frustration can be explained in part by Alice's unwillingness to live for herself (rather than merely existing, like Marie), but also because Marie feels cheated of what she believes is rightfully hers. The narrator reflects: "Because so much money was needed to send Alice to college, her mother was being deprived of the opportunity of a lifetime" (201). Ironically, the "opportunity of a lifetime," Omar's scheme to dupe Marie out of her savings, materializes into a crisis of almost biblical proportions. One troubling issue is how Marie manages to be so easily manipulated by the unctuous Omar Duvall, a traveling salesman who offers nothing in the way of stability. (Like so many of Morris's characters, we find that Omar is hiding a sinister past.) Drawn irresistibly to Omar, Marie rationalizes her attachment to him, telling her children: "It's a terrible feeling to be alone. You have each other, so you don't know what that's like. You don't know how frightening that can be! How lost and desperate you can be!" (189). After revealing the shame she feels at her inability to provide her children with the essentials, Marie displaces her anger onto Sam, exploding in a terrible furor (which she revisits later in even greater waves of self-abasement): "Look at my children. . . . Their shabby clothes, their thin nervous faces. I am a terrible mother. He doesn't know that. He doesn't know this rage" (131).[5]

Here again Morris displays a deft hand in portraying the despair that characters like Marie Fermoyle endure in the face of extreme deprivation.

She also does not shirk from exposing the pressures that characters like Marie face or the delusions to which they often feel forced to resort. Much of what appears to motivate Marie's involvement with Omar is the desire to avoid being ridiculed by her social-climbing neighbors. Her fear of being judged surfaces when she compares her plight to that of Mrs. Mangini, a woman who also has experienced domestic chaos but with different results: "because her husband is dead, she has everything she wants. . . . She doesn't have to work a day or minute for the rest of her life. She can go to a movie with a man on a Saturday night, and the next day, no one looks at her and thinks, Harlot, sinner, as she marches up to the communion rail while I kneel alone . . . judged and condemned for a sin that is not mine, but your father's" (132).

While not a pronounced presence in Morris's early work, Catholicism and the expression (or sometimes inversion) of religious values alluded to in the aforementioned quotation are embodied in the character of Father Gannon, as well as in Alice's response to him. Alice expresses her passion for the older priest in religious terms: "how could she explain this violent commingling of guilt and longing that left her feeling bruised and sore, without it sounding like confession, an admission of the worst sin, desire but not love" (456). As for Gannon, his flaws are numerous and pronounced; whether he is aware of them is another matter. With no apparent sense of irony, he tells the teenaged Alice after professing his love to her: "I realize that my faith has become a wholeness. It's a unity of mind and soul. And flesh . . . I finally feel like a real priest" (415). At the same time, he exhibits some positive characteristics, including his role as an activist rallying his neighborhood in a rent strike. His good works do not go unnoticed, however. He is transferred out of his parish in retribution for buying a jacket for a needy child whose father becomes enraged. In the process he becomes branded as "a pervert and a thief" (412).

The key themes developed by Morris in her earlier works are more fully explored in *Fiona Range*, published in 2000. By the time she wrote *Fiona Range*, rather than patterning her characters after the grotesque models found in Flannery O'Connor's fiction, Morris had matured into a sympathetic contemporary chronicler of lonely, dispossessed women and men. And in part because her two latest works (*A Hole in the Universe* and *The Lost Mother*) are more about the protagonist and less about the settings, *Fiona Range* is a stronger, more character-driven work. Although Maggie Paley takes issue with what she see as the novel's sentimentality (categorizing the novel as "women's romance fiction" and contending that, at times, its "plot contrivances make it hard to take seriously" [7]), Paley suggests that, in the end, *Fiona Range* "exert[s] a much deeper pull" than it initially displays and "become[s] extraordinary" (7). The occasional lapse into sentimentality is counterbalanced by the intensity of the rising action and a desire on Morris's part to locate strength and redemption in the character of Fiona. Clearly, Morris evolves as a stylist from her earliest to latest work, and Fiona is her most fully realized and strongest creation in her early novels.[6]

This tendency toward strength that characterizes Morris's female protagonists is undercut by their tendency toward self-effacement, which, according to Dezell, is a fundamental trait of the Irish: "Self-deprecation is *sine qua non* of the Irish subculture. It is as ubiquitous as humor, fine talk, loyalty, and sympathy for the underdog, as characteristic as a tendency to drink too much, and to harbor trepidations that the light at the end of the tunnel is a train" (3). From the beginning, Fiona is nothing if not self-deprecating, telling George Grimshaw, a prospective suitor, "What I mean, George, is that I can be a raving, flaming bitch, and that's not what you're looking for" (37). She is also a complex character in other ways. When one character inquires of her, "You still a daredevil?" Fiona replies, "Yes. But now it's mostly people I take chances on" (151). At least for Fiona, however, her gritty realism and her painfully acute self-awareness mitigate her self-effacement in places. In other words, she is able to ascertain the limitations of her situation even while being unable to do much if anything to change that situation. These traits, along with the treacherous secret at the story's core, make *Fiona Range* a deeply satisfying read.

Fiona's greatest strength may be her acknowledgment of her weaknesses (including a weakness for men, "bad boys" in particular) and her growing recognition of her vulnerability, both of which lend believability to her character. One example of her vulnerability occurs when she lies to her aunt and uncle about talking to her mother on the phone, in the process deluding herself into believing that her dead mother is still alive. Like a latter-day Jean Rhys heroine, we see Fiona habitually retreating into dysfunctional patterns, succumbing to the allure of old boyfriends, and engaging in continual run-ins with her family members, particularly her uncle, the pompous Judge Hollis, and his beautiful but fragile daughter Elizabeth, Fiona's cousin and foil.

Elizabeth embodies the treacle "good-girl" Fiona knows she can never—nor would want to—resemble but on some level aspires to be. As I have noted, the concept of duality figures prominently in Morris's works. "Irish society paradoxically expected that Irish women should be either 'sweet-good mothers' or young women out in the world doing their duty," according to historian Timothy Meaghan (qtd. in Dezell 93). In Dezell's view this has particular ramifications for self-conceptions of Irish woman-hood: "Irish [American] girls are raised to be respectable, responsible, re-silient and rarely with any expectations that they're going to be taken care of" (89). Fiona, who would undoubtedly chafe if the monikers of "respectable" and "responsible" were applied to her, notes of her cousin Elizabeth: "She thinks everyone has to be happy and everything has to be perfect. And if they're not, well, she's a wreck. She always feels so respon-sible . . . And when we got older it was almost like she was trying to make up for me or something" (212). Fiona is clearly reacting to this model of behavior; through her "bad-girl behavior" (for example, excessive drink-ing, flailing about in successive one-night stands) she attempts to subvert tableaus of domesticity and the fixed notions of proper gender-linked be-havior that she finds so stifling. She also shows, however, that she is more than a bit of an incipient feminist: "Real happiness is what you do for your-self . . . not what some guy does for you" (123). Although Morris's female characters do not most readily come to mind when the term "feminist" is uttered,[7] it could be said that her women hark back to the tradition of the Irish warrior queen Medb, also known as Maeve. When a suitor asks to marry Maeve, she replies, "I was better off without you" (Dezell 99).

Admittedly, Fiona's unwillingness to take advice and her marked pro-pensity toward self-destructive behavior, as well as her inability to control her temper, all work against her at times. But it is her anger at the world and the situation in which she has been placed that becomes her most defining feature. More impatient with herself than she is with others, she struggles to understand the root of this anger. As the narrator notes, "Some-times she didn't know where all this anger came from" (78). One might say, however, that it is Fiona's anger along with her insistence on being an individual that allows her to finally reach her full potential in the end: "Fiona Range could never do things the simple way, the right way" (71). Morris implies, however, that the anger that Fiona expresses in response to the dilemmas she finds herself in is counterproductive. We see Fiona storm-ing away from her job as a waitress and later exiting abruptly in the middle of an exam for a class at the local community college, tearing up her paper angrily before she goes. Sometimes Fiona's tendency to throw up her hands and storm out is entirely justifiable; she recalls "quit[ting] in the middle of a wedding reception because [the caterer] kept screaming at his waitresses" (294). Hers is a defensible rebellion; but others, particularly her uncle, place Fiona in a psychic straitjacket precisely because this makes her more pliable in their hands.

Along with her refusal to be subsumed by inauthentic gender and cultural norms, there are many other positive aspects to Fiona's character, including her dogged persistence and her awareness that she is often the source of her own problems. She does not "make nice" or attempt to ac-commodate someone else's expectations of how a woman should behave. In particular, two telling statement reveal the depth of her self-awareness: "No matter how long or far she ran, she would always be trying to outdistance one person only—Fiona Range" (392); and, "what she hated most was her own weakness, her inability to see anything through to the end" (392). Her tendency to dwell on her failures is another flaw; Fiona is all too human, and therefore she develops into a largely sympathetic character.

Arguably the most disturbing female figure in the book is Elizabeth, in that she violates the integrity of others as much as she violates her own autonomy. Seemingly oblivious to how much their actions wound each other, both Elizabeth and Fiona seek reprisal in petty betrayals involving old boyfriends, but it is only Fiona who has matured enough by the novel's end to take responsibility for her actions. Exposed for the fraud she is, Elizabeth (described as a latter-day golden girl and shown in stark contrast to Fiona's darkly brooding [Irish?] self in both looks and attitude) behaves in too sanctimonious a fashion to be truly good, at least in everyone's eyes except those of her deluded parents. A whimpering mess, Elizabeth is re-duced to acting the part of a trapped female who cannot locate the means to free herself from the socially proscribed role of "the good girl," much like Arlene, her mother, who is the classic example of an enabler who would rather her family wear a sheen of hypocrisy than live in the harsh light of truth.

Not surprisingly, it is Fiona who takes the brunt of the family's criti-cism. Her Uncle Charles's condescending attitude toward her epitomizes the comments strong women like Fiona and Martha Horgan have to con-tinually contend with: "My mistake has been in continuing to deal with you and all your troubles as if they were the mishaps of a child. Always picking up the pieces and patching the holes. But you are a grown woman, and as such, the havoc you wreak is so serious . . . so continuous, that now I see you destroying people's very lives, and I can't continue on in the same way. I just can't!" (222). Like Martha before her, Fiona's behavior regularly puts her in situations in which she becomes captive to almost constant public scrutiny. Nevertheless, it is the judge's actions, not Fiona's, that have placed her in the position of having to reassemble the wreckage of her secret past.

One of the most compelling elements in the novel is its premise that Fiona does not just live in Dearborn—she *is* Dearborn. By the novel's conclusion we learn Fiona is both the judge's daughter *and* his niece; what is more, Charles could be said to be indirectly responsible for the murder of Fiona's mother, Natalie. For most of the novel, however, Fiona is not aware of this secret. Her constant denigration of her abilities and life choices can be traced to her insecurities about her parentage, as well as how she is perceived by others. She is branded by the community as a bastard both because of her lineage and behavior, which negates her ability to see herself positively. As the judge lectures a young alcoholic in his court about making bad choices in "a society of laws where order must prevail," Fiona thinks to herself, "If she closed her eyes, he might be speaking to her" (400). The character of Charles represents a variation of the Learesque patriarch who contorts himself into nightmarish proportions, all the while hiding behind the protection of his judicial robes. In exposing Charles and his behavior, Morris again deflates those characters who present themselves as something other than true selves and those norms that privilege wealth and social class above all else. After Fiona manages to find some happiness in her marriage to the boring but infinitely stable Rudy, she has the bittersweet satisfaction of seeing her uncle exposed as the person he has been all along: a desolate and bitter soul who has refused to acknowledge the extent of his hypocrisy. Of all of Morris's early protagonists, it may be Fiona who is most capable of remaking her life as a "bad girl" into something hopefully stronger and wiser the next time around.

From her days as a nascent writer who has found a way to come into her own, Morris deserves recognition as one of the most absorbing chroniclers of American life, Irish American or otherwise. Morris's real strength may be her ability to keep us absorbed in late-night reading rituals by transforming the age-old clichés of what used to be derisively referred to as "women's fiction" and imparting those clichés with new meaning. As a mark of her apparent humility, Morris describes herself as a rather cautious person, commenting in 1991 that she placed a quote from Flaubert over her writing desk to inspire her: "Be regular and orderly in your life, so that you may be violent and original in your work" (Weinraub). Of said caution, Morris notes: "It's the Irish in me . . . I didn't want to go too far out on a limb. It might break off" (Weinraub). As readers, we should be very glad she has not chosen to craft cautious novels.

Notes

1. One cannot help but think of the Gaelic phrase *"Deravaun Seraun,"* or "The end of pleasure is pain," that Eveline's mother utters on her deathbed in the eponymous tale from James Joyce's *Dubliners*. The latter schema is most apparent for the character of Marie in *Songs in Ordinary Time* and Fiona in *Fiona Range*, but it could equally apply to Martha's delicate predicament at the end of *A Dangerous Woman*. Indeed, Morris notes that *Fiona Range* involves "betrayal on every level" (Penguin, Reading Guide to *Fiona Range*).

2. As Roger Cohen notes, the New England settings in Morris's works are based on her childhood experiences in Rutland, Vermont, which Morris renames Atkinson; the wild country near Rutland becomes "the Flatts."

3. Regarding this point of repressed emotion, Maureen Dezell quotes several psychotherapists who work in the Irish American community, Bill Regan among them (Dezell 127). Both Dezell and Regan suggest the Irish and Irish Americans, like so many displaced cultures, experience great feeling all the while experiencing difficulty in expressing said feelings. This trait could be said to apply to several of Morris's characters, especially *Vanished*'s Aubrey Wallace, whom Posesorski describes as "almost choking with feeling."

4. The film version of *A Dangerous Woman* (released in 1993 with Debra Winger playing Martha) strays from the integrity of the text in several places. Most noticeable is the omission of the sexual assault scene with which the novel begins (a glaring omission indeed, since it describes Martha's situation as a mentally challenged person who finds that the world is unable to meet her on her own terms). The ending of the film also attempts to lighten the mood of the story, resulting in a less than faithful adaptation.

5. Like several other themes, the figure of a mother who worries that she has betrayed her children will be echoed in the absent parent Irene Talcott of Morris's *The Lost Mother*. We learn that Irene has been driven by a distant husband to seek factory work during the Depression. When nothing substantive materializes, Irene turns to prostitution to keep food on the table. This only becomes a conflict within

her value system when her two needy children show up on her doorstep, forcing her to acknowledge their presence to the community and her benefactor.

6. One concern some readers might have is whether Fiona develops believably as a complete character by the novel's conclusion. Arguably, the revelation of Fiona's parentage involves more than a bit of suspension of disbelief on the reader's part.

7. Morris's female protagonists do not embody the tenets of the first or second waves of feminism, in that most put their own needs last, in particular Marie and Alice Fermoyle and Elizabeth, Fiona's cousin. Conversely, those who do act according to their own desires do so in a self-defeating way (for example, Martha Horgan and Fiona Range). Nonetheless, as I have attempted to demonstrate, Martha and Fiona's actions and utterances often work to subvert fixed gender roles and behavior; in the process, Morris creates what might be called tableaus of anti-domesticity.

Works Cited

Carlson, Margaret. "Unloved Ones." *Time* 137. 4 (1991): 89.

Cohen, Roger. "Amid Serenity, Twisted Characters Are Born." *Seattle Post-Intelligencer* 9 Feb. 1991: C1.

Dezell, Maureen. *Irish Americans: Coming into Clover*. New York: Doubleday, 2000.

Edwardsen, Elizabeth. "Author Doesn't Want to Be Pegged." *Cleveland Plain Dealer* 23 Nov. 1995: 3 LL.

Fanning, Charles. *The Irish Voice in America: Irish American Fiction from the 1760s to the 1980s*. Lexington: University Press of Kentucky, 1990.

Gilbert, Matthew. "A First Novel Told in the Spirit of Dickens." *Boston Globe* 19 July 1988: 58.

Harkins, Susan Lynn. "Morris Again Looks in on the World of the Weak." *Orlando Sentinel* 3 Mar. 1991: F8.

Howard, Maureen. Foreward. *Cabbage and Bones: An Anthology of Irish American Women's Fiction*. Ed. Caledonia Kearns. New York: Henry Holt, 1997. xi–xiv.

"Mary McGarry Morris." Andover Authors. 20 Jul. 2003. 1 Aug. 2003 <http://www.mhl.org/community/authors.htm#mary>.

Mehren, Elizabeth. "What? A Nice Writer Like Her with These People?" *Los Angeles Times* 7 Mar. 1991: 1.

Morris, Mary McGarry. *A Dangerous Woman*. New York: Viking, 1991.

———. *Fiona Range*. New York: Viking, 2000.

———. *A Hole in the Universe*. New York: Viking, 2004.

———. *The Lost Mother*. New York: Viking, 2005.

———. *Songs in Ordinary Time*. New York: Penguin Books, 1995.

———. *Vanished*. New York: Viking, 1988.

Paley, Maggie. "Big Girls Don't Cry." *New York Times Book Review* 4 June 2000: 7, 16.

CHAPTER 9

Blurring Boundaries

Eileen Myles and the Irish American Identity

KATHLEEN ANN KREMINS

Charles Fanning's inclusion of Eileen Myles in his seminal *The Irish Voice in America* indicates his recognition of the evolution not only of Irish American realism but also Irish American identity. Much of twentieth-century Irish American writing reflects the dominance of realism and explains why Irish American fiction has both contributed to and dispelled historical and fictional stereotypes of the Irish (Conners 9). Contemporaries of Myles, such as Pete Hamill, Frank McCourt, and Alice McDermott, employ modernist conventions in their recollection of childhood, whereas Myles rejects linearity in narrative, closure, and "straight" realism. Myles writes from the disjointed time of memory, a place that lacks closure (and even defies it at times), thus injecting a suspicion of nostalgia while inhabiting a reality often altered by alcohol and/or drugs. Whether Myles is postmodern is not the focus of this chapter (although it bears deeper conversation). Rather, this chapter focuses on how Myles views "Irish American" as one of her identities and how those identities merge and conform to six thematic domains of the Irish American female writer.

Eileen Myles's Irish American world is Boston (especially the areas of Arlington, Somerville, and Cambridge) in the 1950s through early 1970s. It is a world dominated by Irish democratic politicians and Irish-Catholic mayors: John B. Hynes, John F. Collins, and Kevin H. White. Yet by the mid-1960s, the insular world of Irish-Catholic Boston began to change. City government and white ethnic neighborhoods engaged in a power struggle, while black residents grew increasingly discontented (O'Connor 239). As Myles explains, "My town's identity was in flux when I was growing up, but there were still plenty of ye olde elements that added texture to our play" (*Cool for You* 31). The Myles family represents the second and third generation's attempts to deal with the breakdown of the strict boundaries of ethnic communities, the shifting line between the working and middle classes, the shocking move into mixed ethnic and religious marriages, as well as new opportunities in higher education and white-collar work. Granted, the Catholic Church and schools provided some element of stability in this "mixed" Polish-Irish family, not poor yet not rich; it encouraged education as a means of social mobility, as it had done since the late nineteenth century.

For Eileen Myles, education and reading led to a poet's life and a fictional style that defies categorization. Both of her novels, *Chelsea Girls* and *Cool for You*, blend fiction, memoir, autobiography, and prose poetry. The hybrid style of Myles's works melds with the subtextual layer of shifting identities, a new type of migrating. Rather than moving to another country, Eileen Myles and her family contend with the movement from one social and/or economic level to another. Her father holds a coveted government job—he is a postman—and her mother is a secretary for a toy company. Because of her father's alcoholism, however, the social shift is never smooth, and the money earned is not necessarily applied toward the family's advancement. For the Myles family, social identity vacillates between middle and lower class, despite the white-collar positions of Myles's parents.

Identity also raises issues pertaining to gender, race, and sex—taboo topics in many previous works of Irish American fiction. Myles reveals the turbulent period following World War II when the values of the Irish-Catholic community came into question. Not only does she address the ever-present condition of the "single" Irish American woman (either unmarried, widowed, or "abandoned") but also the racial tensions in Boston:

that apocryphal host of Cambridge ministers who ran little churches on the side streets of Central Square, down by Western Ave, where you weren't supposed to go if you were white—which was a pity because there were plenty of big cheap apartments down there. . . . And I would drive slow through all those special streets, with tons of kids, and hair stores and jazz clubs and crane my white neck all I liked. It was the unwealthy side of the river. (*Cool for You* 21)

Most significantly, Myles explores the previously avoided topics of sexuality and sexual identity, including her own lesbianism. In an Irish-Catholic community, sex was fraught with anxiety and doubt, often devoid of romanticism, and associated with evil; Myles calls it "the obscenity of dating. . . . Though my mother was Polish, the feeling was Irish. I guess it was just Catholic" (*Cool for You* 95). By writing of her own sexual identity, Myles not only confronts the homophobia inherent in the Irish-Catholic community; she also adds new layers of "exile" and "otherness" to the themes of Irish American literature.

By placing Eileen Myles the character—in exile and an "other"—in conversation with common themes in the writing of Irish American women, Eileen Myles the author establishes herself as an Irish American writer. In *Cabbage and Bones,* Caledonia Kearns identifies six themes common to the fiction of Irish American women: levity, nostalgia for childhood, origins of identity, irony, mother as center of the family, disappointing fathers, and Catholicism as an underlying reference. To some extent and with slight variations and additions, Myles includes all of these themes; however, she interweaves them into the fabric of class. These themes and variations are further transfigured by Myles's use of a transgressive narrative, for her works resist convention both in style and subject. As "novels" of transgression, *Chelsea Girls* and *Cool for You* re-imagine the contemporary Irish American experience as "exiled" or "outsider."

In a self-protective gesture, Myles's humor tends toward self-deprecation. She mocks herself before anyone else gets the chance. While she is the main "character" of her works, she often writes about "Eileen" from the distance of authorial perspective, allowing for an intimate objectivity:

Times had changed, however, and so had the definition of cool. Now it was something collegiate, or that was one of the available fashion strains. The widest possible explanation of this look was that you had money. Those who were best at the look did have money, or were thieves. You learned to steal topcoats out of J. Press in Harvard Square, Filene's in Belmont or Anne Taylor's or Casual Corners if you were a girl. I was and I stole. But stealing's another topic and we'll get to that later. (*Chelsea Girls* 84)

Simultaneously, Myles uses the ironic tone of the author and the mocking voice of the character to admit she has succumbed to "coolness." She invites the reader to see one's own self in Eileen without judging either the character or oneself.

Although memories of childhood in Arlington battle memories of young adulthood in New York City, neither pattern of memory can be classified as nostalgic. Any longing for the past seems to rest solely on the loss of a loved one rather than a desire to return "home." Moreover, it is apparent that the paradox of memory envelops the loss of her father, the pain of the moment wrapped in the joy of other moments. In *Chelsea Girls* Myles describes the different kinds of darkness found in her house growing up. Yet a loving portrait of her father emerges in her mind, just as Eileen Myles enters each day.

> The darkest parts of my house were the stairs. You had to come down so the day could begin. My father went to work very early. He was a mailman. Weekends, however, he would hold court in the parlor. Atmosphere would be pumped out on 78s all day. Nelson Eddy and Jeanette MacDonald, Bing. Danny Kaye singing those boisterous, eerie tunes: Oh Thumbaleena don't be dumb-tum, tum, tum. My mother's participation in the weekend music festival was evidence that they loved each other. The occasional dance through the house, my mother's sighs at the appropriate song, as she worked. That this was going on all the time was a fact of life and the weekend, like my Dad. (*Chelsea Girls* 198)

Such remembered moments of domestic bliss are few, however.

Most often in both novels Myles's mother represents authority and distance, although in the above quote the light is clear enough that even her mother receives positive attention. At times it appears as if Myles uses her mother's lack of a mother as an excuse for that distance: "We weren't poor, but I felt that the way to be closest to my mother was to get a job, to do anything to support myself, because now that I was half an orphan, I was more like her" (*Cool for You* 33). Still, Myles dwells in ambiguity. Her relationship with her mother carries with it a deep associative love connected with abandonment and a lack of trust, fueled by issues of authority and power. Myles is aware that perception in the present and memories of the past are often prone to the whims of imagination: "Because she was always angry and he was always sad it's easy to think of my mother as mean in those days" (*Chelsea Girls* 204). In addition, the ambiguous nature of Myles's relationship with her mother rests on the way time manipulates the mind, giving clarity to what was unclear and blurring the boundaries of reality. Her mother's presence—"My mother is still alive" (*Cool for You* 196)—also makes telling the truth a dangerous task.

Myles's father, on the other hand, who died when she was eleven, exists more firmly in the world of memory: "My father wasn't like a parent. He was like an older brother. Kind of, when he was good. . . . At home some nights it was hard to tell if he was good or bad" (*Chelsea Girls* 205). Myles accepts her father's alcoholism, in part because that was all she knew but also because he was a "better" alcoholic than the other fathers she knew:

> Mr. Dolan was something sick. You knew that. Then he was something angry. He was red. Then he was gone. He was a scary-looking man. He was an alcoholic. The bad kind. My father was an alcoholic too but he was more of a sad one, a lamb not a red frightening guy like Mr. Dolan. Whose first name I never learned. He was almost gone as soon as I saw him. The Dolans got separated. It was a Catholic divorce. Things were that bad. (*Chelsea Girls* 174)

Myles portrays two kinds of Irish alcoholic fathers: the warm, gregarious drunk and the violent madman. She also comments on the permanence of Irish Catholic marriages, at least in name only. Therefore, the Dolans' separation, or "Catholic divorce," underscores the abusiveness of their family life.

Often Myles's tone is ironic rather than tragic. Perhaps that is why, as with so many other Irish American writers, the pathos in her work is tempered by her appreciation of life's ironies. For example, Myles understands that, unfortunately, alcoholism is part of her culture: "It's called alcoholism. It runs in my family. We have a genetic disposition towards it and depression. . . . In Arlington the whole town was drunk. It was the only dry town in the state of Massachusetts. So it was one nice thing a drunk could do for his family, buy a house in Arlington" (*Cool for You* 151–52). Irony leaves room for humor and fond reflection on the past. Tragedy oppresses and suppresses humor, which may explain why irony is so often the tone of choice for Irish American writers. Irony recognizes sadness and invites sympathy, but it does not impose itself on the reader as tragedy does. Therefore, Myles is not compelled to see her father as a tragic hero, thereby avoiding any sense of the judgment inherent in tragedy.

The final two themes identified by Kearns—Catholicism as an underlying reference and origins of identity—play prominent roles in *Chelsea Girls* and *Cool for You*; however, Catholicism is more of an institution than a faith, while identity as an Irish-Catholic American woman features the additional dimension of lesbianism. Once the community center of urban ethnic Catholic neighborhoods, the Catholic Church of the 1950s and 1960s experienced a period of transition reflecting the changing socioeconomic dynamics of the period:

> We were border-line working class/middle class. Our school was confused, being merely Catholic, not being utterly elite, but enough wealthy families allowed their children to attend Arlington Catholic because it was a new high school built with the funds from St. Agnes parish, so it behooved the parents who attended the church and had supported it for decades to send their children to this basically free private school. There were poor kids in Arlington Catholic as well. I think in our circle I was the poorest. But I was smart and was very well aquainted with music and was funny. (*Cool for You* 73)

For Myles, the Catholic Church and parochial school were associated with fear. "I went to Catholic schools and it had not so much marked me for life as marked life itself with funny, holy and evil pictures. I was scared then, and I'm still scared now, but I'm flashing these pictures to you" (*Cool for You* 9). In some way fear also becomes associated with her mother, while her belief in God provides the same protection as her father had:

> I was not a bad kid. I always pushed it, but not so far. I had a deal with God. If I failed to do my homework, in the absent-minded way, I wouldn't get caught. If I skipped it on purpose, watching teevee, I would get nailed. God protected my spaciness and innocence. We had an understanding that things would essentially go my way if I was generally good. God was fair, God cut me a margin of error. I was safe. Bad kids got caught. I could never afford to get caught. It was sad in

my house with my father being dead, and my mother now so totally alone, again, after her enormously sad childhood. Also I must admit there was some lingering mystery around his death, his strange fall off the roof. Sometimes I wonder if she killed him, and maybe she would kill me too. I was afraid of her. (*Cool for You* 153)

In a sense, God allows Myles to keep her father alive: "To be real. My father wasn't dead. That's an important thing about that time. The energy was higher in my world, in my life" (*Chelsea Girls* 172). Without her father, God functions *in loco parentis*, and faith becomes the words of gentle guidance on the path to goodness for the adolescent Myles.

The formation of identity, of one's own history, rests at the boundaries of class, ethnicity, and sex. Myles explores how "the child of culture is also culture's victim" (Casey 171). In her reminiscence of the rapidly changing Arlington neighborhood, Myles investigates what Charles Fanning calls "ethnicity as liberating doubleness" (371)—a view of ethnic otherness not as destructive self-estrangement but as creative expansion of possibility. Myles's New England world of the 1950s and 1960s shifts to a suburban world where ethnicity loses ground to class. Eventually, her liberating doubleness has more to do with sexuality than ethnicity or class. It is in the investigation of her grandmother Nellie's life that Myles fears she will find her own reflection, but instead she discovers a window into a world that helps her better understand herself.

In her earlier book, *Chelsea Girls*, Myles spends significant space discussing her father's alcoholism and sadness. As in so many other Irish American novels, she suggests the children are responsible for their father's behavior:

We always thought it was because we had been born. It is our fault. There's a picture of me and Terry in those Pilgrim stocks—you know, heads and wrists poking through holes. It was some day we went to Plymouth or Salem. My father's standing behind us. We're laughing, he looks worse, a prisoner. All the pictures look like that after a point. Me and Terry goofing around in front of an old car, my father in the square of the driver's seat, looking sad, looking trapped. (213–14)

In *Cool for You*, however, which opens in a mental hospital where Myles is working, she begins to explore the connection between alcohol and depression that runs through her family.

Nellie Myles, her paternal grandmother, spent the last seventeen years of her life in a mental institution, Westborough State Hospital. While her father's death provides the narrative link in *Chelsea Girls*, in *Cool for You* her grandmother's institutionalization unites the narrative. "It seems people go nuts from a number of things: being too smart or someone being gone. My father's mother went crazy because her daughter died" (27). In *Erin's Daughters in America* Hasia Diner notes the high rate of hospitalization for insanity for immigrant women in the nineteenth century; even as late as 1908, the Irish made up the largest group of foreign-born in insane asylums (110–11). "On Nellie's death certificate, as well as stating that she had an enlarged heart; it says that she was depressed" (*Cool for You* 151). Ironically, Myles learns about her grandmother and family from the documents and records of the state.

While both books provide a look into the Irish American urban structure of postwar America, the story Myles collates of her grandmother's experience describes immigration at the turn of the century. Born Nellie Riordan in 1880 in County Cork, Ireland, Myles's grandmother came to Boston in 1900 and married her grandfather, Terrance Myles, in 1908. The reports Myles finds concerning her grandmother repeatedly mention that she is older than her husband: "It's an important fact, low-value wife, a worker and a breeder. She was cleaning houses all those years. Between immigration and marriage" (*Cool for You* 143). In many ways, including employment, age, and marriage, her grandmother's life epitomizes the Irish American woman's experience in the nineteenth and early twentieth centuries. Myles provides some commentary on the political causes for massive Irish immigration and blames England's lack of a response to the famines[1]: "I guess I just want to say that Nellie probably came here and cleaned the houses of the relatives of the same people who drove her out of her home, who took all the food except the potatoes, which were rotting that year. Teeth lost: 32" (*Cool for You* 144).

As O'Connor notes in *The Boston Irish*, by the late 1940s and early 1950s many of the old-time neighborhoods had lost their ethnic distinctiveness (216). By the 1950s the Irish immigrants had begun to enter the economic mainstream, even though this move threatened their ethnicity and sense of group unity (Takaki 163). Ted Myles worked as a mailman and his wife worked as a secretary at a toy store. Ted was Irish and his wife was Polish. They lived, as Myles puts it, "in a public school neighborhood. They had stupid and strange beliefs in God" (*Cool for You* 113).

Just as Myles's mother's work as a secretary signaled a rise in status and higher pay for the immigrant woman, Nellie's job as a domestic reflected the propensity for Irish women who immigrated for economic reasons to work in domestic service, earn good wages, and postpone marriage (Diner 90–91). For Eileen Myles, understanding Nellie provides both a window and mirror to understanding herself: "My grandmother and my father were both surrounded by a magic feeling" (*Cool for You* 27). The window provides her with a view of a world of gender, class, and sexuality that she would transgress; the mirror reflects the creativity she would cultivate.

Cool for You is a much more accomplished work than *Chelsea Girls*. As a first novel *Chelsea Girls* is an experiment in form that is more disjointed and vague than necessary. It does introduce Myles's subject matter and themes, however, most of which she deals with in a more detailed and skilled fashion in *Cool for You*.[2]

In an interview in *Provincetown Arts*, Myles discusses her character "Eileen Myles" and the autobiographical elements of her work: Arlington, alcoholism, New York City, Irish Catholic, and lesbianism: "They seem part and parcel with why I write. Writing is just making a mark. It's your mortality, your need to exist. It's probably totally linked to feeling endangered. Arlington, lesbian, et cetera—I'm just constructing a monument to those things" (Richards 29). For Myles, as for many Irish American writers, the autobiographical nature of her work allows her to continue to reinvent the novel form: "There's a tremendous challenge, to take that whole sea of familiar details and make them flow and shift. How can you keep renewing the autobiographical impulse. I'm completely in love with doing that. It seems so dangerous" (Richards 29). Luckily, for her and for us, the novel form gives Eileen Myles the writer permission to continue to reinvent herself.

Notes

1. Myles mentions a catastrophic famine in Ireland in 1900. I have not been able to locate any information on such a famine. It is possible that Myles superimposed the Great Famine of 1847 on the plight and flight of her grandmother from Ireland in 1900.

2. In a number of interviews Myles mentions that she is working on two novels. She makes no mention, however, if she will continue with her previous themes. She does note that her main character will still be "Eileen Myles."

Works Cited

Casey, Daniel J. "Heresy in the Holy Diocese of Brooklyn: An Unholy Trinity." *Irish-American Fiction*. Ed. Daniel J. Casey and Robert E. Rhodes. New York: AMS Press, 1979. 153–72.

Conners, Margaret E. "Historical and Fictional Stereotypes of the Irish." *Irish-American Fiction*. Ed. Daniel J. Casey and Robert E. Rhodes. New York: AMS Press, 1979. 1–12.

Diner, Hasia R. *Erin's Daughters in America: Irish Immigrant Women in the Nineteenth Century*. Baltimore, MD: Johns Hopkins University Press, 1983.

Fanning, Charles. *The Irish Voice in America: 250 Years of Irish-American Fiction*. Kentucky: University Press of Kentucky, 2000.

Kearns, Caledonia, ed. *Cabbage and Bones: An Anthology of Irish-American Fiction*. New York: Henry Holt, 1997.

Myles, Eileen. *Chelsea Girls*. Santa Rosa, CA: Black Sparrow Press, 1994.

———. *Cool for You*. New York: Soft Skull Press, 2000.

O'Connor, Thomas H. *The Boston Irish: A Political History*. Boston: Northeastern University Press, 1995.

Richards, Frances. "Never Real, Always True: An Interview with Eileen Myles." *Provincetown Arts* (2000/01): 24–39.

Takaki, Ronald. *A Different Mirror: A History of Multicultural America*. New York: Little, Brown, 1993.

FEMINISM, CULTURE, AND CRITIQUE

CHAPTER 10

The World of Mary Gordon

Writing from the "Other Side"

SUSANNA HOENESS-KRUPSAW

Among Irish and Irish Americans the "other side" denotes America, the land of plenty on the other side of the Atlantic. It is a place many imbue with dreams and desires, while others associate it with an escape from the persecutions and suffering of their forebears. For those who crossed to the other side, the experience often proved a mixed blessing. Success stories were common, but they occurred at the high cost of cultural assimilation and loss of heritage (Casey and Rhodes 266, 267). Moreover, the immigrant experience positioned the Irish American author—whose native language is English but whose cultural and political affinity rests with those who have historically been oppressed by the English—both inside and outside the mainstream of American life. As Miller and Wagner explain, feelings of alienation among immigrants are not uncommon when emigration from one's homeland is seen as a kind of exile or banishment (17). Thus, the term the "other side" acquires yet another meaning that meshes well with the "doubleness" that scholars have observed in the works of various contemporary Irish American authors (Fanning 358). The literary world of Mary Gordon illustrates well all of these concepts of otherness.

Initially, Mary Gordon's short stories and novels emphasized the plight of Irish American immigrants and the effect of a Catholic upbringing on immigrant women's experience of guilt and shame. Her later works embrace what Casey and Rhodes have called "an intellectualized Catholicism" (272).[1] Gordon's most recent works, however, display the author's increasing interest in connections between literature and art—influenced, as we shall see, by her Catholic upbringing—and between place and identity. Other recurring themes include father-daughter and priest-parishioner relationships, which are related to the master-servant issues in other Irish American fiction, and troubled mother-daughter relationships, echoing the Irish preoccupation with the matriarch. Obviously, Mary Gordon's interests vary widely, and critics have tried to categorize her variously as an Irish American, moral, Catholic, and feminist writer. Although she rejects such labels (Bennett, *Mary Gordon* 1), Gordon's major themes position her firmly within the Irish American literary tradition.

Mary Catherine Gordon, née Davis, was born in Far Rockaway, New York, on December 8, 1949. Her mother, Anna Gagliano, a legal secretary, was the daughter of Italian and Irish immigrants; her father, David Gordon, was a Polish Jew who had converted to Roman Catholicism before his marriage and turned virulently anti-Semitic. A failed writer, he taught his daughter to read when she was only three years old and inspired in her a love of books. After her father's death of a heart attack in 1957, Gordon grew up at her maternal grandmother's house in the working-class neighborhood of Valley Stream on Long Island, New York. It is precisely because of her multiethnic background that Gordon considers herself somewhat of a hybrid, an outsider who writes from the "other side."

Gordon was educated at various parochial schools and entered Barnard College on a scholarship. In 1973 she earned a master's degree in English and creative writing at Syracuse University with a thesis consisting of a collection of poetry. She also began a dissertation on Virginia Woolf. Over the years, Gordon has received many honors: *Final Payments*, one of the *New York Times* outstanding books of 1978, was nominated for the National Book Critics Circle Award; *Men and Angels* received a Literary Lion of the New Public Library Award in 1985; and Gordon was awarded a Guggenheim Fellowship in 1993. Gordon teaches creative writing at Barnard College, where she is the Millicent C. MacIntosh Professor of Writing. Together with her second husband, Arthur Cash, biographer of Laurence Sterne and professor of English at the State University of New York at New Paltz, she resides in Manhattan. They have one daughter, Anna Gordon Cash (born in 1980), and one son, David Dess Gordon Cash (born in 1983).[2]

Although Gordon planned to become a poet, her literary breakthrough occurred after she became a fiction writer; the publication of *Final Payments* in 1978 constituted her first publishing success. This story of a young Irish American woman who needs to rebuild her life after the death of her father, for whom she had cared for many years, underwent multiple drafts. Critic Alma Bennett reports that Gordon eventually changed the narrative point of view from third to first person, a step suggested by her friend and mentor, Elizabeth Hardwick, at Barnard College. The novel's success resulted in a paperback contract with Ballantine. In 1979 it sold 1.25 million copies (Bennett, *Mary Gordon* 11).

This first novel demonstrates several of the criteria Charles Fanning's seminal work, *The Irish Voice in America*, posits as characteristic of contemporary Irish American works: like other domestic novels, it focuses on one character's private life and familial realm, explores the father-daughter relationship, examines the effects of the tradition of a daughter's self-immolation in service to a widowed parent, and looks at the priest-parishioner relationship as a means of redemption (Fanning 328). Plagued by feelings of guilt for not having loved her father enough or perhaps indirectly causing his death, Isabel Moore has built for herself the cocoon of the saintly good girl, which excludes her from sex and other pleasures. Her only contact with real life is her two friends, Liz and Eleanor: one, a withdrawn, artiste divorcée, the other a strong-willed, married lesbian whose husband Isabel has a brief affair with after her father's death. Although highly acclaimed, the novel suffers from minor stylistic weaknesses. Like the protagonist whose ruminations prevent her from taking action, the novel itself never seems to take off and finally arrives at a somewhat unsatisfactory ending when, after conferring with her priest and family friend, Isabel rejects her inheritance and guilt in order to begin a new life with the help of her friends.

Perhaps because of this novel's somewhat stifling setting, Charles Fanning singles out *Final Payments* from other Irish American domestic novels that are "fueled by personal rage and bitterness" for its "movement . . . from a caricatured constriction to an exaggerated escape into the open air" (329) and accuses Gordon of anti-Irish bias. Yet neither in her fiction nor in her essays and interviews has Gordon ever revealed the personal vendetta against the Irish that Fanning suspects. On the contrary, he seems to overlook her respect for her parents, referred to admiringly as "immigrant survivors" in an interview with Patrick Samway (97).

Gordon is keenly aware of the hardships many immigrants overcame and points out that to evade discrimination, immigrants created their own secluded world marked by sexual Puritanism—a potentially limiting environment for budding writers. Gordon credits her father's influence— Jewish scholarship and a broader worldview—with giving her the tools for breaking out of this impasse. Nonetheless, she affirms her Irish American identity and, in an interview with Deiter Keyishian, notes the strong storytellers on her mother's side of the family (63). Indeed, reminiscing about her uncle, Gordon writes, "the Irish-American experience has fed me because my uncle could have thriven [sic] in no soil but the Irish-American. And someone needs to tell about him" ("I Can't Stand Your Books" 218).

Final Payments' Irish American characters foreshadow another important element in Gordon's early publications, in which her major characters, whether orthodox or lapsed, are Catholic. Because of this preoccupation, Gordon has been called a Catholic writer and her works compared to Mary Renault, Mary McCarthy, and Flannery O'Connor. As is the case for many other Irish Americans, Catholicism has, indeed, been a formative influence for Gordon; in fact, she still defines herself as a Catholic ("For One Catholic"). In her novels readers find references to the strengths of a Catholic upbringing, such as the sense of community, distinct values, and strength of convictions that mark Isabel in *Final Payments* and Felicitas in *The Company of Women*. At the same time, examples of religion gone awry abound. Readers may recall Laura's pettiness in *Men and Angels* or the picketing scene in *Spending*. Gordon considers growing up Catholic in a largely Protestant environment an asset: "One of the greatest treasures a novelist can have is a secret world which he or she can open up to his or her readers" ("Getting Here," 34). At the same time, she feels that being a Catholic with Jewish roots has given her an edge, which critic Deiter Keyishian describes as "like you're crossing over to another island" (69).

Many of Gordon's fictional characters struggle with the tenets of their Catholic upbringing. In *Final Payments* Isabel clearly suffers from a "good girl" complex that makes her reticent to step into the world and live her life more fully. Raised, like Gordon herself, on stories of martyrs and their sacrifices, Isabel prefers that people view her in that saintly light rather than as human and sinful. This novel in particular grapples with concepts important to a Catholic woman like Isabel, such as love, charity, and generosity. Gordon has pointed out that she considers generosity the most significant attribute a person can possess because without it love is not possible (Millhaven 52)—a trait manifested in Isabel's parting gift to her nemesis and former housekeeper, Margaret.

Gordon credits the success of *Final Payments* to her ability to afford readers an inside view of Catholic life in America, a world they were curious about yet had rarely read about (Keyishian 69). Catholicism gave her "a rubric," a ready-made "template" from which she could write (Bennett, *Conversations* 123–24). It also gave readers unfamiliar with this aspect of American life a glimpse of the "other side." Gordon believes that Catholicism in America is equivalent to Irish Catholicism ("Getting Here," 47). When Catholic issues are under discussion and the media need a speaker or commentator, she is frequently called upon to voice her opinion: she has criticized the pope's stance on various issues as well as Mel Gibson's film *The Passion of the Christ* ("For One Catholic").

The rituals with which Gordon grew up also left their mark on her dualistic thinking, which, she says, she struggles against and attributes to being Irish and intellectually situated both within and without Christianity (Bennett, *Conversations* viii). In fact, many of her characters struggle with different aspects of their identities, whether it is their Catholic beliefs or their Irish American background. Perhaps one consequence of this struggle is that Gordon cannot merely embrace one position but must explore issues from various points of view.

While Charles Fanning has criticized Gordon's unsympathetic depiction of Irish Americans in *Final Payments* and *The Other Side*—which he argues contain "stereotyping generalities about working-class Catholics" (330)—her stance could also be said to reflect the doubleness of her broadened perspective. The "doubleness" mentioned by critics exists both in Gordon's heritage and in her writing; thus, it manifests itself in characters for whom immigration involves hopes and dreams on the one hand but loss of home and heritage on the other. Fully aware of the "partiality of our knowing" (Samway 102), Gordon realizes the impossibility of ever seeing the whole picture; therefore, she attempts to illuminate the human condition from multiple viewpoints. This technique also helps her transcend an either/or approach to important questions (Gross 176).

This effort is apparent in Gordon's second novel, *The Company of Women* (1981)—initially titled "Fields of Force"—which she dedicated to her mother. This novel introduces several interesting characters, extending the maternal theme to an entire group of caring women. Charlotte, Clare, Muriel, and Mary Rose cluster around a priest, Father Cyprian, and have arranged their otherwise man-less lives to meet his needs. The atmosphere of this work resembles a Roman Catholic Barbara Pym novel with the same emphasis on "excellent women." Felicitas, Charlotte's daughter, is Father Cyprian's special concern. As she grows up, however, she realizes his narrow-mindedness and resents his impositions upon her. Her rebellion against Cyprian consists of a brief fling with an equally paternalistic university professor. Only after the birth of her own daughter is Felicitas strong enough to revisit and come to terms with her past.

Gordon's early novels paint careful pictures of the narrowly defined and closed circles of Irish Catholic life in the United States. In *The Company of Women* the women's outlook is proscribed by their faith, which both sustains and stifles them. The narrative makes it clear that the four women, three of whom come from a working-class background, find their intellectual and spiritual fulfillment through the retreats regularly organized by Father Cyprian. He is shown to be a loving and careful mentor of the young Felicitas (a portrait that perhaps balances the allegedly stereotypical depiction of the priest in *Final Payments*); at the same time, however, his conservative values and refusal to accept change sabotage the girl's healthy mental development and burden her with feelings of guilt and worthlessness. As before, Gordon refuses to see just one angle of Catholicism and emphasizes the difficult duality of the women's faith.

Since both of these novels emphasize the female characters' spiritual lives, Isabel and Felicitas appear inert, as though their biology (in a Freudian sense) had condemned them to being passive vessels that await being (ful)-filled by active male characters. The self-absorbed narrators seem to ruminate endlessly about traditional notions of shame and guilt and how they might liberate themselves and achieve wholeness and fulfillment. The Catholic belief in fate and the American belief in free will and personal independence clash in Gordon's works, as they do in other novels by Irish American writers (Dezell 69).

In both *Final Payments* and *The Company of Women* Gordon explores the lives of Irish American characters. In *Final Payments* the neighborhood in which Isabel grew up is marked by immigrant elements. Together with her girlfriends, she reminisces about their parochial schooling. Vivid descriptive elements include ethnic characteristics, such as Eleanor's mouth, described as "another kind of Irish trick, brimming with mockeries as her eyes flicked up and down, scanning for foolishness like radar" (9). In contrast, the neighborhood in which the much-abhorred Margaret Casey lives has an unattractive Polish priest named Pilkowsi and a grocery store called Baumgartner's where Isabel does not shop because the owner is Jewish (264–65).

Similar ethnic references occur in *The Company of Women*. Mary Rose's good friend Joe Siegel, whom she eventually marries, is Jewish. Mary Rose always takes Felicitas out to lunch at Schrafft's, for she "liked to be loyal because Schrafft's had always hired Irish girls just over from the other side" (131). When Felicitas speaks with Professor Gifford, she regards her beauty in the manner "thought of as belonging only to Protestants" (135). Gordon appears to be keenly aware that her own multiethnic background enables her to shed light on various angles of the "other side."

While *The Company of Women* gave Gordon a chance to develop her narrative technique by exploring the life of more than one female character, in *The Other Side* (1989) she honed this approach in an even more disjunctive fashion by exploring the consciousness of several members of one Irish American family. Gordon's most Irish novel to date, *The Other Side* investigates the fate of several generations of an Irish immigrant family. To do so, she relied on various historical sources about immigration. From their arrival in the United States at the beginning of this century, the members of the MacNamara family entertain high hopes for a more successful life in America, the "other side" of the novel's title. On the day that serves as the focal point of the novel, as the family gathers around the ailing matriarch, Ellen, they reminisce about their family's collective history.

Somewhat self-consciously, this novel employs many of the ingredients Charles Fanning and others have identified as typical of the Irish American literary tradition: a preoccupation with death, fate, the family, and domesticity; themes surrounding the home and the Irish American matriarch; and the pervasiveness of the past in the present. As in Elizabeth Cullinan's *House of Gold,* the novel's setting occurs shortly before the death of Ellen MacNamara when nearly all the members of her family have arrived for this premature wake. Each family member, in turn, reflects on his or her relationship with this headstrong woman who nurtured some and neglected others. In Ellen's own memory looms the large house that her father built for her mother, who went insane after several miscarriages. As the reader gains insight into the thoughts of each character, none ponder the future but all weigh the significance of past events (a danger pointed out in the novels of Maureen Howard). Given this array of traditional Irish American themes, it is somewhat surprising that Fanning dismisses this novel's "skewed perspective" (330).

Fanning's approach, delineated in the introductory chapter to *The Irish Voice in America,* harbors its own risk of bias. Excluding the comic depictions of the "state Irishman" and "the melancholy poetic figure of the suffering exile" (4), Fanning appears to favor the version of the Irish American experience he finds best exemplified in the works of James T. Farrell, to whom he dedicates an entire chapter. We must recognize, however, that Fanning's approach to the Irish American experience bespeaks his own perceptions. Moreover, while acknowledging late-twentieth-century changes in Irish American life and society, Fanning's comprehensive study seeks common rather than divergent patterns—that is, the traits that endure (312) rather than those that cease or deviate.

Shaun O'Connell, reviewing recent works dealing with Irish American issues, comments on Gordon's "striking bitterness" and dismisses *The Other Side* as a "thesis of Irish-American failure in a novel that thwarts all joy" (257). Like Fanning, O'Connell mistakes Gordon's depiction of one family's dramatic situation for a prescriptive documentation of Irish American life. This perception seems as misguided as arguing that all Irish American families must take the same journey into night as Eugene O'Neill's Tyrone family. Gordon's novel (like Mary McCarthy's work, which Fanning also dismisses) merely illustrates the ideas of one Irish American woman writer who does not completely or comfortably fit into his categories. Rather than "skewed," Gordon's approach could be viewed as liberating, for she employs traditional fictional elements to new effects that eventually broaden the parameters of the traditional Irish American novel.

While traditional Irish American novels often investigate the success stories of the newly arrived poor immigrants who eventually rise to middle-class prosperity, *The Other Side* broadens this perspective by introducing Ellen as a well-to-do person who flees not poverty but bleak family circumstances. Gordon actually debunks some Irish American stereotypes by depicting a middle-class Ellen, who, upon her arrival in America, follows the customary career of going into service, always aware, however, that her social position in Ireland ranked above that of her employers. Her strong sense of justice leads Ellen into politics and union activism. Her husband

Vincent corresponds more firmly to the classical Irish stereotype since he comes from a poor farming background in County Cork. With few exceptions, the MacNamaras' children and grandchildren live the American dream of success, particularly Ellen's beloved grandchildren Cam and Dan, who thrive as lawyers.

The immigrant experience lends itself to explorations of such political issues as social class and prejudice. In an article about "composite" ethnicity, June Dwyer comments on the dangers to identity encountered by the immigrant characters in *Temporary Shelter* and discusses Gordon as an author critical of the experience of assimilation into mainstream culture. By depicting Irish American characters who do not live the American dream, perhaps failing so badly in this country that they must return to Ireland, Gordon (like Frank McCourt) actually investigates the "other side" of the more popular immigrant success story.

The MacNamaras evince the political awareness and class-consciousness found in other pieces by Gordon manifesting the constraints of growing up in a working-class environment. In *The Company of Women*, when Robert Cavendish describes Charlotte as "a real peasant," Felicitas immediately becomes defensive and says, "That's right, Robert. My grandfather would have been plowing your grandfather's fields" (178). She clearly identifies with the working class while everything Robert does exudes privilege: "There was nothing second-rate about his knowledge, it was not scratched from the hard earth of immigrant labor" (100). Similarly, despite his business success, Joseph Kasperman cannot dispel the shame of his servant-class upbringing and always remembers in his dealings with Maria that her father was his mother's employer (*Pearl* 256).

Motherhood and maturity as a writer may have helped Gordon break out of customary narrative patterns and embark on a new branch of storytelling—what Fanning refers to as the "stylized novel" (313). Yet her more recent works continue to include modified elements of Irish American fiction. She still investigates religious and spiritual elements of human existence while examining the plight of motherhood and the complexities of domestic life. By exploring an area of modern life that often remains hidden or silenced, Gordon has found yet another element of the "other side" to investigate.

In *Men and Angels* (1985) Gordon returns to a smaller cast of more subtly developed characters. She maintains her previous approach of alternating chapters, each dedicated to the investigation of one of the protagonists. Immigrant and specifically Catholic concerns do not figure overtly in this novel; however, the story of Laura Post, a young, neglected, and unloved woman who deems herself an angel after finding religion, introduces matters of spirituality and otherness. Conflict arises when Laura becomes the nanny of Anne Foster's children. Anne is an art historian who enjoys sensual experiences such as art, food, friendships, love, and motherhood. She is only too human, deeming herself unworthy of the love and admiration of others, yet she emerges as the true angel of the story. Based on the life of Mary Cassatt and correspondence between Cassatt and Paula Modersohn-Becker, the novel deftly explores the motivations of great artists and the personal obstacles—especially for mothers with young children—that interfere with the creation of masterpieces.

Gordon takes the concept of domesticity in the Irish American novel to the next level by not merely describing a matriarch but carefully investigating several aspects of maternity. Critic Suzanne Juhasz discusses at length the various maternal subjectivities developed in this novel and has nothing but praise for Gordon's accomplishment. Frequently silenced in the past, the maternal narrative is fully realized here as Gordon introduces several good and bad mother figures and even allows for a mother's artistic expression.

In *Spending* (1998), somewhat irreverently subtitled "A Utopian Divertimiento," Gordon again explores the realm of women and art. She returns to a limited cast of characters, focusing on Monica Szabo, a painter whose relationships have failed. Her daughters have left home, and she prefers to live alone until she encounters her "muse." Bernard, who at first remains an unnamed benefactor, permits the woman artist all the advantages that in the past only wealthy men possessed. This plot development allows Gordon to explore matters of money and power. As expected, the woman, devoid of all distractions and money problems, suddenly thrives as never before; meanwhile, her wealthy partner, who now spends his time caring for her, encounters financial (and sexual) difficulties. Such reversals of traditional gender roles offer Gordon yet another "other side" to explore.

As if this interesting premise were not enough, Gordon pursues a provocative artistic theme in this novel, inspired by Leo Steinberg's classic 1983 study, *On the Sexuality of Christ in Renaissance Art and Modern Oblivion* (Schuessler). Monica's paintings suggest that the many striking Renaissance and Baroque paintings of the crucifixion could actually show Christ in sexual poses after orgasm. The subsequent outrage that Monica encounters from the religious right permits Gordon once again to ponder the philosophical and political questions in which she previously expressed an interest. At the end of the novel, both male and female characters find themselves in a stable, egalitarian relationship that offers a deep sense of sexual fulfillment.

In many ways *Spending* is a traditional romance novel, featuring various loving couples and their stories. For Gordon, who always likes to look at things from a new perspective, operating within this genre, which is considered less reputable by many writers, means using it for her own purposes and infusing it with philosophical and artistic investigations that provide the novel with considerable depth. On the one hand, she plays on the many associations with the word "spending," as in Bernie's spending money on Monica, expending or spending emotions on another person, and being spent after orgasm. On the other hand, the "divertimiento" playfully contemplates the still utopian "other side" of the woman artist inspired by a male muse and supported by a wealthy patron. Moreover, Gordon ventures into territory rarely seen in women's fiction: she vividly details a fervent sexual relationship in which the older, mature woman takes the initiative.

Power issues in *Spending* are informed by subtly invoked Lacanian elements. When Monica gives an interview to a reporter from the *Village Voice*, Gordon has her reject its implications because Monica does not like the critical jargon. Nonetheless, having introduced this well-known terminology and dismissed it, Gordon plays with and cleverly applies concepts of the gaze throughout the novel. Monica revels in her awareness that she is the one exerting power by gazing at the male subject. Sex in front of a bathroom mirror gives her a disembodied sensation of being someone else who is performing—but for her own eyes. This experience leads her to ask "At what moment the visible became nothing, did I pass through the visible to pure sensation?" (176). The question of how existence is established through someone else's perceptions recurs when Monica and Peggy visit the Russian baths, a scene that vividly illustrates how men look differently at women: "But this was different. This was a woman's world. A world in which the nakedness of bodies was not about being seen, but about the body's own well-being. The nakedness of women, removed from the pleasure of men" (276). Here, Gordon permits her readers a glimpse of female otherness.

The examination of power-driven relationships between men and women in *Spending* echoes Gordon's early novels featuring priests and women who submit to religious doctrine and family dynamics that "entrap" people. While conforming to the social expectations of women, Isabel, Felicitas, and Anne also attempt to define themselves through their actions. This theme also finds resonance in Gordon's partly autobiographical explorations of father-daughter and mother-daughter relationships. Because her early novels focused on the lives of women, male characters were less vividly drawn. Since the publication of *Spending*, however, Gordon has tried to create more appealing and well-rounded men in her fiction. In "The Translator's Husband" she adopts a male point of view, whereas "Raising Sons" comments on the importance of providing appropriate guidance for boys so that they grow up into well-adjusted men.

Although Irish ethnicity is not a concern in *Spending*, it appears that, having explored her Irish heritage in her early works, Gordon continues to investigate the immigrant theme through the introduction of other ethnicities—Monica Szabo is Hungarian—and to investigate other elements of her own ethnic heritage—Monica's lover is Jewish. This approach attests to the flexibility and viability of contemporary Irish American writing. As noted elsewhere, the Irish have long lived in diasporic communities; consequently, Irish literature partakes of the diversity and globalism that we appreciate in contemporary writing (O'Connell 251). A similar pattern may be discerned in the short stories and novellas that Gordon has published in various journals and magazines, some of which have been collected in two volumes titled *Temporary Shelter* (1987) and *The Rest of Life* (1993).

The title story in *The Rest of Life* is particularly impressive. The interweaving of past, present, and place demonstrates the author's awareness of the past's persistence in the present, which connects her with other Irish American authors (Fanning 313). Gordon's own Italian background on her mother's side may have spurred some curiosity about Italian immigrant characters. "The Rest of Life" revisits the troubles of Paola, an Italian immigrant woman who has borne feelings of guilt all her life until she revisits the places of her youth together with her son and future daughter-in-law. She finally realizes that she is not to blame for the suicide of her youthful lover and manages to emerge from the paralyzing silence that has enveloped her all her life. In "Death in Naples" Lorna is also of Italian descent. Her return to Italy with her son and daughter-in-law is less successful than Paola's, however, because she keeps thinking of her deceased husband, and all the places she visits remind her of him. Guilt, lack of voice, and a haunting sense of the past craft these travelogues into a new hybrid Italian-Irish-American fiction.

In *The Shadow Man* (1996), dedicated to Aunt Hattie and Aunt Rose, the paternal aunts she never knew, Gordon struggles with an entirely new genre as well as the legacy of her parents. As she points out in the foreword, the work is part biography and part memoir, but it eludes categorization. Because her father, a published writer and editor, had been so instrumental, despite his early death, in determining Gordon's values and worldview, she finally decided to deal with persistent questions about him. She always said, "His death was the most important thing that could be known about me" (38). Gordon tries not only to come to terms with her memories of her father but also with her uncertainties about her Jewishness; she has "the desire of origins" (197). As she discovers her roots in a Yiddish-speaking family from Vilna and her father's real identity as Israel Gordon, she probes her feelings as an outsider: "I have never felt really American, or assumed that my parents were. Americans were Protestants and we were not" (113). With this, her position on the "other side" finally crystallizes. When her research yields more and more evidence of her father's attempt to "pass" by espousing fascist ideas, Gordon desperately clings to the positive aspects of his legacy.

Because of her interest in women of faith, critic Deiter Keyishian terms Gordon "a secular nun" (64). One of the elements of Roman Catholicism that continues to intrigue her is the church's ability, despite its patriarchal hierarchy, to offer women not only opportunities to serve but also role models of women in positions of power (Millhaven 46). Gordon credits the lives of nuns and other high-ranking women in the church for providing important role models that helped shape her brand of feminism, which she describes as a form of justice (Wachtel 88). Perhaps this fascination with influential Catholic women and "an image of an alternate female world that often had to trick the male world" ("Getting Here" 43) moved Gordon to write *Joan of Arc* in 2000.

Like her biographical piece about Joan of Arc, Gordon's novel, *Seeing Through Places* (2000), reflects a shift in focus from the mysterious father figure of *Shadow Man* to the world of her foremothers. In addition to a powerful attachment to matriarchs, a strong sense of place connects Gordon once more to her Irish heritage. This collection of eight nonfiction essays is "about the places that shaped her sensibility" (Mudge). As Gordon herself points out, they are hastily written impressions, not quite characteristic of an otherwise meticulous stylist. "My Grandmother's House" establishes a link to Gordon's Irish family by examining her grandmother's adherence to Old World customs that wracked her family with guilt. Gordon argues that in this case, the large family does not constitute a strong support system; rather, it stifles individuality. "Girl Child in a Women's World" gives voice to the narrator's feelings of exclusion and superiority when she is left in the care of her neighbor, Mrs. Kirk, a sentiment reinforced by the physical act of violation experienced in "The Country Next Door."

In "Places of Play" Gordon illustrates the difficulty of being the only child of serious older parents. The little girl becomes so absorbed in a world of fiction, saints' lives, and fairy tales that she prefers creating a make-believe world to spending time at a summer camp. "The Architecture of a Life with Priests" explores her parents' courtship and her own interest in priests as perfect men. She remembers wearing her communion dress and reflects on her outsider situation as the child of an intellectual Jewish father in a largely Italian and Irish working-class neighborhood. "The Room in the World" allows Gordon to ponder her misgivings about her own good fortune, while "Boulevards of the Imagination" depicts the role of a Barnard education in helping her transcend the limitations of her upbringing. In a BookPage interview with Alden Mudge, Gordon reveals that "the metaphor of place" mattered so much to her that she "'wanted to meditate on a place being at the center of a consciousness.'" Therefore, she arranged her book like a journey that is physically short but psychologically deep.

Gordon's most recent novel, *Pearl* (2005), takes the reader on a journey to Ireland, but without the sentimental nostalgia one might expect from the more traditional Irish American sense of home described by scholars Kerby Miller and Paul Wagner (125). While the Dublin setting suggests Gordon's return to her Irish heritage, in reality it enlarges her philosophical and religious interests and her explorations of mother-daughter relationships. None of the major characters in this novel have any Irish roots; nevertheless, the cast of characters reaffirms Gordon's interest in the immigrant's hybrid experience. Maria Meyers's father (much like Gordon's) is a Jewish immigrant who converted to Roman Catholicism, while her friend Joseph Kasperman descends from Polish immigrants. Maria's daughter, Pearl, was fathered by a Cambodian doctor. Through family connections and business travel, Joseph and Pearl embody contemporary transnational individuals who inhabit a liminal space unbounded by national borders. It is only Pearl's desire to study the Irish language that causes her travel to Ireland.

Pearl not only extends Mary Gordon's interest in the outsider experience but also broadens her interest in all things Catholic. Although Maria has rejected her Catholic upbringing and stashed away her copy of *Lives of the Saints*, her daughter chooses the path of the religious martyr. Gordon describes Pearl's self-starvation and meditations as luminously as she did the life of Joan of Arc. In fact, Maria, Pearl, and Joseph are deeply preoccupied with staples of Irish American fiction—the themes of sin, guilt, and redemption. Maria experiences pangs of guilt after refusing to reconcile with her estranged father; Pearl shoulders responsibility for the pain of the world and accepts punishment for her lack of charity, seeking redemption though her choice of self-starvation; Joseph feels guilty for not having loved his wife enough and encouraging her estrangement from her Orthodox Jewish family.

While Gordon's past novels, such as *The Other Side* and *The Company of Women*, featured young characters such as Cam and Felicitas who suffer under the repressive rule of the Irish matriarch, *Pearl* represents the maternal perspective more sympathetically. With the Cambodian father conveniently removed through Pol Pot's atrocities, the novel focuses prominently on an intense mother-daughter relationship. Even though Maria realizes the dangers of this close bond, she cannot contain her maternal desire to shelter and protect her child. When Pearl seeks to escape her mother's controlling love by going to Dublin, Pearl nearly perishes. In detailing Pearl's recovery, Gordon seems to confirm Maria's position as correct.

Despite the large number of Irish characters in this novel, the Irish setting remains largely undeveloped. Pearl's friendship with Finbar and his Irish Republican Army (IRA) cronies gives Gordon the opportunity to survey and interpret contemporary Irish politics; however, in comparison to the American transnationals, the Irish remain one-dimensional. Maria's hotel room is as bland and uninspiring as the restaurant food she orders, and Joseph's promenade in the rainy city fails to yield the artistic treasures he finds in Rome. Pearl's acquaintance with Finbar leads to a somewhat unconventional romance and to the young woman's encounter with Irish politics after four hundred years of British colonization. As Gordon parallels Maria's reflections on her own political awakening during the 1960s with Pearl's feeble attempts at making sense of the Troubles, Finbar's— and by extension, all IRA—activities seem rather misguided. The character of Mick Winthrop, an American who vacations in Ireland and supports the IRA, reveals Gordon's attitudes. She characterizes him so negatively that she obviously rejects his naïve and arrogant stance. The death of his son Stevie Donegan after a foolish ploy instigated by his friends fleshes out what Maria and Pearl perceive as the Irish politics of death. Stevie's mother Breeda's pathetic life, stuck in her apartment in front of the television, functions as Gordon's version of Joyce's Irish paralysis.

Pearl's love of languages and her desire to learn Gaelic is reminiscent of Felicitas's excellence in the study of Latin and Greek. One is reminded here of Fanning's observation that the Irish exhibit a love of language (280), a trait Gordon and her characters seem to have inherited. The years of training as a poet certainly manifest themselves in Gordon's lyrical style. Early influences identified by Gordon include Virginia Woolf, Elizabeth Bowen, and Margaret Drabble (Bennett, Mary Gordon 10). Gordon herself has said that Woolf's "rhythms of those . . . incredible sentences—the repetitions, the caesuras, the potent colons, semicolons" (Bennett, Mary Gordon 10) proved significant models for her own writing. In a biographical profile in Ploughshares, Don Lee explains that by copying passages from Woolf's work onto index cards for future use in her dissertation, Gordon assimilated Woolf's prose style. Gordon also claims that it was Woolf's work that allowed her to make the transition from poetry to prose by showing her that prose could possess "poetic and imagistic intensity" (Lee). Other influences include Edith Wharton and Flannery O'Connor. In Good Boys and Dead Girls (1992) Gordon lauds Edith Wharton's technical perfection and hails Flannery O'Connor's work for its "dimension of transcendence that distinguishes it from most contemporary writing" (43).

Such early influences may help explain why postmodern literary experimentation bores Gordon (Cooper-Clark 12). In her view, meaning and message have been abandoned by many contemporary writers for self-reflective experimentation; in fact, she rejects this postmodern trend and is equally critical of minimalists such as Ann Beattie and Raymond Carver (Keyishian 66). Like other writers of Irish descent, Gordon views herself as a realist storyteller. Her aesthetics are simple: she considers the novel a thing of beauty. Exposure to Catholicism's liturgical elements shaped her aesthetics ("Getting Here," 27) and intense formalism (Lee), while her desire for clarity and precision may have been gleaned from medieval scholasticism (Bennett, Conversations viii). In this way, Gordon's artistic achievement parallels that of Monica Szabo in Spending: "In a time of postmodern ironic emptiness, this painter dares to combine wit and feeling, a line that takes its clarity from the Renaissance masters and its intelligence from the feminist revelations of the seventies" (176).

While she aims for formal literary perfection, Gordon maintains a casual relationship with her readers, interspersing her prose with the humor and satire characterizing Irish writing (Casey and Rhodes 273). Monica Szabo's final remarks in *Spending*—"I know you understand. If you didn't understand, there'd be no reason for me to have been talking to you all this time" (301)—illustrate Gordon's typical approach; that is, a first-person narrator who reminisces and shares her life story informally with the reader.

In an interview with Deiter Keyishian, Gordon said that she feels free to write more autobiographically and personally in her essays than she does in her novels (59). This liberty is apparent when she explores issues of Irish American identity. In "I Can't Stand Your Books," for instance, Gordon takes the occasion of her uncle's funeral, at which other relatives found it appropriate to insult her books, as a starting point for a thesis regarding the lack of Irish American writers. She posits that years of colonization have turned the Irish into an oppressed people who like storytelling (Wachtel 85) but will employ cunning to protect their well-guarded secrets. She blames the paucity of Irish American writers on the immigrants' effort to achieve financial success by more commercial means than writing creatively.

In her novels and short stories Gordon does not deny her interest in philosophical and theological questions; her characters are slow to take decisive actions and tend to ruminate and ponder means of overcoming obstacles or subverting encrusted social structures. In the fictional world created by Gordon, we are allowed to see "the other side" while her protagonists struggle toward enlightenment. At the same time, her literary universe embraces many of the themes and ideas we have come to expect from novels by Irish American authors. Using this approach, Mary Gordon has simultaneously expanded the canon while reminding us once again that "these traits endure."

Notes

1. Casey and Rhodes use this phrase in reference to Flannery O'Connor, but their description seems to fit Mary Gordon equally well: "The Irish American quality of her work is sublimated—it is *felt* rather than stated, expressed as an intellectualized Catholicism rather than an Irish consciousness" (272).

2. Biographical data collated from Mary Gordon's *Shadow Man* and Alma Bennett's *Mary Gordon*.

Works Cited

Bennett, Alma, ed. *Conversations with Mary Gordon.* Jackson: University Press of Mississippi, 2002.

———. *Mary Gordon.* New York: Twayne, 1996.

Casey, Daniel J., and Robert E. Rhodes. "Irish-American Literature." *New Immigrant Literature in the United States: A Sourcebook to Our Multicultural Literary Heritage.* Ed. Alpana Sharma Knippling. Westport, CN: Greenwood, 1996. 265–80.

Cooper-Clark, Diana. "An Interview with Mary Gordon." *Conversations with Mary Gordon.* Ed. Alma Bennett. Jackson: University Press of Mississippi, 2002. 9–19.

Dezell, Maureen. *Irish America: Coming into Clover.* New York: Doubleday, 2000.

Dwyer, June. "Unappealing Ethnicity Meets Unwelcoming America: Immigrant Self-Fashioning in Mary Gordon's *Temporary Shelter.*" *Melus* 22.3 (Fall 97): 103–12.

Fanning, Charles. *The Irish Voice in America: 250 Years of Irish-American Fiction.* 2nd ed. Lexington: University Press of Kentucky, 2000.

Gordon, Mary. *The Company of Women.* New York: Random House, 1980.

———. "Death in Naples." *Salmagundi* 137/138 (Winter 2003): 99–119. 30 Sept. 2003 <http://www.proquest.com>.

———. *Final Payments.* New York: Random House, 1978.

———. "Getting Here from There." *Spiritual Quests: The Art and Craft of Religious Writing.* Ed. William Zinsser. Boston: Houghton Mifflin, 1988. 25–53.

———. "For One Catholic, 'Passion' Skews the Meaning of the Crucifixion." *New York Times* 28 Feb. 2004: Section B, 1, 7. 18 May 2004 <http://web.lexis-nexis.com>.

———. *Good Boys and Bad Girls.* New York: Penguin Books, 1992.

———. "I Can't Stand Your Books: A Writer Goes Home." *Visions of America: Personal Narratives from the Promised Land.* Ed. Wesley Brown and Amy Ling. New York: Persea Books, 1993. 212–18.

———. *Joan of Arc.* Penguin Lives. New York: Viking, 2000.

———. *Men and Angels.* New York : Random House, 1985.

———. *The Other Side.* New York: Viking, 1989.

———. *Pearl.* New York: Pantheon, 2005.

———. "Raising Sons." *Ms.* 12.2 (Spring 2002): 89–92. 27 Aug. 2003 <http://www.epscohost.com>.

———. *The Rest of Life: Three Novellas.* New York: Viking, 1993.

———. *Seeing Through Places: Reflections on Geography and Identity.* New York: Scribner, 2000.

———. *The Shadow Man: A Daughter's Search for Her Father.* New York: Random House, 1996.

———. *Spending: A Utopian Divertimiento.* New York: Scribner, 1998.

———. *Temporary Shelter.* New York: Random House, 1987.

———. "The Translator's Husband." *Ms.* 12.4 (Winter 2002): 86–87. 7 Oct. 2003 <http://www.epscohost.com>.

Gross, Terry. "Review of *Spending.*" *Conversations with Mary Gordon.* Ed. Alma Bennett. Jackson: University Press of Mississippi, 2002. 174–80.

Juhasz, Suzanne. "Mother-Writing and the Narrative of Maternal Subjectivity." *Studies in Gender and Sexuality* 4.4 (2003): 395–425.

Keyishian, Deiter. "Radical Damage: An Interview with Mary Gordon." *Conversations with Mary Gordon.* Ed. Alma Bennett. Jackson: University Press of Mississippi, 2002. 57–70.

Lee, Don. "About Mary Gordon." *Ploughshares* (Fall 1997). 2 Feb. 1999 <http://www.emerson.edu/ploughshares/Fall1997/Gordon.profile.html>.

Miller, Kerby, and Paul Wagner. *Out of Ireland: The Story of the Irish Emigration to America.* Washington, DC: Eliott and Clark, 1994.

Millhaven, Annie Lally. "Mary Gordon." *Conversations with Mary Gordon.* Ed. Alma Bennett. Jackson: University Press of Mississippi, 2002. 42–56.

Mudge, Alden. "A Sense of Place: Looking into the Life of Mary Gordon." *First Person Book Page.* January 2000. 10 Sept. 2003 <http://www.bookpage.com/0001bp/mary_gordon.html>.

O'Connell, Shaun. "That Much Credit: Irish-American Identity and Writing." *Massachusetts Review* 44.1/2 (2003): 251–68.

Samway, Patrick. "An Interview with Mary Gordon." *Conversations with Mary Gordon.* Ed. Alma Bennett. Jackson: University Press of Mississippi, 2002. 97–103.

Schuessler, Jennifer. "Mary Gordon: Confessions of a Good Girl." *Publishers Weekly* 9 March 1998: 45–46. 10 Sept. 2003 <http://www.proquest.com>.

Wachtel, Eleanor. "Mary Gordon." *Conversations with Mary Gordon.* Ed. Alma Bennett. Jackson: University Press of Mississippi, 2002. 81–89.

CHAPTER 11

Jean McGarry

Sojourners Between Dreams and Realities

AMY LEE

Jean McGarry is a professor of fiction in the Writing Seminars at Johns Hopkins University. To date she has published six volumes: four collections of short stories and two novels. Brought up in an Irish Catholic community in Providence, Rhode Island (she was born on June 18, 1952), McGarry frequently builds her characters and their background around this familiar community. Both of her novels focus on the experience of a female character who grows up in a working-class community such as that in Rhode Island and who later moves to a large city for work despite discouragement from her immediate family and friends. Instead of enjoying a feeling of achievement in their migration to American cities, McGarry's protagonists find settling in the new environment impossible, for memories of their hometown cannot help them overcome the blazing loneliness they feel in the city. Their subsequent return to their hometown, however, not bring a sense of consolation, for homecoming means a return to the unchanging problems and concerns of working-class people in a persistently grey and uncompromising environment.

Most of the characters in McGarry's stories are leading unsatisfactory lives; the unfolding of the narratives is very often the characters' slow realization of the inadequacy of their lives or an unrewarding attempt to contain or go beyond this unhappy state of affairs. It would be unfair, however, to see McGarry's characters and stories as representations of typical Irish American lives in contemporary society. While McGarry uses "Irishness" frequently via family origins, names, habits, and values, what she has essentially portrayed amidst this setting of Irishness are more inclusive issues of intimate personal problems relevant to ordinary people in their daily lives. The domestic landscape, so much a center of her narratives, is not just the habitat of one single Irish American family but rather a general landscape of all families in contemporary society eaten up by the same problems of isolation, loss, and emptiness.

Trapped between the public world of mundane life and the private world of frustration, these people, although bearing names that show an Irish ancestry, represent all people marginalized by the gap between their expectations of life and their loneliness, which may or may not specifically result from their cultural identities. These people, having grown up in American society, are "homeless" because they cannot understand their experience in a world that does not care enough to make them feel at home. The bright young people who go from their humble small towns to big cities feel shattered by the cold indifference facing them in their new environment, and when they seek consolation from home, they are either misunderstood or seen as traitors to their own community. Similarly, men and women who live and work in their hometowns find no consolation in the familiarity and are often threatened by disappointments.

Small problems in the banal, unchanging daily routines accumulate and form vast pictures of unbearable tediousness in McGarry's works. Rather than say that the works of Irish American McGarry represent the Irish voice in contemporary literature, it would be more appropriate to say that her family and cultural background put her in a position to understand one of the reasons for the immense sense of loneliness human beings feel in our multicultural and multinational communities today. Irishness is part of the small town domesticity from which many of her characters emerge; the separateness inherent to their cultural identity adds to their sense of isolation when they try desperately to seek confirmation from their fellow beings. In this chapter I examine the common settings and recurring themes in Jean McGarry's short stories and novels. I then focus on her re- cent publications for a more detailed discussion of individual pieces and an examination of how they speak about the common human condition through the voices of the younger generations of Irish Americans.

McGarry's first collection, *Airs of Providence* (1985), is set in the town whose name ironically means fate and provisions from God. This fifteen- story collection starts with a deathwatch on a Halloween night, when death is so thick in the air that even the overabundance of sweets cannot wipe away the obsession. The collection contains two series of stories; eight por- tray residents of Providence during the 1950s and 1960s — people who are dead, dying, sick, and hoping and planning to die, as seen through the eyes of young people. The other seven stories describe the life of April and Mar- garet Flanaghan, who spend their childhood trying to live a normal life in Providence amidst the harsh demands of the nuns at the school, surrounded by relatives they fail to understand, and wading through the local gossip.

Credited with "stunning emotional accuracies" (Rev. of *Airs of Provi- dence*) the stories describe Margaret, who finds life undesirable in Provi- dence because its day-to-day normalcy consists of reruns of TV programs, late afternoon confessions, potatoes to peel for the family dinner, and avoid- ing nosy family and relatives. Among these boring and repetitive events, however, the sisters' attempts to lead a normal life by doing their home- work, baby-sitting, and going to the prom fail to protect them from the almost destructive realities of their lives, such as a sarcastic mother and a fa- ther whose mood swings occur without warning. Growing up is an adven- turous enough journey in the best environments; growing up in this Irish Catholic community in Providence means being dragged in all directions, leaving the sisters exhausted and unsure of to whom or where to turn. The indistinguishable Irish families — the Feeneys, Dooleys, Mahoneys, and McGoverns — form in particular a backdrop of stagnant provincial life.

McGarry's detailed depiction of the triviality and banality of life in Providence demonstrates her careful observation of the harshness and crudity of daily life. Richard Orodenker compliments McGarry's ability to translate experience into words; he points specifically to moments in which characters' feelings are enlarged through the events they experi- ence, writing that "in fiction, details must get bigger in extraordinary ways" (31–32). McGarry achieves the identification of a cultural and social ‵cape that harbors enormous possibilities for the exploration of the experience.

McGarry's second book, *The Very Rich Hours* (1987), lies somewhere between a novel and a collection of short stories. In its layout the book is a continuous unfolding of eight units—a prologue and seven chapters. The prologue acts as a guide to the reader by claiming a similarity between the following chapters and the medieval book of hours, *Les Tres riches Heures du duc de Berry.* While the medieval book of hours was used as a prayer book and a holy calendar in keeping the hours of the monastic day with its eight parts, McGarry's fictional version features a record, in eight parts, of the life of a soul—a beginner—entering the world. Each chapter begins with a short piece of prose not directly linked to the text that acts as a miniature narrative to highlight the significance of the portion of Anne Marie Kane's life recorded in the following chapter, just as the illuminations in the book of hours are supposed to enhance and decorate the content.

The chapter titles—"Black-Letter Vulgate," "The Workhouse," "Seven Last Words," "Dream Date," "Four Things," "Solitaire," "I Meet the Family and Show My Mettle," and "The Beating"—together weave a composite picture of the formative years of Anne Marie Kane's life. Anne was a student at a Catholic women's college in Boston and Cambridge during the early 1970s. As she matures physically and intellectually, she moves farther away from her lower-middle-class family and provincial friends in Providence and finds herself isolated in the middle of an intellectual and emotional void. Every step she advances, either intellectually or emotionally, takes her further from those around her. Whatever progress she makes is accompanied by her realization of more faults and shallowness in her fellow companions. Girls at the Catholic college are boy-chasers; students at Harvard are obsessive narcissists. Her yearning for life is not fulfilled even in her post-college career and her marriage, and we see the end of the narrative marking possibly the beginning of a series of exit points in her life journey.

The Very Rich Hours is indeed rich in terms of its composition. Although it is not a complete picture of Anne's life from beginning to end, a sense of completeness emerges from the complex layering of her memories and experiences from different periods of her life. Lyons sees this work as a *bildungsroman*—"a coming of age fiction told in a cycle of interrelated stories" (84)—for Anne's youth, her years in college, and her married life are all knitted together in a complex and overlapping space of time. Indeed, her discomfort when studying at the Catholic college is only a precursor for her sense of isolation and mismatch at Radcliffe, where she finds herself surrounded by pampered girls from rich backgrounds. Anne's career in a mental hospital is in many ways a continuation of her university days, when she saw a psychiatrist every day for hours. Each new stage of her life is a reentering of the world, and each time she feels disappointed because of her failure to belong and be satisfied. At the end of the narrative, Anne's "first getaway" seems to promise a new beginning.

The Courage of Girls (1992) is McGarry's first full-length novel. Once more she bases her narrative on the centrality of memory and isolation. Loretta Costello is a native of Providence, Rhode Island, living with her working-class parents. Loretta does not have an idyllic childhood, but as an only child she often misses her mother's companionship. When a tragic accident kills her parents, she goes to live with her relatives, the Gillis family. Her parents' death brings not only the end of her childhood but more importantly, the end of her sense of security. With the loss of her rightful home, she no longer belongs anywhere; she finds herself unable to feel emotionally connected to people around her.

During her high school years she meets Daniel St. Cyr, a philosophy student studying Kant. Eventually they marry and live together in a flat in Greenwich Village, where Loretta starts sketching under the influence of a friend who is an art student. Art becomes her connection to the world, but it is a connection at a distance, for the more she observes the more she feels unable to identify with her surroundings. This intense observation of the world isolates Loretta from her husband and leads to the deterioration of their marriage. A subsequent miscarriage and the resulting depression force her to leave her newly established home with Daniel and return to her hometown to recuperate. The narrative's conclusion does not indicate whether Loretta's problems are resolved, but the centrality of memory in this narrative suggests that the loss of a sense of comfort and security early in her life is not redeemable.

A review of the novel in Kirkus Review states that it contains considerable charm and the wit of Mary McCarthy. Other critics commend McGarry on her careful depiction of Loretta's complicated mental journeys. Sally Eckhoff writes in the Village Voice that one falls in love with Loretta when "she's watching the blue cat on her fire escape" and starts to "hate everybody who hurts her." In Loretta, McGarry creates a keen-eyed girl who wins readers' sympathy through her wonderfully brave observations and her ability to receive attention from other people. Jan Blodgett of Library Journal considers the novel a story of "courage found," writing that "this well-crafted work should appeal to readers of serious fiction." Loretta's ability to overcome her undesirable reality by creating a future out of memories once again reminds us of McGarry's recurrent theme of the interaction between one's past and present.

Home at Last (1994), McGarry's next collection of short stories, looks at the various meanings of coming home. The twelve stories portray people who are homeless in different senses. Although most of the characters are residents of Rhode Island, this Catholic community cannot provide them with the security of feeling at home, especially when returning is closely followed by leaving again. Even with the presence of familiar things such as cities, local streets, hospitals, amusement parks, and well-known consumer products, this local gathering of Irish Americans does not make an ideal home for its characters in either the public or private domains. What strikes the reader is the emotional drain and identity void facing characters of different ages.

True to the name of the collection, "home" is the center of the stories. A ten-year-old boy, Jimmy McGinnis, has the haunting experience of seeing his father fall off the local Westminster Building and having to call the operator to inform his family. His father's inability to cope with the demands of career and home deprives the boy of his home and shatters his wife's sense of domestic security. McGarry's attention to detail here creates a special "feminine" sensitivity. In "The Sacrifice" Anne Angell, a mature woman living with her middle-aged unwed daughter, has to face daily challenges from her friends and daughter to her sense of security. After an unsatisfactory marriage, during which her home was just a place to do housework, Anne looks forward to life with her daughter as compensation. But domestic insecurity has affected not only the mother but the daughter as well. Sharing the same roof does not mean sharing a home; both mother and daughter become deeply frustrated by their lack of communication, which intensifies their feelings of homelessness.

In this collection children, teenagers, young people, and the old are all described within their domestic environment, yet this environment—which is supposed to be their safest abode—provides neither comfort nor confidence. The number of deaths contained in the stories cannot help but challenge the meaning of home and domesticity. By baring the deficient emotional and spiritual lives these characters endure, the stories invite not only attention and sympathy—factors contributing to the quality of life—but also engage readers with the courage and toughness with which some of

the characters battle their undesirable conditions. Bracing against the circumstances of their lives, the characters may be able to pierce through the
darkness of homelessness and march toward light through their endurance.

Gallagher's Travels (1997) is McGarry's second novel. Once again she
sets the story in a small Irish Catholic community, Wampanoag, Rhode Island, in the early 1970s. The protagonist, Catherine Gallagher, is a college
graduate originating from this small community. Eager to bid farewell to her
protected college years, where her most professional piece of work is the
thesis "Crazy Eights: The Mid-Career of Federico Fellini," Catherine joins a
local paper, the Wampanoag Times. To her dismay, she is put to work on the
women's page, where her daily work centers on fashion, weddings, births,
recipes, and other domestic concerns. Even in a small local newspaper such
as the Wampanoag Times, she has a glimpse of the politics involved in professional work, which she finds very disappointing.

Catherine's chance to show her journalistic potential comes when the
city editor "borrows" her to write a few feature articles. These articles outrage the local residents, including her parents, but the attention she captures gives her a sense of real work and success. Not long after, urged by
her mentor and lover, she applies for a job at Michigan Depointe Bullet, a
much more successful paper. After a trial period she is finally hired, but she
is again disillusioned to find herself working in the entertainment section
rather than hard news. Together with her disappointment in work, Gallagher has to deal with advances from different men, leaving her exhausted
and disturbed.

The 1970s was a time when newspapers, like many other industries,
entered a period of dramatic change because of the changes in the mode
of production. One of the challenges both Gallagher and news reporting
had to face during this time is the full automation of the process of production; the older ideals and ethics related to news reporting are either
considered inefficient or downright valueless in the face of this new tech-
nological advancement. With the changing face of reporting, personali-
ties involved in the profession also undergo a major transformation. Old
hands, such as Gallagher's mentor, feel so disillusioned that they quit; others become totally detached. Even Gallagher, newer to the industry, feels
that the passion of reporting has died in the new system introduced by the
new technology.

Although Gallagher's Travels portrays the last days of an ideal and a
passion and includes a number of disillusioned characters, it does not

exclude the possibility of change. Unhappy with her work, Gallagher manages to make a few waves and impact the local people and her newspaper cronies. The awareness with which people in the profession receive the changes makes their life a bitter but hopeful battle. Viewed as a part of McGarry's *oeuvre*, this picture of life in Wampanoag informs a recurrent theme of characters' struggles to create a sense of belonging and rootedness. Whether it is domestic life, career life, or love life, McGarry consistently reveals the dismal reality in a relatively light-hearted manner.

Dream Date (2002), McGarry's latest collection, continues previous themes and breaks new ground stylistically. The volume is a collection of thirteen short stories divided into two sections—"His" and "Hers"—seemingly featuring romantic dreams by men and women, respectively. In McGarry's own words, "The book is about prospects for men and women in a postdivorce era" (McGarry, "Time Out"). While the stories in the two sections are oriented toward either sex, the dreams are not entirely romantic in the strictest sense of the word. Rather, this is a collection of stories about people who dream in various ways and at various levels. Linda Simon divides the stories into three categories: "anxiety," "temptations," and "inner landscape." In these stories dreams are given a central position because they are the space in which the characters seek to hide or express their feelings about life.

Juxtaposed with McGarry's previous fictional work, *Dream Date* is different from her other works in that the stories do not take place in a specific setting. The usual Irish Catholic community forming the background of the protagonists' lives does not exert a significant presence. Characters bear no distinctive features to reveal their cultural backgrounds. Readers who regard McGarry as one of the representative contemporary Irish American voices might feel her work is moving away from such a direction. Interestingly, however, the emphasis on dreams and dreaming not only retains McGarry's concerns with cultural and national identity but also extends these concerns from a particular group of people to the human condition in general.

In her review of the collection Linda Simon suggests that the title can be understood in a number of ways, one of which is "a time for dreaming" (234). It is useful to look at the stories as a series of dream narratives concerning characters who are somehow entwined in the grip of a dream, willingly or not willingly, in order to approach or to avoid something outside of the dream world. "Dream date" may refer to an ideal companion, but it may also refer to a date with dreams, for some of the characters find their realities so unbearable that they yearn for a date with a dream to escape. Yet other characters find themselves so lost in the middle of non-being that they have difficulty identifying themselves and their location. Whether desirable as alternative worlds or as empty vessels providing no foothold, dreams become a common language shared by these lonely individuals.

A need for recognition is one of the main concerns in the stories, especially in the "His" section. In "Among the Philistines" Alex Morgan obviously needs more to have a meaningful life than what his students in an evening literature class can provide. Although he was a promising scholar in his youth, at middle age he has become a "shallow scholar, not important, a mean person, trying to get hold of somebody to become important" (20). This somebody is Professor LeDuc, who is about to retire and needs to bequeath his research projects and funds to someone in the same field— a successor. In this sense, what Alex is seeking can be simply described as an acquired ownership of "the old greatness that had been American classics" (20), a position that automatically gives him the right to belong to a specific community. To acquire his right to belong, he is willing to sell not only ideas he borrowed from his evening students but also his wife.

Morgan wants to belong to an elite academic group whose names are big enough to go down in literary history. Other male characters in the collection share a similar kind of yearning. Both LaSalle of "The Thin Man" and George McCoy in "The Secret of His Sleep" have gone through a fantastic journey of waking up from a special dream. Although their experiences are very different in material, the results are similar: both feel that they have been accepted into a new identity—manhood. Dreams in their experience are not the fulfillment of their wishes but rather nightmares that immobilize and prevent them from becoming the type of person into which they desire to develop.

In LaSalle's case he realizes he has to become his father, ironically retreating into a past that is more like a dream. Whereas LaSalle's past is a dream, George McCoy has awakened from an equally long dream. The story begins with a Kafka-esque statement: "George McCoy spent the first forty years of his life in a deep sleep. He woke up on a Friday in the month of March" (67). Upon waking, he needs to learn everything about his life again, for he has had no communication whatsoever with his family and no memory at all of what happened before his long sleep. His forty-year sleep makes him even more isolated from others than does LaSalle's un-happiness with his weight, for at least LaSalle has been conscious of what he has done with his forty-year life, whereas George seems totally uncon-scious of himself and the people around him. Waking up after forty years offers George the opportunity to make a choice about how he will live his life in the future. The questions he asks himself are real—"Why wake up now?" and "Would he sleep again?"—because he has to decide whether to join his forefathers in a deeper permanent sleep or to wake up and only sleep at the end of each day. Living each of his new days consciously, George gradually comes to realize that it is a choice he can make and that he is fully responsible for events related to this choice.

Apart from recognition, dreams in these stories often have to do with love, probably one of the most frequent obsessions people have in their ordinary lives. In this collection a number of "his" and "hers" stories rep-resent "dream dates," though not all of them appear in a positive light. "Landing" and "Body and Soul" are both perfect dreams in the sense that the end of the story fulfills the most sincere wishes of the characters. John does not understand very much of what is going on in Abigail's mind, although he is very careful to show that he cares and respects her as his dream woman. After a miserable period of not communicating, at the end of the story Abigail (whether in reality or in John's dream) has accepted the feverish John: "It was late for happiness, but happiness was here" (66). The same kind of movement from miscommunication to understanding and acceptance can be found in Joann and Edward's relationship in "Body and Soul." Although the end of the story does not indicate definite happi-ness, Edward's willingness to express his love creates trust and confidence in Joann so that she can think "He would come; this was his part" (138).

The protagonists of "With Her," "The Maestro," and "Better than Real" have all encountered seductive temptations either in their dreams or real life, and their reactions have given them very different knowledge about themselves. Dr. Green, a middle-aged neurologist, bumps into one of his patients at a concert and lets his desire rule in his fantasy world. The temp-tation is so obvious that his wife notices a special intimacy between the two that is beyond that of doctor and patient. At the same time, his wife also meets a gay artist friend of hers, about which Dr. Green makes a re-mark. This couple, who has been married for fifteen years, is suddenly at-tacked by this dreamy realm, from which they may or may not emerge un-harmed. Although his mind has already flown to be with the actress-patient, through a most banal conversational exchange the husband has come face to face with the woman he has loved for fifteen years. As if to remind himself of this fact, he says to his wife "you're a beautiful china doll . . . to explain why he was here with her and not high up on that platform with the artist" (51).

While some characters enjoy an imaginary relationship with an ideal image or recreate their past, other characters find excitement in establishing relationships with total strangers or through chance encounters. "Moon, June" and "Lavara" feature women who spend their emotional efforts in relationships with people they meet by chance. June likes to buy clothes from second-hand stores; in particular, she imagines what the original owners of the clothes did with them and what their lives were like. Curious about the comments her boyfriend makes about a purple dress she gets from the store, June starts to buy all the clothes this owner sells to the store. This creates a sort of understood relationship between the two women, until one day the two meet at a party and June realizes that not only has she inherited the clothes but also her boyfriend from the same woman!

Paris is the dream setting for the last two stories of the collection. In "Paris" the wife discovers her husband's affair, flies to Paris, waits for the lovers to appear, and creates a fuss. What happens in Paris is such a dream that she cannot find words to talk about it when she gets home: "Here I sit. What did you say? Speak up. Oh, yeah, you took the words right out of my mouth" (224). Apparently it is not easy to find words to talk about the dream state, not even easy to distinguish between the dream and the reality.

Dream Date explores many of the issues that appear in McGarry's previous works. By separating the stories into "His" and "Hers," the collection emphasizes the narrators, as well as their relationships with the stories. Even though McGarry's previous fiction has always been set in small towns in America where the regional population includes an Irish community that is upholding a sort of tradition and identity, the focus has always been on the people of these towns. In all of the previous stories, the protagonist bears the burden of the traditional identity inherited from the family yet has to face the reality of new opportunities and new challenges, which leave no place for the traditional side of the protagonist's being. Both inside the local community and the protagonist, therefore, a battle for recognition is fought between the traditional and the new, the marginal and the global, and self and the other.

Although the regional details and cultural specificity included in *Dream Date* are not significant, this collection is no less McGarry-like than her previous works. While a specific community of Irish American people has been inserted into most of her previous writing, the center of attention has always been the characters going through personal dilemmas. These are lonely people who have no way to deal with their isolation or detachment from the external world. Some of them do not even understand what they are feeling and resort to the most illogical way to endure. Women seek a sense of security in domesticity but discover it is not a safe abode; men may find solace in drinking when they feel that reality is coming at them too quickly. These human conditions are not unique to any particular group of people but rather a general picture of our society. Although it could be argued that the characters in McGarry's fiction might have felt more intensely about these issues because their Irish heritage makes those conditions a part of their identity, as *Kirkus Reviews* comments on her writing: "when she's at her strongest, McGarry's prose is flesh [*sic*], her plots unpredictable, and her dialogue shimmeringly wry—as in the pointed exchange between George and his dead father in an empty afternoon bar; at her weakest, she is oblique and abruptly elliptical" (*"The Courage of Girls"* 9). In many ways McGarry's writing does for the Irish American identity what Shena Mackay does for the Anglo-Scottish: by not specifying a cultural identity, they nonetheless incorporate the sentiments of that identity into a general human narrative.

Works Cited

Blodgett, Jan. Rev. of *The Courage of Girls*, by Jean McGarry. *Library Journal* 117.6 (1 April 1992): 148.

Eckhoff, Sally. "Brief Encounters—*The Courage of Girls* by Jean McGarry." *Village Voice* 12 May 1992: S7, 19.

Lyons, Bonnie. "The Very Rich Hours." *Studies in Short Fiction* 25.1 (Winter 1988): 83–84.

McGarry, Jean. "Time Out with . . . Jean McGarry in Her Writer's Hideaway." *Gazette Online: The Newspaper of the Johns Hopkins University* 32 (7 Oct. 2002): 6.

———. *Airs of Providence*. Baltimore, MD: Johns Hopkins University Press, 1985.

———. *The Courage of Girls*. New Brunswick, NJ: Rutgers University Press, 1992

———. *Dream Date*. Baltimore, MD: Johns Hopkins University Press, 2002.

———. *Gallagher's Travels*. Baltimore, MD: Johns Hopkins University Press, 1997.

CHAPTER 12

Erin McGraw

Expanding the Tradition of
Irish American Women Writers

SALLY BARR EBEST

An armless, legless sixteen-year-old girl elopes with a love-sick farm boy. A middle-aged professor graduates from picking her students' pockets to kidnapping a baby. An elderly woman takes voice lessons so she will speak clearly when she calls the man of her dreams—a talk-radio host. Such plot lines do not fit our conceptions of Irish American fiction. While some readers accept Francis Phelan flitting in and out of William Kennedy's books, or others dispute the degrading poverty in *Angela's Ashes*, most readers have come to expect relatively straightforward renderings from Irish American women's novels. Maureen Howard's Mary Agnes Keely may perch on the edge of sanity, Joyce Carol Oates's Corrine Mulvaney may abandon her raped daughter, and Alice McDermott's charming Billy may waste his life on a lie, but these acts maintain a semblance of reality. They also fit the categories Charles Fanning established over a decade ago in *The Irish Voice in America*.

As Fanning has noted, Irish American novels can be categorized into "past lives, public lives, private lives, and stylized lives" (Fanning 313). Past lives are usually represented in historical novels, while authors of stylized lives elevate style so that it becomes "a willed, obtrusive element of meaning" (342). More prevalent are novels centering on public and private lives. Public lives are "novels largely concerned with Irish-American experience on the job and outside the home, novels about priests, politicians, businessmen, policemen and firemen, and other civil servants" (316)—topics usually the domain of male authors—whereas novels celebrating private lives center around family, relationships, and domesticity, often exploding the myth of the "saintly matriarch" (329) to deconstruct relationships, thus "bring[ing] the fresh air of considered moral perspective to Irish-American life" (334). The vast majority of Irish American women writers fall into this latter category. Among them, Erin McGraw is a notable exception; her works crisscross the boundaries between public and private lives while adding unexpected twists in moral perspective.

Bodies At Sea

At the ripe old age of forty-five, McGraw has produced four bodies of work, each of which further expands the boundaries of Irish American women's fiction. Her first book, *Bodies at Sea* (1989), winner of the Illinois short fiction award, was described by *Kirkus Reviews* as displaying "a sure hand and an even voice busily at work documenting the struggles of regular people trying to lead ordinary lives. At her best, McGraw encourages us to see sainthood in its human context, relevant to the most mundane experiences . . . Without rancor, these poignant moral tales gently go beyond most family fiction; they would merit our attention even if that were their only distinction" (Rev. of *Lies of the Saints*). McGraw puts a twist on traditional Irish American themes by applying them to nontraditional subjects, whom she describes as "on the edge of madness" (McGraw, email interview). The most startling of these subjects, summarized at the opening of this chapter, fall into the category of private lives and play on the themes of family loyalty, yet they do so by echoing Flannery O'Connor's sympathetic depictions of grotesques.[1]

All of the stories in this collection display a theme common in Irish American literature: alienation. As Elaine Fowler Palencia writes: "Mc-

Graw is good at showing the despair that lies beneath the smooth surfaces of people's lives. In that regard, the overarching metaphor of drowning in this collection recalls Stevie Smith's poem about the man who 'was much farther out than you thought/And not waving but drowning.'" At the same time, McGraw's stories often turn familiar themes upside down. "Accepted Wisdom" and "Finding Sally" reverse the traditional Irish theme of a child's self-immolation in the service of her abandoned or widowed parent: in these stories, it is the parents who center their lives around their children to no avail. An abandoned husband, dependent on his teenaged daughter, discovers the girl is having an affair with the town's married butcher; friends of drug-addicted Sally search for her, believing they must save her from her own mother.

Unlike most Irish American women writers, McGraw also features prominent male characters, but they too reverse the norm. In "Tule Fogs" she combines the stylistic convention established by James T. Farrell with Maureen Howard's tendency for "self-defining rebellion," writing realistically about the problems gripping the Catholic Church in the story of an idealistic young priest ostensibly bent on saving his secretary from slipping into madness if not promiscuity. Yet as the story concludes, he vows to "take her to a safe place and talk to her about love. He would wait until her pulse quieted, and then he would hold her so that she could not touch her hair, and when she slept he would stroke the blue shadows of her white throat" (*Bodies* 113). "Legs" explores the postmodern theme of alienation through the story of a young man so mesmerized by tales of his famous show-business aunt that he devotes his life to designing retro artwork, evoking images of Norma Shearer, Theda Bara, and Marlene Dietrich in order to reproduce their elegance, beauty, and heroism. Asked why he does not try anything new, his response echoes William Kennedy's explanation of Irish American writing: "It's in my blood" (qtd. in Quinn 126).

Lies of the Saints

These themes grow more obvious in McGraw's second book of short stories, *Lies of the Saints*, named a Notable Book for 1996 by the *New York Times*. The book's title, which unites the volume's last three stories, firmly positions it as a member of the traditional Irish American canon via explicit images, places, and names while simultaneously introducing the feminist themes characterizing contemporary Irish American women's writing. Wendy Dorsel Fisher argues that

> McGraw's strength stems from being both Catholic and catholic. . . . Saying she stresses her faith as framework does not mean you'll find priests appearing in pivotal roles or drives to and from the confessional as settings for character revelation. . . . McGraw doesn't write from the pew or the pulpit, and yet her stories possess a steady assurance, the pulse of someone fingering the decades of a rosary. The movement from one bead or moment to the next has the seamless practiced progression of known prayer—with all its power to redeem the reader. . . . [H]er religious practice strengthens her fiction.

"I was raised Catholic," McGraw explains, "and those stories are a kind of love song to the women I grew up among. They were funny and energetic and practical, I always knew I could trust them, and I almost never meet women like them anymore" (email interview). The purpose in this volume, says McGraw, was to examine "characters who were fully sane, often irritable, and rooted in the everyday world. I wanted to start exploring the costs of daily living, costs that we are generally too busy to tally until life, one way or another, presents us with the bill: sometimes divorce, sometimes addiction, sometimes simply a relationship overdue for an overhaul and sometimes, blissfully, unexpected delight" (email interview). Each story deals with relationships, but again, McGraw presents them with a twist. "As in Flannery O'Connor's stories," writes reviewer Ann Harleman, "the only irony is dramatic irony, brought about by the actions of the characters themselves" (239).

Two of the stories, "Blue Skies" and "Her Father's House," mix alcoholism with relationships, always a combustible topic; yet each story views the problem from an unexpected perspective. In "Blue Skies" Ray and Constance deal with the aftermath of alcoholism—including issues of sobriety and trust. As Anne Owens Weekes has detailed, Irish women's fiction, especially that from North Ireland, is rife with the horrors of alcoholism; however, few if any writers have addressed the "hangover" this induces in the sober, codependent spouse. The aptly named Constance has remained true to Ray throughout his drinking days, but she is no less constant in her vigilance to detect the first whiff of alcohol or to remind Ray of her ongoing distrust. McGraw takes a realistic look at the damage a sus-

picious spouse can wreak on a relationship, as well as the difficulties of letting go and rebuilding trust. Conversely, in "Her Father's House" McGraw
follows the lead of William Kennedy's *Ironweed* by describing a woman's
descent into alcoholism[2]; however, by setting the story in the house where
the protagonist's father died from alcoholism, McGraw deftly questions
Irish stereotypes regarding heredity and environment in producing alcoholic behavior.

McGraw similarly breaks new ground in her placement of contemporary Irish American women protagonists in public lives. Gwen, the main
character in "The Return of the Argentine Tango Masters," hosts a call-
in talk show on a local radio station in southern Indiana; Della, the flawed
heroine in "Stars," sells real estate. Both characters' public lives are complicated by their private lives. Gwen's husband grows jealous at the public-
ity surrounding the return of her ex-husband, Rafe, while divorcée Della
must weigh her desire for an exciting sexual life with her need for financial stability. Although the particulars of each plot might seem foreign to
traditional scholars of Irish studies, such characters certainly fall within
the parameters of Maureen Howards's description of Irish American women
defined by "a culture of commerce as much as the duties and privileges of
home and of proud, self-defining rebellion" (xiii).

The collection's second story, "A Suburban Story," also deserves mention, for although its characters are named Iris and Jack, their domestic
situation, the Irish American themes of motherhood and relationships,
and explicit references to Irish American customs and manners make it a
clear precursor to the last three stories bearing the book's title, *Lies of the
Saints*. "Mary Grace," "Saint Tracy," and "Russ" are three interconnected
stories about the same Irish Catholic family told over a forty-year period.
The stories, says McGraw, "reflect a lot of households I visited, but they
aren't directly autobiographical. I remember coming home from friends'
houses when I was a kid and thinking about how loud and rambunctious
other people's homes were." These stories "reflect those memories—more
warmly than not, I hope" (email interview).

Set in 1958, the first story revolves around thirty-nine-year-old Mary
Grace's suspicions that her son's female tutor has a crush on her husband.
McGraw juxtaposes the love and frustration of parenting five children
with the tutor's rosy image of one big happy family. Despite the frustrations of reality, the overriding themes celebrate family, faith, and loyalty. Explaining her relationship with her husband, Mary Grace tells the

tutor bitterly, "We hold each other in place" (*Lies* 151). Ironically, as the story closes, Russ repeats the phrase to reassure Mary Grace, telling her, "You keep me in place" (155). The second story, "Saint Tracy," is set in 1968 and delves more deeply into Catholic themes through the use of Catholic language. It is Tracy's tenth birthday, but she is no longer Russ's affectionate baby: having just read a book about St. Therese, she has taken on a more restrained, "saintly" demeanor based on what Russ views as "her mother's aggravating air of sanctity" (*Lies* 160). To atone for the "IOU" he gave her for her birthday, Russ buys Tracy a basset puppy, which shakes Tracy out of her martyrdom. But just as he starts to fit in, the dog develops distemper, and the family draws together to pray for his recovery. This time McGraw reminds us to be careful what we pray for: the dog survives, but he has lost his sight and, consequently, Tracy has lost her faith.

The final story jumps twenty-three years to Russ's death to find Mary Grace, despite her lifelong professions of faith, bitter and angry to be the surviving spouse. In this story McGraw further explores the Catholic themes of suffering, penance, prayer, and forgiveness, traditionally associated with Mary Grace's generation of Irish American women. McGraw then contrasts these characteristics with the guilt, repression, exploration, and rejection of traditional roles experienced by the younger generation as exemplified in her granddaughter, Kate, who has run away from school.[3] When Kate's father arrives to reclaim his daughter, he recalls the summer Mary Grace made him memorize *The Lives of the Saints*, which helps her realize she got her faith from her husband. "'If a goal is worth anything, it should be the hardest thing you've ever done,' he'd say. 'Then he'd tell me that was why he married me'" (*Lies* 191).

As the story closes it is clear that Mary Grace's faith has returned and will sustain her—an extremely Catholic theme for the twenty-first century but not surprising in a book of stories by a contemporary Irish American woman writer who freely admits that her work is primarily influenced by her reading:

> Although the 20th Century was famously the century of the death of God, it is filled with wonderful fiction about clergy and other kinds of religious characters. Look at the fiction of (for starters) Flannery O'Connor, Bernard Malamud, Shusako Endo, J. F. Powers, Georges Bernanos, Graham Greene—and there are many more. Some of these characters are charlatans, some holy fools, some (especially with

Greene) figures of intelligence and despair. But the fact that we're seeing fiction in the last fifteen years from Ron Hansen, Oscar Hijuelos, Gail Godwin and other writers that focuses on religious characters doesn't seem to me a break from 20th-Century convention. I'd say it's a continuation. (qtd. in Wicket)

The Good Life

Traditional Irish American themes and characters return in McGraw's third book, ironically titled *The Good Life* (2004). Indeed, Joseph J. Feeney describes this good life as "brittle, fragile, ironic, impermanent. And it is often Catholic. . . . Catholic stories—or stories with Catholic touches—make up over half of this collection." Yet Feeney does not altogether care for McGraw's attempts. In the story "A Whole New Man," Feeney claims "religion is just a few passing phrases: 'Sweet Jesus,' 'the answer to my prayers,' 'Jesus Christ, that's enough,'" whereas later stories, he maintains, "are more overt, being set in seminaries. . . . I'm not sure she understands priests, and her laypeople are often shallow, with responses more psychological than religious." McGraw refutes this contention:

> I am terrifically interested in faith—which is sometimes represented by organized religion, sometimes not—and the ways that faith can change a life, for better or worse. Humans, I think, yearn to believe in things, whether those things are structures or systems (paranoiacs, for instance, have a deep faith in a world gone wrong) or paths to immanence. We long for ways to understand ourselves and our place in the world, and one of the most interesting and sometimes heartbreaking things I know is to put faith to the test, and see at what point faith snaps. This is one reason that martyrs are interesting. Are they fools or saints? There is no firm answer, which makes this material ideal for fictional investigation. (qtd. in Wicket)

Feeney's review appears to reflect its source—*America Magazine: The National Catholic Weekly*—more than an understanding of contemporary Irish American women's writing or the inroads McGraw has made into the Irish American canon as a whole. More perceptive (and less parochial) is the review in *Image Update: A Journal of the Arts and Religion*:

Engaging as car-wrecks, [McGraw's] stories are ferocious little moral exercises, and the lesson again and again is humility, new eyes, transformation through weakness, and more humility. In nearly every story there's a turn where the weak become strong, the first become last, the bottom rung goes on the top, the underdog becomes terrifying, and always at the expense of the smart-mouthed, quick-minded character, who is also the character you have the most sympathy for.

"Daily Affirmations" is a prime example. Taking place sequentially before "Russ," the final story in Lies of the Saints, Tracy has never regained her religious faith and thus has lost her early affinity with her mother. Perceiving her mother as the cause of her problems, Tracy reads daily affirmations and writes best-selling psycho babble prescribing self-love, exemplified in the mantra, "I have nothing to apologize for" (Good Life 107). Such lines may have led the New York Times Book Review to describe McGraw's efforts as "put[ting] wisdom in the mouths of flakes. . . . [T]here is humor and compassion, and an understanding that diminished expectations might be better than shattered dreams" (Zeidner).

Called home to help her father care for Mary Grace, who has broken her ankle, Tracy finds that the daily affirmations now "feel absurdly childish" (Good Life 108) against Mary Grace's barrage of guilt trips. Ultimately, she finds peace after attending mass, where she weeps uncontrollably and forgives her mother. This response—recounted much more humorously than this rendering—sounds suspiciously like a return to the Catholic Church, or at least an awareness of the need for faith in a higher power. Similar messages resound throughout this collection. McGraw explains:

> The new book takes those rooted lives and gives them a yank. These stories explore characters who have undergone big life changes. I'm interested in looking at what will prompt us to take the risk of making big changes in our lives, and in particular, I'm interested in seeing what happens after the change is made. Life, in all of its trivial particulars, does not stop just because we have made a decision. This fact holds both promise and threat, and the new stories explore that seam.

"Ax of the Apostles," "Appearance of Scandal," and "The Penance Practicum" reenter a venue generally avoided by Irish American women writers.[4] "I've been writing about priests," McGraw explains, "who are not, in my mind, models of strength or power." Other stories in the collection address the traditionally Irish American theme of private lives—the vicissitudes of relationships before and during married life. In "The Beautiful Tennessee Waltz" a couple realizes the strength of their marital ties even as they recognize the wife's crush on someone else. Similarly, in a plot reminiscent of *Charming Billy*, "One for My Baby" traces the love triangle formed by Patrick, Aless, and Patrick's dead wife, Eleanora.

All of the women in these stories are strong, reflecting McGraw's ongoing affiliation with feminism's second wave as well as her Irish American heritage. "The women I grew up with were funny, feisty, and as far as I could tell, did whatever they wanted," she recounts. "I loved the women's slapdash grace and easy assurance." Perhaps most memorable was her grandmother, Bess McGraw, who married at fifteen and left her abusive husband (and two daughters) at age seventeen, moving from Kansas to Oregon. "I see my grandmother's ruthlessness as a kind of courage," McGraw writes. "Having decided to start afresh, she did the job right. No one knows if she was ever overcome with homesickness, or dread, or the hunger to smell her young daughters' hair. She knew that a decision, if it's going to mean anything, must be kept. A large part of whatever made up my grandmother was steel." After moving to Los Angeles, Bess met her second husband, Clarence McGraw. A good Catholic, she played the organ at mass and "as president of the Altar Society oversaw the laundering of altar cloths." "Rebellious Bess" moved to California "to create the exact repressed, status-conscious life that many people fled the Midwest to escape." McGraw sums up her grandmother's choices, noting, "We go where we have to in order to grasp happiness, a truth any Californian could tell you."

Bess McGraw and women like her provide models for Erin McGraw's female characters, who are "articulate, as smart as I can manage to make them, and empowered, particularly in the last two books, with women ministers, accountants, business women of various stripes." In creating these characters, McGraw moves out of the territory primarily identified with Irish American women writers. Moreover, while her female characters' strengths are evident throughout her *oeuvre*, they are most evident in her first novel, *The Baby Tree* (2002).

The Baby Tree

Kate Gussey is a Methodist pastor living at the buckle of the Bible Belt, southern Indiana; she is the wife of compassionate-conservative physician

Ned and ex-wife of the manipulative Bill-o (short for Bill O'Grady), whom she has not seen in fifteen years. Obviously, Kate's character is designed to make a political statement. If she were Catholic, she could not be a priest, divorced, *or* remarried. "But at a practical level," writes McGraw, "I made Kate a Methodist minister because I wanted to write about a woman in ministry. As it happens, I think the Church's position on the ordination is about as wrong-headed as most of its social positions, but I was less concerned about the book making a statement than having the opportunity to explore some issues. The Methodist church was the first to ordain women (in the 1930s), and the Methodist position on abortion is explicitly pro-choice" (Wicket). Yet McGraw did not have an "explicit political agenda." As she explains in an interview with Dan Wicket: "To write well, it seems to me, means respecting the characters. They do not exist as soundboards for me. And just as I resist sermons when people in life direct them at me, why should I expect readers to want to hear them from my characters?" Thus, although she uses the novel as a vehicle to point out the inequities of the Catholic Church's restrictions, McGraw does not neglect to detail the challenges and frustrations engendered (pun intended) by change.

Booklist praises McGraw's "deceptively simple prose [because it] turns each story over to her characters. Her loosely woven narration—light but with great tensile strength—lets their voices come through unimpeded; as in Flannery O'Connor's stories, the only irony is dramatic irony, brought about by the actions of the characters themselves" (Wilkinson). *The Baby Tree* revolves around three seemingly unrelated subplots. As pastor, Kate feels it is her duty to take in Mindy, a pregnant teen kicked out of her home by her parents. At the same time, Kate's husband, Ned, believes it his Christian duty to invite newly arrived ex-husband Bill-o to stay with them in the parsonage until his new house is built. Meanwhile, an ultraconservative fundamentalist group—the Sanctuary Christians—has decided it is their duty to question the existence and beliefs of a female minister and, if possible, lure away Kate's congregation. These plots are complicated by and ultimately intertwined around a single issue: abortion.

In the first half of the novel, the various relationships are explored and expanded: childless Kate and Ned find Mindy's blissfully ignorant pregnancy irritating, while they gradually decide that former reprobate Bill-o has reformed. Meanwhile, the Sanctuary Christians have succeeded in attracting supporters, among them Ned, which has naturally caused a rift in the marriage. Everything comes to a head when Mindy decides to abort her pregnancy. Kate initially supports the decision, whereas Ned, despite his belief that Mindy is unfit to be a mother, is so firmly against abortion that he moves out of the parsonage. At this, the Sanctuary Christians escalate their activities, picketing outside the church and even challenging Kate during a sermon.

Throughout the novel Kate's inner turmoil is foregrounded, thus positioning the book within the genres of the feminist novel and Irish American private lives. At the same time, Kate's external actions as pastor and protector of her flock cross the boundary into the traditionally masculine Irish American arena of public life. Kate continues in her role as "priest," described by Fanning as perceiving "religion as an active force, literal as well as symbolic, in their lives" (326). Indeed, in her "insistence on life's religious import and [her] avowed moral purposes" (Fanning 326), Pastor Kate continues the pattern established in the works of Andrew Greeley, which Fanning notes "recall the work of his nineteenth-century priest-novelist forerunners, Father John Roddan, John Boyce, William McDermott, and John Talbot Smith" (326). None of these men would be likely to defend a young woman's right to have an abortion—and that is the crux of The Baby Tree.

When Kate learns that Bill-o fathered Mindy's child, she realizes the girl will never receive emotional or financial support. Consequently, rather than continuing to ignore the girl's platitudes, she begins hammering home the realities and responsibilities of motherhood: prenatal nutrition, colic, tardy development, juvenile delinquency, the "money, the plans, the youth slipping daily away" (Baby Tree 186). Finally, Mindy makes her decision: "What else can I do? It's sad, but like you keep saying, I'm not ready for this" (187).

Once Mindy decides to abort her pregnancy, Kate supports her. Although the Sanctuary Christians have made her stance public and threatened her standing among her parishioners, and even though Ned has flatly declared "if you help this girl to get rid of her baby, that will be the end" (Baby Tree 179), Kate maintains her "avowed moral purposes"—a woman's right to choose. She drives Mindy to the clinic, signs her in, and sits with her. But as they converse, the girl admits she is there because of Bill-o: "It isn't that he doesn't want a baby; this just isn't the time," she tells Kate. "A baby now would bring us unhappiness. . . . It may not seem like it to some, but coming here [to the clinic] is our stake in tomorrow. . . . He said I could think of it as the path to our future" (195). Mindy has not made this choice; Bill-o has coerced it. With this knowledge, Kate switches gears. "Put your pants on," she tells Mindy. "If you knew what you were doing, you'd be crying now, hating me. You'd be hating Bill-o too, or at least you wouldn't be loving him. You need to wait. You need to remember what you're doing" (196). So they leave the clinic, fighting their way through protestors mistakenly calling them "killers" and "enemies of the innocents." As the book concludes, Mindy, who has had time to make her own choices, decides to put the baby up for adoption.

Although the abortion plot drives the novel, this multilayered work takes pains to detail the depth and breadth, the frustrations and challenges, of a pastor's duties in order to show that women *can* be married and serve the church. Moreover, despite—or perhaps because of—McGraw's feminist beliefs, Kate and Ned are given equal attention in the novel. "I strongly believe in the need to play fair," McGraw explains, "and if I happen to agree with one character—say Kate Gussey—I do my utmost to make sure that her foil—say, Ned—is at least as smart and his arguments as sensible as hers. To do less, I'm afraid, would be to allow the work to skirt propaganda for whatever causes I happen to believe in" (email interview).

Expanding the Irish American Tradition

Despite their twists and topics, Erin McGraw's works are clearly Irish American. Emigrating from Ireland in the nineteenth century, her father's family recalled little of their roots. But like her own characters, McGraw has reversed this situation. Born and raised in Redondo Beach, California, she eschewed the stereotypical association with beaches and bikinis, preferring instead the California characterized by "the sense of possibility, that life is infinitely renewable, that the past can be shed as if it were a coat" ("Not from Here"). At seventeen, she overtly self-identified with her Irish heritage: she officially changed her name from Susan to Susan *Erin* McGraw, then chose to be called by her middle name and proudly embraced her Irishness. "I liked its hint of the brogue," she writes, "its suggestion of fey humor and a certain wildness at the core." Despite growing up in California—the epitome of cool—McGraw has embraced life in what most see as the "nerdy" Midwest, attending graduate school at Indiana University and living in Ohio. She appreciates "the new sense of spaciousness" and defends "the culture—insular, yes, and self-protective, yes, but quick to see and respond to people's needs. Hoosiers," she writes, "knew how to demonstrate a personal interest without being intrusive. This was real sophistication, as opposed to the brittleness of fast-paced coastal culture." She makes Indiana sound like Ireland.

Although these themes and understanding characterize the works of Erin McGraw, she has used them to move beyond the constricted realm of private lives most often associated with Irish American women writers. Despite their Vassar degrees, suave conversations, and hopes for the future, the women in Mary McCarthy's *The Group* could not overcome McCarthy's own antifeminist beliefs; apart from the occasional dalliance, their lives remained constrained by their husbands and children. Maeve Brennan was similarly ensconced within the familiar world of the disenfranchised shanty Irish. This Old World view was shattered when Elizabeth Cullinan overturned the myth of the saintly matriarch. Shortly thereafter, Maureen Howard and Mary Gordon broke further away, taking their heroines out of the shackles of self-immolation in service to one's parent and sending these young women to the big city to fend for themselves—with a little help from a boyfriend or two. Mary McGarry Morris took readers further into the real world through her depictions of confused and alienated young women.

With the backlash against feminism, Irish American women writers such as Alice McDermott, Tess Gallagher, and Jean McGarry brought their characters back home. McDermott and Gallagher focus more on family than feminism, while McGarry examines male-female relationships and the too often resultant feelings of alienation. Not surprisingly, Joyce Carol Oates pulls together all of these traits in *What I Lived For*, but always with her characteristically unique approach, this time in the tale of an Irish American male protagonist. Eileen Myles has renewed the attention to feminism, but she added another dimension by introducing lesbian characters while experimenting with the novel's traditional form. Yet overall the predominant emphasis has been on private lives—family and relationships.

Erin McGraw has thoroughly broken those boundaries. Her Irish American women are no longer content to stay at home and raise a family, nor are they willing to accept or ignore the restrictions handed down by the Catholic Church. McGraw has taken us "public," drawing complex, thoughtful characters unafraid to address the issues that have plagued and restricted women for years. Through her stories, she attempts to reconcile past and present, Irish and American, realism and postmodernism, feminism and Catholicism. In so doing, she has expanded both the genre and the expectations associated with Irish American women writers and provided a vision of new literary possibilities for the twenty-first century.

Notes

1. Comparisons to Flannery O'Connor recur throughout reviews of McGraw's work. O'Connor's work, as Charles Fanning explains in *The Irish Voice in America*, is clearly Irish American, although she preferred to be identified as Southern Gothic (4).

2. Although female alcoholics are relatively rare in Irish American fiction, this character trait follows a literary type established earlier in James T. Farrell's *Studs Lonigan* and taken further into drug addiction by Eugene O'Neill in *Long Day's Journey into Night*.

3. This generational split echoes the differences between Elizabeth Cullinan's Mrs. Devlin and her granddaughter Winnie in *House of Gold*.

4. Both Elizabeth Cullinan and Mary Gordon feature priests as characters in *House of Gold* and *Final Payments*, respectively; however, they are not the protagonists of these works. The plot of Colleen McCullough's *The Thorn Birds* is driven by the relationship between Meggie and Father Ralph de Bricasart; however, McCullough is Irish Australian.

Works Cited

Fanning, Charles. *The Irish Voice in America*. Lexington: University Press of Kentucky, 1990.

Feeney, Joseph J. "Woe Are They." Rev. of *The Good Life*, by Erin McGraw. *America* 19.8 27 Sept. 2004 <http://www.americamagazine.org/content/article.cfm?article_id=3773>.

Fisher, Wendy Dorsel. Rev. of *Lies of the Saints*, by Erin McGraw. *pif Magazine*. 16 May 2005 <http://www.pifmagazine.com/SID/695/?page=2&>.

Harleman, Ann. Rev. of *Lies of the Saints*, by Erin McGraw. *Ploughshares* (Fall 1996): 239.

Howard, Maureen. Foreword. *Cabbage and Bones: An Anthology of Irish-American Fiction*. Ed. Caledonia Kearns. New York: Holt, 1997. xi–xiv.

McGraw, Erin. *The Baby Tree*. Ashland, OR: Storyline Press, 2002.

———. *Bodies at Sea*. Urbana: University of Illinois Press, 1989.

———. Email Interview. 29 June 2004.

———. *The Good Life*. Boston: Houghton Mifflin, 2004.

———. *Lies of the Saints*. San Francisco: Chronicle Books, 1996.

————. "Not from Here." *In the Middle of the Middle West*. Ed. Becky Bradway. Bloomington: Indiana University Press, 2003. 119–29.

Oates, Joyce Carol. *What I Lived For*. 2nd ed. New York: Signet, 1995.

Palencia, Elaine Fowler. "Short Stories in a Tradition of Excellence." *Illinois Periodicals Online*. (June 1990). 16 May 2005 <http://www.lib.niu.edu/ipo/ii900634.htm?.

Quinn, Peter. "William Kennedy: An Interview." *Recorder* 1.1 (Winter 1985): 65–81.

Rev. of *Lies of the Saints*, by Erin McGraw. *ImageUpdate: The Biweekly Newsletter from Image: A Journal of the Arts and Religion* 52 (15 June 2004). 16 May 2005 <http://www.imagejournal.org/imageupdate/52_040615.htm>.

Rev. of *Lies of the Saints*, by Erin McGraw. *Kirkus Review*. 1996.

Weekes, Anne Owens. "Ordinary Women: Themes in Contemporary Fiction by Irish Women." *Colby Quarterly: Contemporary Irish Fiction* 31.1 (March 1995): 88–99.

Wicket, Dan. "Interview with Erin McGraw." *Emerging Writers Forum*. 16 May 2005 <http://www.breaktech.net/emergingwritersforum/View_Interview.aspx?id=32>.

Wilkinson, Joanne. Rev. of *Lies of the Saints*, by Erin McGraw. *Booklist* 92.19–20 (1996): 1673.

Zeidner, Lisa. "Stumbling into Happiness: *Lies of the Saints*." *New York Times Book Review* 1 Sept. 1996. 3 Nov. 2006 <http://query.nytimes.com/gst/fullpage.html?res=9A07E3DA1139F932A3575AC0A960958260>.

About the Contributors

SUSANA ARAÚJO teaches literature and film at the University of Sussex (UK), where she holds a FCT Postdoctoral Research Fellowship. She received her D. Phil. in American literature from the University of Sussex, UK, was awarded an M.A. with Distinction from University of Warwick, UK, and received a B.A. (First Class Honours) from Faculty of Letters, University of Lisbon, Portugal. She has written widely on Joyce Carol Oates, and her articles have been published in academic journals as well as edited collections. Araújo is currently considering publication offers for her book manuscript, *Rewriting Literary Genre: Joyce Carol Oates*.

PATRICIA KEEFE DURSO received her Ph.D. in English from George Washington University. She has taught at George Washington University, Rutgers University at Newark, and Montclair State University. She currently teaches at Fairleigh Dickinson University. She has published essays on Mary Gordon, Alice Walker, and other women writers. Recent publications include a chapter on the impact of the Internet on U.S. multiethnic literature and the "canon" in *Multiethnic Literature and Canon Debates* (SUNY Press, 2006). Current projects include the design and development of a Web site devoted to Irish American women writers.

SALLY BARR EBEST is professor of English at the University of Missouri–St. Louis, where she teaches courses in Irish and Irish American women writers, feminist theory, and pedagogy for the English Department and the Institute for Women's and Gender Studies. Her publications include *Changing the Way We Teach* (Southern Illinois University Press, 2005) and *Reconciling Catholicism and Feminism?* (University of Notre Dame Press, 2003).

PATRICIA GOTT teaches a variety of British and American literature courses, as well as composition and women's studies courses, in the English Department at the University of Wisconsin–Stevens Point. In addition to Mary McGarry Morris, her research interests include Jean Rhys, Daphne du Maurier, Jeannette Winterson, Stevie Smith, and Edna O'Brien.

SUSANNA HOENESS-KRUPSAW is an associate professor of English at the University of Southern Indiana in Evansville. She earned her doctorate at Southern Illinois University–Carbondale with a dissertation on the role of the family in the novels of E. L. Doctorow. She teaches contemporary American and Canadian literature and has recently published on Ann Petry, Joy Kogawa, and Amy Tan.

BEATRICE JACOBSON is professor of English and director of the Women's Studies Program at St. Ambrose University in Davenport, Iowa. She earned her doctorate at the University of Iowa, where she wrote a dissertation on Emily Dickinson. Her M.A. is from Pennsylvania State University and her B.A. is from Seton Hall University. Her specializations in early American literature, women's literature, and ethnic literature are complemented by her focus on global feminism, especially women in development and women's literacy. She is a member of the board of directors of Centro de Estudios Interamericanos in Cuenca, Ecuador, where she teaches courses in Latin American women's issues and Teaching English as a Foreign Language.

A daughter of an Irish immigrant, **KATHLEEN ANN KREMINS** (neé Lahey) grew up in Newark, New Jersey. She teaches high school in New Jersey and is an adjunct professor at the College of St. Elizabeth. She has an M.F.A. in writing from Goddard College and recently completed her doctoral studies at Drew University. Her dissertation is entitled "An Ethics of Reading: The Broken Beauties of Toni Morrison, Nawal El Saadawai, and Arundhati Roy."

AMY LEE has a Ph.D. in comparative literature from the University of Warwick, UK. Her research interests include the Chinese diaspora, female self-writing, contemporary fiction and culture, and narratives of marginal experiences. She has published on women's diasporic writing, gender issues in contemporary fiction, witchery and witchcraft, and detective fiction. Currently she is an assistant professor in the Humanities Programme and the Department of English Language and Literature at Hong Kong Baptist University.

KATHLEEN HANLEY MCINERNEY is a faculty member of the Bilingual Education Program at Chicago State University as well as the Center for Interamerican Studies in Cuenca, Ecuador. Her research interests include applied linguistics in language education as well as diaspora/immigrant literature. Kathleen earned her Ph.D. in language, literacy, and culture at the University of Iowa.

JOHN M. MENAGHAN received a B.A. in English from Boston College, an M.A. in creative writing from Syracuse University, and a Ph.D. in English from the University of California–Berkeley. He teaches in the Department of English at Loyola Marymount University, where he also directs both the Irish Studies Minor and Summer in Ireland Programs. Menaghan has published scholarly articles on Joyce, Beckett, and Browning, as well as numerous poems in a range of journals. His first book of poetry, *All the Money in the World*, was published by Salmon Poetry, County Clare, Ireland, in 1999. His second book, *She Alone*, was published by Salmon in 2006. Menaghan has given readings of his poetry in London, Debrecen (Hungary), Dublin, Galway, Donegal, and Cork, and at venues across the United States, including New York, Boston, Philadelphia, Berkeley, and Los Angeles, among others. He has received a number of awards for his poetry, including an Academy of American Poets prize.

MARY ANN RYAN is writing a dissertation, with an emphasis on twentieth-century Irish literature, in the doctoral program in English at the University of Wisconsin–Milwaukee. Her academic work has focused on contemporary Irish drama and women's fiction, particularly the short stories of Mary Lavin and women writers of her genre and era. In her work on drama and short fiction, Ryan explores the intersections of postcolonial and psychological theory within a feminist critical discourse, concentrating on performativity, ritual, and spectacle in representations of gender, race, and nationalism in the construction of Irish identity. She has been teaching at Chicago State University for the past fifteen years and is also currently teaching at St. Xavier University in its new Irish Studies Certificate Program. In her previous life, she was a Chicago police officer.

Index